Pakistan's Quagmire

PAKISTAN'S QUAGMIRE

Security, Strategy, and the Future of the Islamic-nuclear Nation

Edited by
Usama Butt
and by N. Elahi

continuum

The Continuum International Publishing Group
80 Maiden Lane, New York, NY 10038
The Tower Building, 11 York Road, London SE1 7NX

www.continuumbooks.com

Library of Congress Cataloging-in-Publication Data
Pakistan's quagmire : security, strategy, and the future of the Islamic-nuclear nation /
edited by Usama Butt.
    p. cm.
  Includes bibliographical references.
  ISBN-13: 978-1-4411-4431-7 (hardcover : alk. paper)
  ISBN-10: 1-4411-4431-5 (hardcover : alk. paper)
  ISBN-13: 978-0-8264-3300-8 (pbk. : alk. paper)
  ISBN-10: 0-8264-3300-6 (pbk. : alk. paper) 1. Pakistan—Politics and
government—1988- 2. National security—Pakistan. 3. Nuclear weapons—Pakistan. 4.
Islam and politics—Pakistan. I. Butt, Usama. II. Title.
  JQ629.A58P365 2010
  355'.03305491—dc22   2010002807

ISBN: 978-1-4411-4431-7 (Hardback)
         978-0-8264-3300-8 (Paperback)

Typeset by Pindar NZ, Auckland, New Zealand
Printed in the United States of America by Sheridan Books, Inc

Contents

Figures and Tables

Figures

Contributors

Ishtiaq Ahmad is an Associate Professor of International Relations at Quaid-i-Azam University in Islamabad. He is the author of *Pakistan in a Changing World: Foreign Policy Options*.

Rabia Akhtar is the Chairperson of the Department of Defence and Diplomatic Studies at Fatima Jinnah Women University, Rawalpindi, Pakistan.

Sartaj Aziz is a former finance and foreign minister of Pakistan and a leading economist. He is currently Vice Chancellor of Beaconhouse National University, Lahore, Pakistan.

Usama Butt is a security analyst and a specialist on the Islamist phenomenon. His book *The Dynamics of US-Pakistan Relations in the Backdrop of US-led War on Terror* is co-edited by Professor Julian Schofield.

Brian Cloughley is the South Asia defense analyst for Jane's Sentinel and also analyzes aspects of nuclear, biological and chemical weapons proliferation for Jane's Information Group, as well as working as a researcher at the Pakistan Security Research Unit of Bradford University. He is a reputed expert on the Pakistani Army and is the author of *War, Coups and Terror: Pakistan's Army in the Years of Turmoil*.

N. Elahi is a doctoral candidate at the Department of War Studies at King's College London. He also holds a Masters Degree in Intelligence and International Security from King's College London.

Rohan Gunaratna is the head of the International Centre for Political Violence and Terrorism Research (ICPVTR) at Nanyang Technological University in Singapore. He is a member of the Steering Committee of George Washington University's Homeland Security Policy Institute and Senior Fellow both at Fletcher School of Law and Diplomacy's Jebsen Center for Counter Terrorism Studies and the Memorial Institute for the Prevention of Terrorism, Oklahoma. He is author of the international bestseller *Inside Al Qaeda: Global Network of Terror*.

Nazir Hussain is associated with the Department of Defence and Strategic Studies, Quaid-i-Azam University, Islamabad. He is the author of *Defence Production in the Muslim World: Limitation and Prospects* and *Strategic Dynamics of West Asia*, a textbook for post-graduate studies.

Sajjad Nasser is a Senior Fellow and Professor of Political Science at Lahore School of Economics and has served twice as a chairman of the Political Science Department at the University of the Punjab, Lahore, Pakistan.

Julian Schofield is an Associate Professor at Concordia University, Canada. His research focuses on security and strategic studies in South and Southeast Asia. He is the author of *Militarization and War*.

Simon Valentine is a religious consultant and freelance writer specializing in Comparative Religions, particularly Islamic Studies. He is also an Associate Lecturer at the University of Bradford and a researcher at the Pakistan Centre at the same university.

Samina Yasmeen is the Director of the Centre for Muslim States and Societies at the University of Western Australia, Perth, and lectures in Political Science and International Relations in the School of Social and Cultural Studies in the same university. Dr. Yasmeen is a specialist in political and strategic developments in South Asia (particularly Pakistan), the role of Islam in world politics and gender issues. She is the author of *Understanding Muslim Identities: From Perceived Relative Exclusion to Inclusion*.

Preface

Another book on Pakistan in the light of recent developments needs no justification, particularly when there is such a dearth of quality on the topic. Pakistan has remained in the headlines since 9/11, but the last few years, when the war came "home," have been particularly crucial. It may be questionable, even with the looming anarchy, to state that Pakistan is going through an existential crisis but it is undoubtedly in a pit of "quagmire," as the book's title suggests; not of mud and water, but of blood, human corpses, terrorism, confusion, disarray, identity crisis and anarchy. At the time of writing, Pakistan has reached a point where almost all news is bad news — its insurgency is out of control amidst continuous military crack-downs, its civilian government is out of public touch and unable to perform national reconciliation on the matter, its populace are frightened by the almost daily brazen terrorists attacks and its civil society is at best disenfranchised on the issue.

Therefore, it is absolutely crucial that Pakistani strategists and civil society, as well as the general populace, grasp the situation fully and understand its dynamics. Similarly, it is very important that the international concerns; however "questionable" they may be, are analyzed and addressed. This book first establishes the fact that Pakistan is already in or steadily moving towards a "quagmire" that consists of the aforementioned elements, second, it analyzes the genesis of this quagmire by attempting to identify factors and actors involved in this phenomenon, and finally, it establishes further recommendations for the future strategic discourses.

The target readership of this book is much wider than the currently available (mostly journalistic) published material engages, i.e. mainly Western readers; this book aims to break such trends and includes renowned academics and specialist contributors to not only educate Western readers, but also to stimulate Pakistani strategists, policy-makers, academics and the general public alike on the matter.

The idea of the book was developed earlier this year amidst a backdrop of turmoil. While it focused my attention from areas I am particularly interested in — Islamism and the West and related issues of global security — towards the situation in Pakistan, I found the available literature mostly journalistic (with few exceptions) and one-sided, tilting towards a particular readership. I also felt that there was a yawning gap in coherent enquiry in the existing literature, which blames all that is wrong on either Islamic ideology or on the lack of liberal democracy based on the Western model, while wilfully failing to explain what Islamic ideology is or ought to be and why liberal democracy in an Islamic ideological state such as Pakistan is crucially important. Hence, instead of generalizing the phenomenon, this book distinguishes between the different factors involved and presents a comparative analysis on each important phenomenon. In order to do so, I have invited a set of contributors and experts of both inclinations, both proponents and critics of "Pakistan's war on terror," in order to present a comparative, coherent and critical analysis of the issue. With both Pakistani and Western experts on board, the book presents a truly critical and academic study of the issue and breaks from the currently predominant one-sided, descriptive and chronological style of writing that most Pakistani authors have so far employed.

Although the "quagmire" referred to is of a multi-dimensional character, its most important dimensions are national and transnational Jihadism, US-led war on terror and the ideologically developed "identity crisis," hence the book's framework (although also exploring other important phenomenons) generally revolves around them. Each contributor is a renowned expert in their respective field and each essay covers a major phenomenon. The hope in the end is to stimulate the readers" interest and quench their intellectual thirst on the matter.

Finally, it remains for me to start the acknowledgements with the Almighty, who provided me with the necessary strength, and my parents, particularly my father, who has constantly encouraged me, as well as my wife Alema and my children, Shifa, Hashir and Safa, who have been kind enough to put up with my extensive writing schedule. I am also hugely indebted to all the contributors, not only for their agreement to write at mostly short notice, but also for their continuous extended support. I am particularly thankful to Professor Julian Schofield and Dr. Simon Valentine, who very kindly encouraged and supported me throughout the whole process, N. Elahi, who helped me with some of the editing, and Dr. Nazir Hussain, Dr. Rabia Akhtar and Brian Cloughley, who agreed to write their very important essays in a very limited time period and finally to Muhammad Rizwan whom helped voluntarily to initially promote the book. I am also indebted to the academics, writers and publishers who to my surprise, showed a huge interest in the project.

Last but not the least, I am very much obliged to the Continuum International Publishing Group, particularly acquisition editor Marie-Claire Antoine, who fully endorsed and supported this project from the outset. Her help and extended support led to the realization and materialization of this very important project.

Usama Butt
December 2009
London

Map 1 Map of the Federally administered Tribal areas (FATA) in Pakistan

Source: Creative Common, public domain

Introduction

Usama Butt

There are many questions surrounding the state of Pakistan, with the ultimate question being, "Will Pakistan survive the *existential* threat emancipating from its tribal region and win its own 'war on terror'?" Everyone, nationally, regionally and globally is anxiously waiting to see, as the Arabian proverb denotes, "which side will the camel sit?" But is this really an "existential crisis," as Western media and governments have strongly suggested earlier this year, or just another phase of anarchy and bloodshed that will eventually pass? Is Pakistan fighting its own "war on terror" or serving as a proxy to Western, particularly US, interests? To what extent is Pakistan sincere in its efforts to eliminate terrorists groups? What are the US interests in Pakistan and do they necessarily serve Pakistani interests? Is Pakistan capable and willing to root out the insurgency once and for all amid "fears" that some elements within its security and military apparatus still continue to support some of the Jihadist elements? Can and will Pakistan survive this turmoil and what will the future hold for the nuclear-armed country? What sort of tomorrow can be expected to emerge from today's ashes? The list of questions only grows and the answers are not short in supply either, everyone, at least within Pakistan, has some sort of opinion on these questions, may they be the secularists, so-called democrats, Islamists, fundamentalists religious parties or Jihadists. This has only blurred the whole picture further. There is no real national debate on the topic, as the government has its own point of view, the opposition is surprisingly quiet or purposefully laid-back amid half-hearted announcements and is at best unclear on the issue, and the army has its own reservation with the civilian apparatus. Similarly, the Western powers, particularly the US, claim to be a "friend" and "ally" of Pakistan's "war on terror," but have so far failed to convince such disparate Pakistani groups of their "sincerity" on the issue, as the recent Kerry-Lugar Bill and an increasing wave of anti-Americanism have demonstrated.

International concerns about the situation are plenty and were all too visible in President Barack Obama's Af-Pak policy review of early December 2009, where, although the importance of partnership with Pakistan was stressed, the focus remained on fighting al-Qaeda, whose location has been tirelessly and continuously pointed towards Pakistan by his administration without providing any solid proof. As almost all of the future US-Afghanistan strategic goals — fighting al-Qaeda, routing the Taliban and stopping the acquisition of nuclear weapon by the terrorists — are directly linked to Pakistan, the "pressure" can only be expected to grow further. Hence, the Pakistani government is constantly reminded by the US that al-Qaeda is within its geographical boundaries and that Pakistan needs to do "much more" than it has so far done. Similarly, the issue of "Quetta Shura" is handily raised whenever things are unsettled in Afghanistan and the pressure is increasingly mounted amid fears of the nuclear arsenal falling into the terrorists hands. All of the above, coupled with the doubts over the Kerry-Lugar Bill, a renewed US-Indian "friendship" and Obama's unrealistic "exit strategy" from Afghanistan have only helped in creating a big question mark over the role, aims and strategy of the US towards Pakistan, which has resulted not only in increasing anti-US sentiments, but also in creating a division within the civilian government and the all-powerful Pakistani army.

Nearly eight years into Pakistan's "war on terror," the government is still unable to defeat the insurgency or meaningfully minimize its strength and capabilities to strike. Amidst the governmental claim that it has successfully routed the insurgents in Swat and is now "winning" in South Waziristan, terrorist attacks brazenly continue all over the country. The militants have shown great resilience even in the aftermath of Baitullah Mehsud's death, which was followed by a strong propaganda campaign by the government that claimed to have "broken the back of the insurgency." The militants, however, are now united under a young and even more "energetic" and furious leader, Hakimullah Mehsud. The recent carnage in many Pakistani cities only affirms

Hakimullah's "zeal" to fight "American proxies" in Pakistan. On the other hand, the government's and military's claims of "victory" cannot yet be verified, as the army remains the only source of information coming out from the battle front, apart from Tehreek-e-Taliban's (TTP) spokesmen.

Besides the death toll, which is well into the thousands, the country's economy is in shatters, its public is frightened and its security apparatus seems unable to control the situation, as the militants have been able to strike almost freely at scores of targets that include the most "secure" sites — offices of different intelligence agencies and even the Army's general headquarters (GHQ) in Rawalpindi. Another grim outcome of Pakistan's "war on terror" is the millions of refugees or internally displaced persons (IDPs), whose number is only growing amid South Waziristan operation. With no end to the conflict in sight, the outcome of the ongoing operations (at the time of writing) in South Waziristan and the government's and military's claim to success, stand amid scores of previous known failures and many broken peace treaties.

The Pakistani public, international audiences and even strategists are stunned by the severity of this crisis, with many asking, "how did it come to this?" and "is there a way out from this turmoil?" Again, people have different opinions — that the root of the current crisis goes as far back as the country's foundations itself and is directly linked with its ideological discourses, or it's the army-backed Afghan Jihad that brought the "foreign" elements into the country and planted the seed of militancy; some link this to Pakistan's foreign policy, particularly in the backdrop of containing India, and others to the military's adventurism by supporting militants under the banner of "Kashmiri Jihad." However, the failure to recognize that each theory may have an element of truth in it has led to a fog of confusion that anti-US sentiments and the lack of government national reconciliatory efforts only exacerbate. The roots of the current crisis not only go as deep as the country's foundations itself, but are also ridden with the hardcore geo-political realities — the Indian threat, US interests in the region; first to "eliminate" communism and then to fight transnational Jihadists under the umbrella of "global war on terror" and al-Qaeda's presence in the tribal belt.

An often-ignored dimension among such explanations, however, is the fact that Pakistan is a classic case of a weak southern state that has both the symptoms of "third world and regime security" and is currently going through its "historical state formation" process, which may be as bloody as the European state formation once was.[1] However, it faces another set of problems that were absent during European state formation: colonialist legacy, globalization, corruption, feudalism and an unjust global system, which only hinders its transition to be a modern nation state. By this prism of "security studies," it becomes all to important to observe the current trends leading to the future, which many European security institutes commonly agree to be even more bloody, particularly in the south where the current prevalent unjust world order may be challenged. The terms "twenty years" crisis" and "great reckoning,"[2] used by Ken Booth of the Welsh School branch of Critical Security Studies, denote that the coming turmoil of the mid-twentieth century that consists of strategic challenges (the "cold war" between US and China or the rise of India, a Russian revival or indeed a further spread of transnational terrorism or chaos in the Middle East), the population stress, environmental crisis that may create a migratory process on an unimaginable level, or ideological battles fought in the name of religion, will create a very dangerous world, particularly in the south. Even a superficial analysis of such conditions puts Pakistan right in the centre of this coming anarchy. Its population stress, natural resources shortages and its geographical location and ideological background leave it wide open to both strategic and ideological challenges in the very near future.

It is, therefore, absolutely crucial that Pakistan comes out of the "quagmire" it is presently stuck in. I have deliberately chosen to use the term "quagmire" here for two main reasons; first, without an end in sight, any steps the current and previous governments have so far taken to avoid or end this crisis (which includes many broken peace accords and different military operations), has further increased the intensity of the problem, resulting in the phenomenon of IDPs, urban warfare, different insurgencies — Punjabi Taliban — and the merger of different national Jihadists organizations. Second, the lack of national reconciliation amongst political parties, religious groups and security apparatus has created a fog of confusion and disarray. This "quagmire" is multi-dimensional, made up of terrorism, identity crisis, ideology, disarray, confusion, anarchy and last but not least, Western strategic interests in Pakistan and the region. The nature of this quagmire is thus synonymous to the weak state's "insecurity dilemma" where "the inability of the state to provide peace and order creates a contentious environment where each component of society — including the ruling elite or regime — competes to preserve and protect its own well being . . . this condition of insecurity is self perpetuating because every effort by the regime to secure its own security through force provokes greater resistance and further undermines the institutional basis of the state and the security of the society as a whole."[3] The irony is that the current civilian government, following in the footsteps of its predecessor military regime, is mostly concerned only with its "regime security," which has furthered a lingering "insecurity dilemma" that was first created by the Musharraf regime, and has now turned into a "quagmire" by even more contentious ideological discourses of both national and transnational Jihadists and by the Western interests in the region under the pretext of "war on terror."

Pakistan's war on terror, whether fought in its name or as a US proxy, will only delay addressing such vital problems that the "twenty years' crisis" is set to throw upon it, which indeed will pose a *real* existential crisis, in the very near future. Pakistan, being a victim of southern weak state syndrome, cannot prolong this crisis any further, as it doesn't have the luxury or the resources to prepare for the coming anarchy, as the First World may.

The purpose of this book, hence, is to discuss, explain and analyze three important dimensions: that of "security," "strategy" and "future" of Pakistan, through the prism of this "quagmire." The "security" aspect will analyze and explain both internal and external security challenges, i.e. Jihadists insurgency in Pakistan, US-led global war on terror, problems at the borders etc., while the "strategy" aspect, reflecting on the above, will explain and analyze what Pakistan must do today and tomorrow to escape this quagmire. Finally, through the "security" and "strategy" prisms possible "future" discourses will be evaluated.

The book aims to discuss the all-important set of issues that are part of this quagmire. The book's overall framework evolves around the genesis, fact, factors and actors of the current crisis. This is then used to analyze possible current and future strategic discourses. Each contributor has written on a particular set of issues that is directly relevant to the overall framework of the book and each chapter analyses all three dimensions — the "security," "strategy" and "future" of Pakistan. Hence, most of the chapters discuss the most relevant phenomenons: nationalist and transnationalist Jihadist ideologies and their capability to invoke an "existential threat" as well as the role and capability of both the government and the army to root out the insurgency; the role of the US and the implications of its foreign policy in Pakistan; the global war on terror and the implications of war in Afghanistan. However, an attempt is also made to include wider relevant phenomena — the existence of IDPs, the rise of Jihadist ideologies within women's in Pakistan, the economic situation concerning US aid packages and the analysis of the nuclear security issue amid mounting international concerns. The Epilogue then summarizes and concludes the debate, and makes further recommendations. Readers are stimulated to draw their own conclusions by comparing and analyzing the debates covered in this book.

One of the many benefits of this book is its uniqueness from other published material. It is the first serious, edited volume that includes both Pakistani and Western experts writing on this issue, and it offers an academic and coherent format of enquiry, with a critical perspective. Most of the material published on the topic, the predominant journalistic discourse and the few worthy academic books, cover some aspects of the current crisis but remain more selective in their nature — a selective or exclusive focus on the militancy, the Pakistan army, Afghan Jihad, or the origin and ideology of Pakistani state — and don't adequately provide an in-depth and thorough analysis of each phenomenon that has contributed to the current crisis. This book provides a unique chance for the reader to indulge in a wider analysis of different aspects of this crisis. The book is also an easy read; after reading the Introduction, readers can choose the topics they most desire to read about, as each phenomenon is discussed in its exclusivity. Hence, instead of dividing the book into different parts, I have purposely left it open for the reader to choose as they desire. The reader, however, must engage fully with each chapter of the book as each of them cover a very important dimension and aspect of the crisis. To make things even easier, each chapter starts with an "abstract" that summarizes the main theme and key discussions of the chapter.

Chapter 1 starts with a discussion of the "identity crisis" that has plagued Pakistan since its foundation. The chapter discusses and explains the larger debate on Islam and democracy and explores how ideologically driven "identity crisis" is one of the fundamental components of this crisis. Chapter 2 evaluates the outcome of the US Af-Pak policy and Pakistan's counter-terrorism response and discusses the current and future discourses of the Obama administration's foreign policy and the US-led war on terror and its implications in Pakistan. Chapter 3 analyzes the current and future effects of the war on terror on Pakistan's economy and evaluates the role and impacts of international aid packages. Chapter 4 deals in detail with the problems, failures and successes of the army in tackling Pakistan's most serious threat, that of enraging militancy and evaluates the previous, current and future capabilities of the Pakistani army to fight urban warfare. Chapter 5 provides the genesis of both nationalist and transnationalist Jihadism in Pakistan, and looks into the history, repercussions and dangers of these elements" presence and activities in Pakistan. Chapter 6 exclusively focuses on al-Qaeda's network in the Federally Administered Tribal Areas (FATA) and evaluates its repercussions domestically, regionally and globally. Chapter 7 analyzes the safety and security of Pakistan's nuclear arsenal in the light of international concerns and propaganda and evaluates Pakistan's command and control system, the multilayered safety mechanisms and contingency planning. Chapter 8 discusses the "politics of IDPs" in this wider conflict and evaluates the impacts of previous, current and future wave of IDPs and its fallouts in Pakistan, and evaluates the wider framework of the "US-led war on terror." Chapter 9 addresses the wider concerns of an "existential threat" to Pakistan and the prospect of an Islamist takeover of the country, and considers the likelihood of three possible paths to this outcome: Islamist civil war (the current situation in the North-West Frontier Province [NWFP]), Islamist revolution (the Iranian model), or an Islamist electoral victory (the Algerian model). Chapter 10 analyzes the psyche and ideology of Tehreek-e-Taliban Pakistan [TTP], and, by placing TTP in its geo-political context, considers the emergence of Islamic extremism generally in Pakistan, and also explains the origins of TTP as a distinct faction. Chapter 11 looks at how women in Pakistan have gradually contributed to notions of divine will as being paramount in determining social and political structures, and, in the process, have promoted orthodox understandings of Islamic identities and Jihadist ideologies. The Epilogue summarizes the whole debate.

Notes

1   Mohammad Ayoob. *The Third World Security Predicament: State Making, Regional Conflict, and the International System*. Lynne Rienner Publishers, 1995.
2   Ken Booth. *Theory of World Security*. Cambridge University Press, 2007.
3   Richard Jackson. "Regime security," in Alan Collins (ed.), *Contemporary Security Studies*. Oxford University Press, 2007.

CHAPTER ONE

Pakistan's Salvation: Islam or Western Inspired Secular-liberal Democracy?

Usama Butt

Abstract

Pakistan has been the victim of an "identity crisis" since its foundation. The only supposedly Islamic ideological state by birth cannot yet decide whether it's an Islamic state par excellence or a Western-modelled secularist democracy, where the majority of the populace happen to practice Islam. The author, while considering the larger debate on Islam, secularism and democracy, explains why neither Islamic and secularist experiences in their totality have been successful either in Pakistan or elsewhere in the Islamic world and how this has led to the formation of the current crisis that the country is facing today. The overall argument is that the ideologically driven identity crisis, deepened by the usage of "Islam" in the services of different regimes, has led to the current turmoil, and that Pakistan's salvation lies in addressing hardcore realist questions — the role of religion in the running of state, Islam vs. secularism democracy and the ultimate question of identity.

Introduction

The events of 9/11 reshaped global politics and re-ignited the question of identity in Pakistan. Musharraf's supposed U-turn amid successful US coercion and his admiration towards Kemalism while simultaneously taking part in back-door diplomacy with the religious parties only exacerbated that dilemma. In the years that followed, the issue of identity unfolded wide open with the birth of Tehreek-e-Taliban Pakistan (TTP), who demanded their own version of "Sharia and nothing but Sharia" in the guise of fighting the "US collaborating" Pakistani state. This demand went hand in hand with other such groups, like Tehreek-e-Nifaz-e-Shariat-e-Muhammadi (TNSM), who had already been fighting for a Sharia-based system in their respective territorial settings. The short-lived Nizam-e-Adl Regulation, coupled with Taliban's "capture" of cities "very close to Islamabad" sent shock waves globally, with a media frenzy focusing on the possible "Shariatisation" of Pakistan.

The post-9/11 era in Pakistan has been directly and indirectly mired with the issue of "identity" based on the Islamic ideology. The more liberated media, which broke the old taboos and "openly" discussed issues like the secularist Pakistani state, liberal democratic model and of course a complete Islamic theocracy, highlighted the simmering issue of an identity crisis. This went hand in hand with the first ever religious and Islamist opposition in the Pakistani Parliament, where Muttahida Majlis-e-Amal (MMA), while achieving around 11 percent of the popular vote, succeeded to form two provincial governments. The country was once again divided over the issue of its identity. Its ruler was a Kemalist-inspired "liberal" dictator who ruled with a loose alliance of feudalistic and opportunistic secular politicians, while its opposition consisted of a religious and Islamist-based alliance, and its mountains were filled with both transnationalist Jihadists — al-Qaeda — and nationalist Jihadists — TTP. This epoch probably sums up the wider issue of "identity" in Pakistan. There are and have been at any given time Islamists, fundamentalists, secularists and ethnic groups, contesting each other over the ideological boundaries of the Islamic Republic, a trend that started as early as the country's foundation.

However, in the centre of this debate is a larger issue of Islam and secularism or Islam and Western-inspired secular democracy. Once more, the contemporary debate in Pakistan loosely revolves around Islam and liberal democracy, where neither Islam nor democracy is properly defined. Almost everyone, including the government, the political parties, Ulema, the Islamists, the Jihadists, and ethnic-based groups have their set of explanations for both phenomenons. The Afghan Jihad, the country, which had already experienced a wave of radical Islam, is now facing a radical attitude towards secularism or Western-inspired democracy as well. Almost all of the noteworthy material published by Pakistani academics and journalists alike comes to the conclusion of the dire need of a liberal/secular democratic Western model. Radical Islamists or Jihadists, on the other hand, call the very notion "kufr" (non-belief), and are furiously engaged in promoting their own brand of Sharia as the solution. Overwhelmed by the struggle of these two radicals are the mainstream Islamists, Jamaat-e-Islami (JI) and its ilk, who have been unable to openly condemn or endorse either side.

Contemporary Pakistani writers like Hussain Haqqani[1] and his ilk rightly observe that the Islamic ideological discourses were "fiercely" used by the elite for the state foundation and cementation, but either willingly or ignorantly forget to observe that the same phenomenon had and was about to occur elsewhere in the Muslim world too. Although Pakistan does stand uniquely as the "only" modern Islamic nation state founded in the name of Islam, almost all other Muslim states from the Middle East to Southeast Asia also used Islamic discourse in their freedom struggles from their respective colonialist powers; even the staunchest of secular regimes like Algeria, Tunisia and Egypt.[2] Similarly, these ideologies are not only being contested in Pakistan; almost every other Muslim country is facing a similar "dilemma."

The equation of this identity crisis cannot then be successfully explained and analyzed if we constrain ourselves to the territorial setting of Pakistan. We must also pay attention to the rest of the Islamic world, not only because of the religious affiliations and the shared histories between us, but also because most Muslim countries, particularly in the Middle Eastern region, have struggled under the same or similar colonial powers as Pakistan. If Pakistan is to be a Western-modelled secularly democratic state, then a brief analysis of such experience in the other Muslim countries will provide some answers to both proponents and opponents of such a system in Pakistan. This chapter, thus, while discussing the larger debates on religion, Islam and secularism in the contemporary world, starts looking briefly at the secularist's experiences of other Muslim nation states and the response in the shape of Islamist resurgences. The chapter also analyzes different epochs of this identity crisis in Pakistan, starting from its foundation until the current time. The findings are then applied to the current turmoil, while discussing how and why the current crisis was created from the composition of the ideologically driven identity crisis, Islam in the service of regimes and the Western, particularly US, "interests" in the region. This is followed by a conclusion that discusses the future fallouts of this phenomenon.

Revival of Religion and the Making of Secularism in the Islamic and Western world

The world today is not secular but furiously religious.[3] The Christian world itself is divided on the issue of religion and secularism. A quick review of the non-monolith Christian world reveals a wave of renewed religiosity/ Evangelicalism, that has now expanded from North America (around 40–50 million Evangelists)[4] to Southeast Asia. Even Western Europe is not fully immune to this phenomenon, as the Church still retains its capability to influence society (although without reasonable successes), through independent educational and charitable projects in which the state does not interfere. In fact a vital ingredient of Western secularism is the "compromise" between the Church and the state, where the Church retains semi-total autonomy on the matters of religion by staying apolitical. Even the "beacon of democracy," the US, is by any comparison one of the most religious nations in the world, with avowed Evangelists and committed Christian Zionists who affect both its domestic and foreign policy agendas.

The other major religious revival is the Islamic resurgence or Islamism that swept through most of the Muslim capitals in the post-Caliphate era. We will turn to Islamism later in the paper but here we will note that the political vacuum left by the fall of Caliphate, deep awareness of Islamic decline, together with anti-colonial sentiments helped in creating this modern-religious resurgence. Today, Islamism is a major force to be reckoned with in almost all Muslim countries, as well as with Muslims in the West.

Amid this renewed religiosity in both the Muslim and Christian worlds, the fact, however, remains that modern political entities are predominantly secularists and their "secularism" is unequivocally translated and related to modernism to such an extent that any anti-secular motion is promptly considered anti-modern and regressive. This secularism is coupled with the "liberalist age," which seeks to promote its own version of secularist "democracy" in order to control the "anarchy" in the world, while believing in the "democratic peace" theory, which denotes that "democracies do not fight with other democracies"; a fair statement that quite happily ignores the fact that "democracies" are always more than happy and to jump in to a fight with "non-democracies." This liberalist-promoted secularism is seen as the only real alternative to modernity and progress in the contemporary world, and as mentioned above, any anti- or non-secular polity is considered anti-modern, regressive and fundamentalist. In practise, however, the situation is somewhat different. Evangelicals and Christian Zionists for instance are not considered "anti-modern," no matter how radically religious or anti-secular they may be, neither is Zionist Israel, which has a considerable majority of right-wing, extremely religious Jews. But when it comes to the Islamic world the labels are many. These labels are coupled with a virtual and practical onslaught of Western-style "democracy," by the leverages of both "soft" and "hard" powers.

So how and why is the Islamic world seen as anti-modern and regressive; in dire need of Western liberal/secular "democracy"? The answer is multi-faceted; first, secularism is the measure through which the Islamic world is weighed, which completely overlooks the historical process of state formation and nationhood in the Muslim world. This is due to the very fact that secularism is "timeless" in essence and history; historical sociology plays almost no part in its philosophy. Second, "anti-Muslimism" plays another vital role in this equation. The Christian West, as Fred Halliday notes, remains fearful of Islam, as it once was against the Medieval Islamic Spain and the Ottoman Empire.[5] This fear is then systematically translated by Islamophobic scholars like Bernard Lewis, Samuel Huntington and Daniel Pipes. Third, extreme forms of Islamist Jihadist ideology and practices, which unsurprisingly are extremely anti-secular, only affirm the notion of many in the West that the Islamic world is anti-modern and in dire need of a Western "democracy." Finally, complete ignorance of the historical processes of the contemporary construct of both Islamic and Western civilizations creates further ambiguities. The Western secularism, for instance, was constructed in the post-Renaissance and Enlightenment era, against an extremely anti-reason and anti-science church. Islamic historical experience on the contrary is completely different. The Islamic world has always been, at least until the gunpowder revolution, extremely pro-reason and pro-science. The practice of reason that outdated "qiyas" (the traditional set frame of thinking), initiated by Ibn-e-Hazm in the tenth century, for example, saw its glory through Ibn-e-Rushd (or Averroes), whose writings founded the very basis of Western renaissance. Lets not forget, when the whole of Europe was stuck in the "Dark Ages," the Islamic world was the epicenter of science, rationalism and reason.

So why should the Islamic world borrow a liberal secular model from the West? Surely it ought to look at its own experiences of reason, rationality and scientific enquiry first? Islamic political theory and philosophy have different points of origin and enquiry and cannot be expected to conform to Western-inspired models. Islam's early experience of reason, rationality and scientific enquiry shows that reason does not have to be irreligious and Godless to achieve "modernity" and scientific success. After all, it was not a Muslim practice to burn men of science as "heretics" but Muslim regimes, no matter how dynastical, did encourage scientific enquiry and reason, and so did Muslim civil society.

We also must pay attention to Europe's secularist journey to its contemporary construct. The answer, as we briefly noted earlier, lies in the Western historical journey out of the Dark Ages towards reason that resulted in an imminent clash with the religion that was then represented by the Catholic Church. The Christian West had to pay a very high price for this transition — countless religious wars that finally led to the Treaty of Westphalia. This whole experience created an anti-Church and anti-religious behaviour that was only cemented by the fallout of the French Revolution. Islamic civilization, on the other hand, did not have to fight for reason and modernity; it reinvented it through cultural and academic revolutions like the age of translations.

To summarize, if the point of "secularism" is modernity and reason, then the Islamic world has a much better and quite different historical experience than the West. Almost all recent Islamic reformers, (Afghani, Abduh, Sir Syed Ahmed) were inherent modernists. The resurgence of religion in both the Islamic and Christian worlds also means that the world isn't profoundly secular either, as it is often portrayed. Religion has now undoubtedly become one of the most dynamic features of global politics. With such contradictory historical constructs and today's profoundly religious world, the proponents of Western-inspired secular democracy in Pakistan either have no rationality in their argument or no argument in their rationality. Irreligious secularism in the Muslim world has only produced dictatorial Bolshevik-style rulers, as the following pages will portray.

Radicalism Begets Radicalism: Secularism in
the Post-Caliphate Muslim World

Today, with the backdrop of raging fundamentalisms and radicalisms, the question of a secular Pakistan is contended more than ever. Although Pakistan was formed as an ideological state, secularism did manage to get some hold within the Pakistani elite, however, Pakistani secularist experience wasn't in totality as it was in some other Muslim countries in North Africa, Levant and Central Asia. It did nonetheless play a significant role along with the Islamic ideology in the post-independence era. The question of a "truly" secularly democratic Pakistani must consider the experiences and outcomes of other Islamic states, not only because they share a common religion but also because, as we noted above, they went through the same independence struggle (against the very same or similar colonial powers) as Pakistan. The result of secular experiences in other Muslim states can provide ample answers for the proponents and indeed opponents of the secularized democratic model in Pakistan.

Unlike the Pakistani state, which was solely formed on ideological grounds, most Muslim states applied Islamic rhetoric for their nationalist struggles. States such as Egypt, Tunisia, Algeria and even Turkey (where Said Nuri's mixed nationalist-cum-Islamist discourse was adopted by Mustapha Kemal Atatürk)[6] that are staunchly secular today nonetheless applied Islamic themes to their independence struggles. The Algerian independence struggle was called a "Jihad" and was wholly supported by the Ulema, and the Egyptian struggle had the full support and backing of Islamists and the Muslim Brotherhood (MB). However, after independence, the ruling elites decided to turn to the "secularist" model, based on the West, under the guise of pursuing "modernity." This secularism, however, was starkly different from the Western secularism that enhanced a compromising stance between the Church and the state, as explained earlier. The "secularism" that many Muslim states adopted was nothing less than radical in its nature, as it saw a radical break from centuries of strong Islamic tendencies and practices. As François Burgat states:

> Paradoxically, immediately after political independence, the culture of the coloniser enjoyed a new success . . . Mass education mean that 20 years after independence there were 10 times more French speakers in the Maghreb, installed with western philosophy than there had been during colonial times . . . the prestigious Zeitouna University was closed. The nationalists Habib Bourguiba was not afraid to sacrifice 12 centuries of local university tradition, something that even the colonisers would not have dared to do.[7]

Apart from the cultural onslaught that continues now, political onslaught labeled any opponents of the regime "enemies of democracy and freedom." This resulted in a Bolshevik-style radical and militant secularism that would provide dictator after dictator, a chance to suppress any political opposition in the name of protecting "freedom" and "democracy."

To start with, in Egypt, which obtained its independence from the very same British rule as Pakistan, Hassan al-Banna's social movement was seen as a severe threat by the King's government. His Muslim Brotherhood (MB) joined the independence struggle with the Free Officers Movement, which used strong Islamic rhetoric for its independence movement. The alliance, however, would soon fall apart, with the Islamists quickly becoming sceptical of leader Gamal Abdel Nasser's socialist pan-Arabism and realizing that he was only interested in "Islam" to legitimize his coup against the King's government. What followed was the severe suppression of the MB's members by the state, including a ban on its political activities, and a socialist dictatorship headed by Nasser that suppressed any political opposition and lasted till his death. The MB, however, would accumulate enough social capital through its charity and welfare work to make it the only viable political opposition in the country within a few years of its independence.[8]

The continuous repression of the movement, however, led to an already existent hardcore and disenfranchised faction within the MB to become even more ultra-radical. Syed Qutb's ideology of "Jahiliyya" and his execution by the state started a chain reaction that resulted in the creation of more ultra-radical groups, like the Society of Muslims and "Takfir wal Hijra" (Excommunication and Exodus), Islamic Jihad and Abdel Salam Al-Faraj's "Jama'a al-Jihad." Nasser's humiliating defeat in the Six-Day War finally crushed pan-Arab ideology, and in his early years his predecessor Anwar el Sadat did what most of his counterparts in Pakistan had been doing all along — "out Islaming the Islamists." He portrayed himself as a "believing president" and gave free reign in his early era to "Islamic Jihad" to function in the universities as a countermeasure against the leftist influence.[9] What followed was a similar "identity crisis" amid Sadat's shift from Eastern to Western Bloc. The country was now simultaneously fighting over its Arab, Islamic, Ancient Egyptian and modern secularist "identity" fronts. Sadat's fallout with the Islamists even before his "historical" visit to Israel started the circle of repression once again, only this time, the radical groups within the MB splintered from the mother organization and formed militant movements, ending in President Sadat's assassination in 1981. Amongst these radical slinter groups was Ayman al-Zawahiri, who would later become al-Qaeda's chief ideologue.

The radical secularism in Maghreb also helped in producing radical Jihadism. As noted earlier, although Islamic ideological discourses were extensively used during the independence struggles, they were soon to be replaced by authoritarianism under the cloak of "secularism" and "modernity" after independence. During the early years this was confined to the cultural and political onslaughts, but things were to change dramatically, particularly in Algeria after the massive victory of the Islamist Salvation Front (FIS) in the early 90s. The military regime, fully supported by the West (particularly France), not only denied the FIS its well-deserved victory but also used mass imprisonment and torture in the name of saving "democracy" and "freedom." A circle of violence ensued, and the Algerian state accused Islamists of rampaging into villages and killing innocent civilians, while the same allegation was levied on the army and the state by the Islamists and many other independent observers. The violence in Algeria continues today, although Islamists who were once a political entity are now sidelined by the radicals — al-Qaeda sympathizers, splinter groups, etc. It is the same story in Morocco and in Tunisia, where Al-Nahda's political persecution and the exile of its leader, Sheikh Rachid Al-Ghannouchi (who is a leading pro-democracy Islamist), has created further radical and Jihadists factions, which are now loosely or totally in alliance with al-Qaeda, whilst Al-Nahda, amid continuous state repression, finds it hard to contain or challenge such radical splinter groups.

The experience of Turkey was quite different. Although Nuri and Kemal used Islamic rhetoric in the beginning, Atatürk would soon break with anything that was affiliated with religion and abolish the political institution of Caliphate, which had started after the death of the Prophet some 13 centuries ago. What followed was the establishment of a radical secular state that persecuted people for anything that was deemed "religious" — the wearing of traditional fez, or the call to prayers in Arabic, which was changed to Turkish language, and changed its script from Arabic to Latin. Although radical Kemalism did not create such a radical response as that in Egypt or in Maghreb for instance, Islamism as a major political force was back within a few decades of the country's modern foundation. The process of Islamism that started in the '70s reached its climax with Refah, under Necmettin Erbakan, in power in the early '90s. Refah's dismissal by the radical-secularist military didn't stop this process but helped only in bringing the AK Party to the power corridors, that has ruled Turkey for the last few years and has consolidated its hold on power by appointing Abdullah Gul as President and by putting the ultra-radical secularist network, "Ergenekon," that consists of retired army generals, businessmen and politicians, amongst others, on trial.

It is pretty much the same picture in the newly independent Central Asian states such as Uzbekistan, where "secularist" dictatorships have persecuted any religion-oriented parties on the grounds of "defending freedom." With thousands imprisoned and murdered, it is no surprise that radical militant reactionary groups like the Islamic Movement of Uzbekistan (IMUs) and its ilk are now in arms with al-Qaeda.

In short, whenever the secularist model has been followed in the Muslim world the results are the same — dictatorial and tyrannical regimes, political and cultural suppression, and the birth of radicalism and militancy. From Syria, where Hafiz Al Assad killed thousands of "Islamists" in Hama, to Iraq, where Saddam Hussein's dictatorship lasted for nearly three decades, to the Central Asian tyrannical regimes that continue in their heavy-handed political suppression and the North African and Turkish experiences; secularism has only brought dictatorship, tyranny and cultural genocide to the Muslim world and is directly responsible for the creation of ultra-radical Jihadist reactionary groups. The only feasible exception may have been the Indonesian Nahdatul Ulama under President Wahid, but that secularist experience was starkly different from those mentioned above and included strong Islamic discourses, political pluralism and a religious freedom to a certain extent. However it still failed to accumulate a vibrant "secular" society and radical Jihadism has now taken its toll. The country has recently seen a renewed battle of Islamic "identity" and an extension of radical and Jihadists groups.

Secular Liberal or "Islamic" Democracy?

The question of democracy and Islam deserves much more space than is available, and it is required for the purpose of our study. Today almost all political parties in Pakistan, even the Islamist Jemaah Islamiah (JI) or traditionalist Jamiat Ulema-e-Islam (JUI), accept the "legitimacy of democracy," at least in theory. When the Pakistani politician Benazir Bhutto was killed in 2008, her widower (the President) and son declared democracy to be the best "revenge." So are we today witnessing the "revenge" of democracy at its best in Pakistan, where (at the time of writing) the only real concern of the regime is associated with maintaining its hold on the power? The failure of this (Pakistan Peoples Party) government's "democracy" is not limited to the "regime security," a stance that it shares with all previous "democratic" governments, but it also includes dynastical politics, failure of national reconciliation amid out of control insurgency and failing economic policies.

Pakistan is one of the few "Islamic" countries where "democracy" seems to be somewhat "Islamised" by the elite and the political parties. The role model for this "democracy" is the West, where its most important ingredient, of course, is "secularism." Pakistan's stance on democracy is, however, unusual in comparison to other fellow Muslim "democratic" countries, where democracy is mostly staunchly secular in nature, as we explored above. Similarly, the question of secular democracy in Pakistan always remained purposefully ambiguous, as it suited most political entities, but it kept popping up time and again. Today there are three predominant groups regarding the issue: the primary group, who are called "Muslim democrats" by Peter Mandaville and others,[10] includes mainstream political parties such as Muslim League Nawaz and Muslim League Quaid-e-Azam and can even include the Islamists and religious parties such as JI and JUI in a sense of political participation; the second group is led by the "secular democrats" and includes the ruling

Peoples Party, Awami National Party (ANP) and the Muttahida Qaumi Movement (MQM); and the third group consists of "anti-democrats," which is a loose alliance of both nationalists and transnationalist Jihadist groups like al-Qaeda, TTP and sectarian groups like the banned Sipah-e-Sahaba Pakistan (SSP), Sipah-e-Muhammad Pakistan (SMP) and Lashkar-e-Taiba. All aforementioned groups nonetheless use Islamic discourses in their respective political struggles. The definition of "democracy," however, is contested by each group. Muslim democrats, for instance, see Islam being compatible to democracy and are often happy to work within the system, whereas secular democrats do not necessarily share the radical views of their peers in other Islamic countries. However, the last group is by definition and by practice "anti-democratic," and falls under the general "rejectionists" category.

Therefore, the question of "democracy" is absolutely crucial for Pakistan's future and the current situation requires serious and urgent answers of "whose Islam" and "which democracy," which isn't possible without defining "democracy" in its contemporary sense. Today's democracy, projected by the West, is entirely different in theory and practice. In theory it derives its power from the people or through the majority rule and includes freedom of speech, rule of law, equality and justice, but in practice it is consumerist, capitalist and mercantilist in nature.[11] Today's democracy is synonymous with statism and capitalism and thrives on liberalist ideology that seeks to "control" anarchy in the world by the "spread of democracy." But as Ken Booth rightly points out, "today powerful democracies have become associated with a 'Galbraith's culture of contentment' in which protecting the well-off few (western states) has become the 'essential business of elections, the economy and foreign and defence policy, as the 'rich world, living in their culture of contentment, look(ed) increasingly the smug occupation of a lifeboat, while all around thrash(ed) about for survival, or sank, with screams unheard."[12]

Today we live in a world that is ruled by a "democratic West," which works exclusively for itself, and it is the West that is ultimately "civilized," while the South, as the West or North sees it, is inherently "violent" by nature and is ridden with conflict, war and diseases. Western armies are only too keen to "keep the violent peace" by threatening to launch its armed forces anywhere in the world where their "interest" are affected.[13] There is no sense of "responsibility" towards the "violent South" in the West either, as it has shrugged off its colonial past and imperialistic present that contributed/contributes toward the South's problems of poverty, hunger and conflicts. Another theory asserts that the Western world has gone through centuries of bloodshed to achieve its "democracy," but expects the South to do so within years, but does it really? Even a superficial analysis of the Western-promoted "democratic model" would demonstrate that this "export" is not all-encompassing but is only imposed when Western interests are threatened. Africa, Maghreb, Central Asia and Southeast Asia for instance, are usually left out by such export of "democracy." The West, for instance, was only too keen to protect Algerian dictator General Pervez Musharraf's "democracy," but when Hamas came to power through a very fair democratic process, it collaborated with Israel to overthrow the government with an economic embargo that crippled the Gazan population and renewed a radical and Jihadist tendency in the region and beyond.

What sort of "democracy" does the West wish to see in the East, particularly in the Muslim world? The Western-projected model of "democracy" as we noted above only serves its own interests in the world, while the rest of humanity suffers. Similarly, the Islamic world, in another common perception, has all too often been subjected to this "democratic" onslaught — but has it really? What about the tyrannical regimes in Maghreb, North Africa, the Middle East and Central Asia, where despite paying lip service to "democracy," the West is all too happy to continue supporting dictators and tyrants?

Therefore, if Pakistan is to be a Western-modelled "democracy" then it has to be for the right reasons and it must include Islam in the equation. On the other hand, if Pakistan is to be an "Islamic-democracy" then this cannot be so unless the equation of "Islam and democracy" is defined. This leads us to analyze the "Islamic" nature of "democracy," as it is commonly portrayed (except by rejectionists and anti-democratic Jihadists) by various groups in Pakistan. To do so, we must examine both philosophical and operational aspects of democracy and their compatibility with Islam. To start with the Islamic concepts of "shura" (consultation) and "ijma" (consensus), some mainstream Islamists or jurists, Shiekh al-Ghannouchi, Adel Hussain and Sheikh Qardawi for example, see no issue in democracy's compatibility with Islam besides "language" or "grammar," as the principles of shura and ijma to them are very close to contemporary "democratic" practices.[14] It is a similar discourse to that of other mainstream Islamist parties, such as the MB, which proclaims that "Umma is the base of Sulta [political power],"[15] the JI, which is only too happy to participate in a democratic process, the AK Party, which works within the system, or the Malaysian Parti Islam Se-Malaysia (PAS), which actively promotes pluralism.

However, this discourse is predominantly operational or institutional, philosophically there is some degree of controversy over the question of Islam and democracy.[16] This is the result of the aforementioned "secular" nature of democracy and the issue of the "sovereignty" of God over people. The confusion only grows, as throughout history "sovereignty" in Muslim countries in theory belonged to God, but in practice belonged to the "ruler," with few exceptions. There is also the question of Sharia law and its place in Muslim societies and politics. Again, throughout Islamic history Sharia remained an integral ingredient of both civil society and politics, however, it was both the civil society and the state that implemented Sharia rather than the state on its own; most rulers would rather have their own "laws" implemented, as a strict adherence to Sharia would have denied them total "regime security" and would have left them open to "muhasiba" (accountability).[17] Hence, the "philosophical" aspect has often played out not only amongst Islamists, i.e. formation of a "moderate" AK Party from the "traditionalist" Refah led by Erbakan, a split up of JI and the creation of Tehreek-e-Islami in Pakistan, emergence of a pro-democratic "Wasat party" in Egypt that splintered from MB on such issue, a recent reported resignation of MB's supreme guide Muhammad Akef to a more moderate al-Erian et; but on a larger scale encompassing jurists, ulema, governments etc. as well.

To summarize the "philosophical" aspect and the larger debate on the issue, the fact remains that on the "philosophical" question, both groups (the former that see Islam being compatible to democracy and the latter who have serious concerns over its secular nature) are somewhat correct in their assertions. Islamic concepts like shura and ijma are very close to contemporary democratic principles. On the other hand, it is also true, as we explained earlier, that irreligious secularity remains an important part of Western democracy. "Operationally," however, we must also consider the assertions of European security schools like the Welsh and Copenhagen schools, that the liberalist "democratic model" is exclusively working for the

West and is directly responsible for most of the world's problems today. As we explained above, today's democracy is very much about "liberalists" and "consumerists," and it is absolutely correct to question the motives behind the Western "democratic" onslaught on the Muslim world, particularly with its overwhelming support of almost all Muslim tyrants and dictators who proclaim to be "democrats."

Pakistanis that still believe in a dominant role of religion in politics[18] are now bombarded with the extreme ideologies of the secularists, who are becoming more and more radical, on par with "rejectionists" (such as TTP, who view any kind of democracy as "haram" [forbidden]). The question of Islam and democracy urgently needs clarity. When considering the possibility of "democracy" in Pakistan, one should look to the worst secular experiences in other Muslim countries. One should also address the Western motives behind its projection and consider operational and philosophical experiences and debates on the matter, but above all it should not blindly follow the West, whose secularist "democracy" is historically all too different, irreligious, power hungry and selfish, and has been used and continues to be used as a pretext for the advancements of its own interests. In short, democracy is neither "Islamic" nor "un-Islamic" but contains elements of both within it. It is this complex nature that creates complexities for both proponents and opponents of it in Pakistan, who, in most cases, possess a very peripheral knowledge of this very ambiguous debate.

However, the role of Islam and democracy cannot be debated and established in Pakistan unless the role and the ideal of the state is established first — is Pakistan an Islamic state or a secularist "democratic" state that happens to have a predominantly Muslim population? It is this identity crisis to which we will turn to next.

Pakistan: Identity Crisis or Identity of "Crisis"?

Pakistan, amongst many other Muslim countries, has been and still is faced with an ideologically driven "identity crisis" — so much so that the issue of "identity" has virtually created a lingering state of "crisis," which started as early as its foundation and continues to haunt the country today in the form of different insurgencies, political ambiguities and calls for complete

Islamization or secularisation. One of the main reasons for this crisis is Pakistan's ideological formation under the pretext of the "two nation theory" (or the Ideology of Pakistan), which asserted that Muslims in India have a distinctive Islamic identity and are so inherently different from Hindus both culturally and religiously that they would not have been able to live together in the post-colonial period. The architect of this theory was the Islamic-oriented philosopher and poet Muhammad Iqbal; however, it was also an indirect result of the Aligarh movement started by a leading reformer Sir Syed Ahmed Khan as well as the foundation of the Muslim League in 1906. Sir Syed, like other Islamist-oriented reformers such as Jamal-ud-Din al-Afghani and Muhammed Abduh, launched his reformist movement against the backdrop of the declining Islamic civilization in general and the fading Muslim power base in the subcontinent in particular.

The Pakistani state was then carved out from the Muslim majority areas, which resulted in the creation of a Western and Eastern Pakistan whose populations were at best heterogeneous. Islamic ideology, by any account, was the best available "combining factor" and a unifier that the Muslim League used extensively during and after the independence in its political struggle. Islamic ideological discourses, therefore, were at the forefront of Muhammed Ali Jinnah's many pre-independence speeches and statements, such as his famous "two nation theory" speech, delivered in Lahore on March 23, 1940, which echoed Iqbal's cultural argument:

> The Hindus and Muslims belong to two different religious philosophies, social customs, and litterateurs. They neither intermarry nor intertwine together and, indeed, they belong to two different civilizations which are based mainly on conflicting ideas and conceptions. Their aspect on life and of life is different. It is quite clear that Hindus and Mussalmans derive their inspiration from different sources of history. They have different epics, different heroes, and different episodes.[19]

He went on to say, "We do not want any flag excepting the league flag of Crescent and star. Islam is our guide and complete core of our life. We do not want any red or yellow flags. We do not want any isms, Socialism, Communism or nationalist's socialism."[20]

Jinnah and his party the Muslim League also clearly emphasized and defined the role of religion and the Islamic ideology in the running of the future state. In another one of his pre-independence speeches, for instance, he noted:

> The injunctions of the Qur'an are not confined to religious and moral duties. The Qur'an is a complete code for the Muslims — a religious, social, civil, commercial, military, judicial, and criminal and penal code. It regulates every thing.[21]

Yet immediately after independence, he tried to water down the Islamic ideological dimension that he himself had fiercely promulgated earlier on, in favor of a Western-style state. His August 11, 1948 speech is often quoted today by secularists:

> You may belong to any religion or caste or creed that has nothing to do with the business of the state. As you know, history shows that in England conditions some time ago were much worse than those prevailing in India today. The Roman Catholics and the protestants persecuted each other ... Thank God, we are not starting in those days, we are starting in the days when there is no discrimination, no distinction between one caste or creed and another. We are starting with this fundamental principle that we are all citizens and equal citizens of one state ... Now I think we should keep that in front of us as our ideal and you will find that in course of time Hindus would cease to be Hindus and Muslim would cease to be Muslims, not in the religious sense, because that is the personal faith of each individual, but in the political sense as citizens of the state.[22]

Without going into a debate about whether Jinnah was an avowed secularist, Islamic-oriented or a mixture of both, two things are very clear; first, that the primary force behind both Jinnah's and the Muslim League's independence struggle was Islamic ideology and second, his early death in 1948, shortly after the above noted speech, left many questions unanswered, particularly to what extent was Islam to play a role in the running of the state? This ideological equation has since been contested by Islamists, secularists and Muslim democrats alike for their respective political purposes.

In the post-independence period, the absence of the "great leader" and the confusion left behind him by his ambiguous statements on the matter and the question of the extent of the role of religion in the running of state, started to play out in the open. Islamic scholar Maulana Maududi, for instance, after initially rejecting Jinnah's "religious nationalism"[23] moved to the "land of pure" nonetheless to join hands with the Ahrars, for the Islamization of the country. Liaquat Ali Khan, Pakistan's first premier, was similarly all too eager to continue to promote Pakistan's Islamic ideology, but at the same time decided to align the country with the US as per strategic requirements. The army was not behind in its usage of the Islamic identity either, although being a "secular" institution in itself, it keenly promoted Islamic ideological discourses. In short, Islamic ideological discourses were strongly used not only by the Islamists but by army generals and politicians alike.

Islamic ideology, however, was severely contested by the secularist elements, which consisted of a loose alliance of the country's powerful bureaucrats, such as the Governor-General Ghulam Muhammad, and some Bengali and Pushtun politicians, such as Suharwardi and Abdul Ghaffar Khan. Together they led a chunk of both the Eastern and the Western halves of the Pakistani population onto a "secular" base by forming secular political parties like the Awami National Party in the West and the Awami League in the East. This, however, isn't to say that either the army or the Muslim League were "Islamists" or even Islamic-oriented, but both of the institutions have had a strong secularist representation (some of whom, such as General Ayub Khan, later came to power). The real difference, however, amongst the secularists and non-secularists (with the exception of a loose alliance of the Islamists and religious parties) was to do with the usage of Islamic ideological discourses, where the secularists rejected the notion of Islam as a "unifier" and the non-secularists (the Muslim League, the army, etc.) were somehow "compelled" to use the Islamic card, in order to unify hugely diverse and disparate groups and to create a Pakistani "nation."

In summary, the country that was created with fierce Islamic ideological discourses was divided soon after its independence, on the issue of its Islamic or secular identity. Maududi and his peers were soon to find out (in the first constitution of 1956) after their severe Islamization campaign, that Islamic ideology was the only available "unifier" that was used, first for the country's foundation, and second to create a "nation" that was ethnically, linguistically and culturally extremely diverse and divided. The failure of the Muslim League in the early years of independence to constructively and openly debate the issue, its unwillingness to create an open political atmosphere and its inability to address the concerns of its disenfranchised population would soon develop into a form of "identify crisis," where the Islamists felt betrayed (after a fierce Islamic ideological independence struggle and a severe Islamization campaign) on the extent of the role of religion involved in the running of the state, and the secularists similarly became annoyed at the inclusion of a part-Islamic ideology in the country's first constitution. This consitution was delayed for nearly a decade due to the very question of identity, and its emergence in the aftermath of a severe Islamist campaign against the Ahmadi sect gave the ruling secularist bureaucratic elite a chance first, to crackdown on the Islamists and second, to bring about a constitution that pleased nobody but themselves.

The usage of Islamic ideological discourses didn't stop there either, however, as almost every regime therein used Islam in the service of their regime security, which only exacerbated the question of identity because none of them were sincere in answering and addressing the all-important question of the role of Islam in the running of the Pakistani state.

Out-Islaming the Islamists: Islam in the Services of Regime Security

Throughout Islamic history, the Islamic card has been played by different regimes, whenever it suited or was required. Islamic ideological discourses were used extensively by dynastical, tyrannical and authoritative regimes to legitimize and protect their power bases and that trend continued during the anti-colonial struggle, as we explored earlier. Pakistan was no exception either, however, it departed from its contemporaries with the extent of its usage; where other Muslim countries used partial Islamic discourse in their respective independence struggles, the Pakistani elite relied solely on Islamic ideology for the country's foundations and for nation-building. Pakistan was founded "exclusively" for Muslims, a place where they could practice their religion freely, and it remains the only modern "Islamic" nation state founded in the name of Islam. However, the fact remains, as we explored above, that the Islamic ideology was at best politically motivated and used as a unifier. After its independence, Jinnah expected it to be a Western-modelled modern state, ignoring the strong Islamic ideological sentiments that he himself helped to create, while Maududi and his peers expected a "citadel of Islam" or an Islamic ideological state, while ignoring and overlooking the fact that most of the military, political and bureaucratic establishment had predominantly secular tendencies. Both sides continued their respective struggles nonetheless and were soon locked in an ideological contest that was to repeat itself over the course of the country's short history.

Amid the battle over the country's ideological boundaries, different regimes, including the secularists — Ayub, Bhutto, Yahya — as well as the so-called Islamic-oriented — Zia, Sharif — continually used the Islamic card. The country's first military ruler, Ayub Khan, for instance, started on a secularist bent, even removing the word "Islamic" from the country's official name (later reinstated as the Islamic Republic of Pakistan) but soon paid homage to the all-too-familiar Islamic ideological discourses during the Pakistan-India war in 1965, and promoted a pan-Islamic ideology in his foreign policy in order to gain strategic ground against India, while strengthening his alliance with the US. His predecessor, General Yahya, despite being an infamous drunk, used rigorous Islamic ideological statements against Bengali rioters, while his generals in East Pakistan fought an "ideological" battle against the "enemies of Islam," which worsened the already existent secular-Islamic ideological gulf, as the secular Mujeeb-ur-Rehman and his Awami National Party contested Islam's role as a unifier. Zulfikar Ali Bhutto, who became the new Pakistani premier in the aftermath of Eastern Pakistan's breakup, introduced "Islamic socialism" and now stands accused of giving in too too much to the Islamists.[24] Although an avowed secularist himself, he soon leaned towards an Islamic orientation, not only on strategic and economic grounds — to garner greater Arab support in the oil-boom period — but also to out-Islam the Islamists in their own game. His strategy of extended Islamic gestures — the Islamic summit in Lahore, declaring the "Ahmadi" sect non-Muslim in 1973 and declaring the country law a "Sharia law" — was very close to the strategy of the "believing President" Anwar el Sadat in Egypt, who hoped to reverse the affects of Nasserism by encouraging Islamist activists in the university campuses releasing them from prison. However, where both Sadat and Bhutto's real interest laid, as it was proved later on in their short-lived regimes, was the security of their regimes above all others. The ideological discourses and gestured concessions to the Islamists were given in the hope of keeping Islamists at bay and there was never any intention to address Islamic and ideological boundaries in either state. This strategy only backfired as the Islamists soon realized what was at play — the repercussions for both of the presidents were nothing less than fatal.

General Zia-ul-Haq was promoted by Bhutto over many of his superior officers because of his known religiosity, which Bhutto hoped would keep him away from a political power-grab, but in fact did exactly the opposite. Zia declared martial law and undertook what many commentators today refer to the "wave of severe Islamization." He furthered his predecessor's gestured Islamization process, but with the stark difference of being himself religious. He started off with the criminal code, which was still Anglo-Indian in nature, and introduced Islamic punishments — stoning for adulterers, amputation for thieves, whipping and finally the death penalty for blasphemous individuals. These punishments were hardly implemented at all, however, and family law remained outside their remit, as Marc Gaborieau notes:

> These decrees covered only a small — albeit very public — part of the legal system. Anglo-Indian law was still in force and ordinary courts continued to sit; the power of Sharia branches, attached to provincial courts to ensure that laws were in conformity with the Sharia-was limited to certain aspects of the law, mainly criminal law. Outside their remit were family law (where the Sharia had an elective status, as a result-strangely enough of Ayub Khan's modernist ordinances in 1961), tax and financial legislation and most procedural code.[25]

Zia's short-lived affair with the Islamists Jamaat-e-Islami (JI) was similarly against the backdrop of his regime's security, as JI, who initially joined very enthusiastically, soon realized that Zia was not necessarily truly interested in "Islamizing" Pakistan. However, JI and other religious parties soon reinstated their extended cooperation against the backdrop of Afghan Jihad, which gave Zia a free platform to play his Islamic card out. In Afghan Jihad not only Zia, but all other Muslim dictatorial and tyrannical regimes — Egypt, Algeria, etc. — saw a golden opportunity to dump their problems and

Afghanistan soon became the first real platform for modern transnational Jihadism. During Afghan Jihad, Islamic ideology was not only used by the Muslim regimes but also by the US, who equated Mujahideen to America's forefathers and only helped in further complicating the question of ideology and identity in Pakistan and Afghanistan. Zia's mysterious assassination brought back so-called "democratic" rule in Pakistan, and civilian premiers, particularly Nawaz Sharif, continued to play the Islamic card during the 1988 and 1990 elections and in the form of the Sharia Bill later on. Despite being "religious-minded," Sharif's style of politics was not only dynastical but also "commercial," as he was one of the country's leading businessmen. His government's authoritarian style led to his fallout with the judiciary, army and the Islamists alike.

Musharraf, despite being a proud Kemalist, played on the Islamic ideological discourses nonetheless, not only during the Kargil conflict, but even beyond 9/11, with a back-channel religious and Islamist alliance that continued until just before his departure. The current Asif Ali Zardari government has also played on the Islamic ideology but with a difference; it is in league with the Western governments' attempts to fight the "war on terror" on "religious grounds," by promoting the so-called "modernist" factions against the "fundamentalist" or "extremist" groups. The theory that is promoted by US think tanks like RAND and the Heritage Foundation[26] is now openly at play not only in the Western countries with meaningful Muslim minorities, like the UK where "radical modernists" such as Ed Husain and his ilk are being strongly promoted by the government, but also in Pakistan in the shape of the Sufi Advisory Council, where its fallouts have so far included numerous attacks on the Sufi's monasteries by the Taliban, the destruction of Sufi shrines, sectarianism and a further increase of ideological clashes. The Pakistani army, on a similar footing to the rejectionist TTP, calls its fight a "jihad" as well.

To summarize, the Islamic ideological card, used by almost every Pakistani regime in the services of their regime security, which has nothing to do with Islam or the Islamic ideology in itself and is one of the major reasons why the question of identity has become more ambiguous in Pakistan, particularly when neither of the regimes mentioned above were at all interested in seriously addressing the question of Islamic ideology or a secular democracy.

This exploitation of Islam has had, and will have, a major impact in Pakistan (amongst other Muslim countries) and its fallout includes the emergence and expansion of both national and transnational Jihadism, which we will discuss in detail below.

From Identity to Existential Crisis

Although contemporary Pakistani writers like Hussain Haqqani, Zahid Hussain, Ahmed Rashid and their ilk would be quick to name all that is wrong with the Islamic ideological discourses and with the lack of "liberal democracy," their analysis is seriously flawed, as it isn't the Islamic ideology, as we explored above, that has created the current turmoil, but it's the ad hoc usage of it by the different regimes for their specific needs. It is also not the lack of liberal democracy they would promulgate but the absence of defining what democracy would mean in a Muslim country in general, and in an ideological country like Pakistan in particular, that has further complicated things. Furthermore, the current crisis cannot be attributed to the usage of Islam as a "unifier," but Islam has always been the only viable unifier and it will remain so in the times to come. But when Muslim states use Islam for their regime security, they forget that a viable portion of their civil society consists of both religious-oriented people as well as the Islamists, who know exactly through their previous experiences what's at play, and they also ignore the fact that the "democracy" they wish to promulgate is severely dependent on that very civil society, so they end up either completely backtracking from any role of Islam in the state or society, or try to "out-Islam the Islamists," such as what has happened in places like Pakistan, Egypt and Jordan. Both roots, however, eventually end in further infuriating the existent identity crisis, as their sincerity only lay with the interests of their regime's security.

In short, the question of identity, not of Islamic ideology is the main reason behind the current turmoil. Almost all Muslim regimes, including Pakistan, are facing a tough identity crisis, which is a composite result of the unsettled question of whether the country should be Islamic or a secularist liberalist democracy, the usage of Islamic ideological discourses in the services of regime's security, the radical secularist elite who suppress anything that is synonymous with Islam to protect their authoritarian regimes and the

Western forces, who are only too keen to implement their brand of "democracy" in the Muslim countries, while playing openly on the question of "religion."

Hence, the nationalist and transnational Jihadist organizations operating within Pakistan are not there because Pakistan is an "ideological Islamic state" but because the question of identity was never properly addressed by any of the regimes, which only served their particular set of interests. It is also completely foolish to assert, in the light of our short case study of secularism in other Muslim countries, that if Pakistan became a secular state instead of an "ideological state" at the juncture of its foundation, the question of "Islam" would have simply disappeared. Pakistan cannot disassociate itself from the greater Middle East either, as a big chunk of its current territory became part of an Islamic empire as early as the eighth century.

We also cannot say with certainty that this identity crisis would have been averted if Pakistan was a practical Islamic ideological state, as there isn't any direct comparison so far to be made (the Iranian Revolution cannot be considered as it wasn't an Islamist but jurist revolution). However, some partial comparison can be drawn with the Ottoman Empire and its Vilayat system, where one's main identity was Muslim, and the extreme disparate groups spread from Central Asia to the greater Middle East could all somewhat affiliate themselves with the Caliphate. In the modern "sovereign" nation state context, however, the closest we got to an Islamist or Islamic regime was in Algeria. The Turkish AK Party is a questionable example — it can be argued that it has successfully used Islamic ideological discourses in its modern context but it cannot be made "the" example because the Turkish military and bureaucracy remains radically secularist, as does a portion of its civil society, and the AK Party works within that system. The Turkish Islamist experience will be interesting to observe in the future.

But can we confidently predict what would have happened if Pakistan was made a completely secular state, like other Muslim countries in Maghreb, the Middle East and Central Asia? Founded in the name of Islam, it could never be a truly "secularized" state; this would result in further chaos, as a majority of its population sees a very large role for Islam in the running of the Pakistani state, and its civil society consists of a vibrant Islamic-oriented community. The Islamists would undoubtedly challenge any acts of extreme irreligious secularity that may lead to further authoritarian regimes, such as that in Maghreb and North Africa, as the historical experiences have so far shown.

Similarly, equating Islamic ideology with the radical and Jihadists ideologies, as is the fashion today with Pakistani writers like Hussain Haqqani and Zahid Hussain, is to completely overlook and ignore the facts and the developments of the Islamist and Jihadist phenomenon in the greater Middle East. The radical and Jihadist ideologies were not developed in Pakistan but, as we explored above, are a combined result of radical secularism and the radical Islamist reaction in the heart of the Middle East. It was Syed Qutb, Abdel Salam al-Faraj, Shukri Mustafa, Al-Shiqaqi, Ayman Al-Zawahiri and Osama bin Laden (inspired by Maududi's teaching) and Egypt, Algeria and Saudi Arabia, not Pakistan, where the roots of current Jihadism and radicalism lie. It also completely ignores the role of Western colonialism and imperialism, which created a necessary space for the Islamist resurgence. Haqqani and his ilk find an easy scapegoat in Islamic ideology, as do most Western writers, without trying to engage in a necessary overall analysis of the historiography and historic sociology of the phenomenon.

And what about the Afghan Jihad and the Iranian Revolution, the two most important factors that helped in creating the radicalism and Jihadism of today? Was it not the Iranian Revolution (that occurred in the aftermath of strong Western interference in the country to secure its oil interests, while simultaneously installing one of the most brutal of regimes) that inspired plenty of Jihadists groups, the Islamic Jihad in Palestine and Egypt, the formation of Hamas and of Hizbullah and AMAL and the Iranian clerical regime? And by the same account no wonder then, that the Afghan Jihad is only with "Zia-ul-Haq as per Haqqani's genius, as well; which again overlooks the fact that the US and dictatorial Muslim regimes were only too happy to dump the 'problems' that they themselves had created, to fight the Communist 'threat.' Finally, as the Muslim dictatorial regimes, including Pakistan, have set the 'example' of using the Islamic card whenever required and dumping it later, the US was only too happy to follow suit, leaving the Afghans to the hell created by the CIA's proxy war and the Soviet invasion. Today, the Obama administration is 'sorry' for what happened during the Afghan Jihad era, but turns its heat on Pakistan to 'do more.'"

In the end, the identity crisis that has haunted Pakistan since its creation gives excuses to different militants, secularists, Islamists, fundamentalists and political groups alike to manipulate it further. Whether it is ethnicist national Jihadists militants like the Pakistani Taliban, radical like the Lashker-e-Tayyiba, transnational Jihadists like al-Qaeda, Muslim "democrats" like the Muslim League N and Q, secularists; the Pakistan Peoples Party (PPP) and Awami National Party (ANP) or sectarian Muttahida Quami Movement (MQM), Sipah-e-Sahaba (SSP) or Sipah-e-Muhammad (SMP), the Islamic card has always been, and is constantly, in play.

Conclusion

It may be questionable to conclude that Pakistan's existence is severely threatened. It is, however, surely in a quagmire when it comes to politics and security, which is mostly the result of the identity crisis that we have explored extensively in this chapter. The question of Pakistan's salvation therefore cannot be addressed without including its identity crisis, which loosely evolves around its ideological spectrum and the struggle for Islam or secular-liberal democracy. Pakistani strategists, in order to salvage the country's future, will have to consider serious burning issues, for which a stalemate is no longer possible. Pakistan can no longer linger on holding both ideals and will have to decide whether its an Islamic state or a secular-liberal state inspired by the West, and that decision among others will ultimately decide its future.

In this chapter we started by looking at the "furiously" religious world that we live in today, where religion has once more established itself as a dynamic political force. However, secularism still holds sway in the Western capitals, which are also the "power centers" of the world. We also established the "compromising" nature of Western secularism, while discussing its comparative historiography, which is marred by an "anti-reason church," the opposite of the Islamic world, which encouraged reason and scientific enquiry and contributed hugely to the Western Renaissance and Enlightenment. We also discussed what the secularist experience meant for the Islamic world in the post-Caliphate era, which resulted in brutal tyrannical and dictatorial regimes. Western-sponsored secularism that is irreligious, which has a complete reverse historiography than the experience of the Islamic world and has produced tyrannical regimes the Islamic world over, surely cannot salvage Pakistan from its contemporary crisis.

Similarly, philosophical ambiguities regarding the secular nature of Western-modelled democracy, its liberalist and consumerist nature and the West's use of it for its selfish and arrogant interests alone, suggest that a Western-modelled liberal democracy cannot and should not be a part of this salvation. However, the operational and institutional aspects of democracy that are already implemented in many Muslim countries, and are generally accepted even by the Islamists and Jurists alike, can and should contribute towards Pakistan's future. Pakistan could be the first Muslim country to excel in establishing an operational role of democratic principle in an Islamic state without giving in to irreligious secularism or liberalist propaganda.

We also explained that the question of Islam or democracy that created an identity debate in Pakistan was only furthered by the different regimes that played the Islamic card in the service of their regimes. We discussed that both Muslim and non-Muslim regimes were only too happy to play the Islamic ideological card, which we explained was purely for political and strategic purposes. This merciless usage of "Islam" for political purposes would only backfire and further confuse the situation. If those regimes had not played the Islamic card or were sincere in their efforts towards defining the role of Islam in the running of a state, Pakistan would not have been in the current turmoil, where the highjacking of Islamic ideology by different regimes has now created different ethnicist, fundamentalist, Jihadist and sectarian groups, all of whom claim to be "defending" Islam. Even a superficial analysis of the state of different Muslim countries would reveal the same ambiguity all around, where the state is forcing its way to implement its own version of "Islam," which has mostly resulted in political and cultural suppressions, lack of political participation and tyrannical and authoritarian-style regimes, while different groups including Jihadists are striving against it with their particular versions of "Islam." This phenomenon is the direct result of "Islam in the service of regimes" and the ambiguity over the issues of secularism, democracy and the role of Islam in the running of state, which has resulted in creating an ideological vacuum that different actors including the state itself have been manipulating in the past and continue to do so.

In the end, it comes down to defining and addressing the ultimate question

— is Pakistan an Islamic state or a liberal-cum-secular "democracy" modelled on the West? The only way to stop this bloodbath in the name of Islam is to seriously address the above question on a national level, which should ultimately include the state machinery, the civil society, the Islamists, the religious parties and of course the *moderate* Jihadist elements. The answer to this question must exclude the irreligious secularism that creates dictatorial and tyrannical regimes and the liberalist "democratic" propaganda that is selfish and arrogant. But it must include a true appreciation of the role of Islam, not only in the running of state but also its directional route within the society itself, or else different sectarian, ethnicist or Jihadists groups will keep popping up time and again and create a turmoil from which Pakistan may not be able to recover.

Notes

1   Husain Haqqani, *Pakistan: Between Mosque and Military.* Carnegie Endowment Press, 2005.

2   John L. Esposito "Introduction: Islam and Secularism in the Twenty-First Century" in *Islam and Secularism in the Middle East*, John L. Esposito and Azzam Tamimi (eds). Tamimi Hurst & Co., 2000.

3   Peter L. Berger, "Secularism in Retreat" in *Islam and Secularism in the Middle East.*

4   Ibid.

5   Fred Halliday, *Islam and the Myth of Confrontation.* I.B. Taurus, 1996.

6   Tariq Ramadan, quoted by François Burgat in *Face to Face with Political Islam.* I.B. Taurus, 2003.

7   François Burgat, *Face to Face with Political Islam.* p. 47.

8   Peter Mandaville, *Global Political Islam.* Routledge, 2007.

9   Gilles Kepel, *The Roots of Radical Islam.* Saqi Publishing, 2005.

10   Peter Mandaville, *Global Political Islam.*

11   Patrick Morgan, "Security in International Politics: Traditional Approach," in *Contemporary Security Studies*, Alan Collins (ed.). Oxford University Press, 2007.

12   Ken Booth, *Theory of World Security.* Cambridge University Press, 2007, p. 25.

13   Paul Roger, *Losing Control.* Pluto Press, 2000.

14   François Burgat, *Face to Face with Political Islam.*

15   Peter Mandaville, *Global Political Islam.*

16   An interview conducted with Professor Khurshid Ahmed, General Secretary of Jamaat-e-Islami Pakistan.

17   Munir Shafiq, "Secularism and the Arab-Muslim Condition," in *Islam and Secularism in the Middle East*.

18   A survey held in October 2009 by the Washington-based think tank "International Republican Institute" (IRI) asked Pakistani participants "to what extent should religion play a role in politics?" The majority replied in favour of a "dominant" role. This survey is just another of many surveys with similar results. The PEW survey conducted on the same topic showed that 75 percent of participants preferred religion to have a "very large role" in politics (quoted in Peter Mandaville, *Global Political Islam*. p. 18.

19   http://wapedia.mobi/en/Two-Nation_Theory (accessed November 2009).

20   Quoted in Akbar S. Ahmed, *Jinnah, Pakistan and Islamic Identity: the Search for Saladin*. Routlegde, 1997, p. 77.

21   Ibid.

22   Jinnah's speech as Governor General of Pakistan in August 1948, quoted in Haqqani, *Pakistan: Between Mosque and Military*. p. 12.

23   Christophe Jaffrelot, "Islamic Identity and Ethnic Tensions" in *A History of Pakistan and its Origins*, Christophe Jaffrelot (ed.). Anthem Publishers, 2002.

24   Ahmed Rashid, *Descent into Chaos*. Penguin, 2008.

25   Marc Gaborieau, "Islam and politics" in *A History of Pakistan and its origins*.

26   Ali Eteraz, "State sponsored Sufism," available online at: http://www.foreignpolicy.com/story/cms.php?story_id=4993 (accessed November 2009).

CHAPTER TWO

Promising Partnership? American Af-Pak Strategy and Pakistan's Counter-terrorism Response

Ishtiaq Ahmad

Abstract

This chapter seeks to evaluate the Obama Administration's evolving strategy towards Afghanistan and Pakistan, including its salient features and implications for Pakistan. It also attempts to analyze Pakistan's counter-terrorism response, which has evolved in synchronicity with the new US policy. The study makes four principal arguments: first, the Af-Pak strategy is a great departure from the Bush Administration's counter-terrorism approach in the region, in terms of the US strategic goal, threat perception, counter-insurgency options, resource allocation, and the level commitment. Second, this strategy is presumed to evolve in accordance with the changing political and security realities in the two countries, although the review and policies formulated thus far are largely in conformity with the originally pronounced strategic principles. Third, given its evolutionary nature, and the fact that it aims to defeat al-Qaeda and its terrorist allies simultaneously in both Afghanistan and Pakistan, the new US strategy has a greater scope for adapting to new political and security realities of the two countries, besides reinforcing and reshaping their respective counter-insurgency campaigns through a variety of cooperative mechanisms. Finally, Pakistan's perception of the enormity of threat from largely homegrown terrorism and its recent successes against the Taliban has enhanced the level of compatibility between the country's counter-terrorism policy and new US counter-terrorism interests in the region. Given that, the chapter concludes by foreseeing a promising strategic relationship between the US and Pakistan, if the two countries are able to overcome the remaining areas of potential friction between them on the issue of tackling terrorism.

The pages ahead will first discuss in detail the salient features of the Af-Pak strategy, its evolutionary nature, review and scope of success. This will be followed by an analysis of the implications of the Af-Pak strategy for Pakistan, Pakistan's counter-terrorism response to it and the areas of compatibility between the two. The concluding discussion will focus on the points of potential friction in US-Pakistan relations on the issue of tackling terrorism and the possibility of their resolution.

Af-Pak Strategy

That Barack Obama would bring about a qualitative shift in the US strategy towards Afghanistan and Pakistan was clear during the US election campaign. As a Democratic presidential contender, he had declared to make the war in Afghanistan his administration's top most priority. For winning this war, he promised to increase the number of US troops in Afghanistan and allow US forces to strike al-Qaeda terrorist targets in Pakistan's tribal areas. In his opinion, the US was fighting a "war of necessity" in Afghanistan. He criticized the Bush Administration for waging a "war of choice" in Iraq, because of which Taliban-led insurgency in Afghanistan had intensified in recent years. But he shared the Bush Administration's growing concern about Pakistan's tribal areas having become a safe haven for al-Qaeda and its terrorist allies, fuelling Afghan insurgency and threatening international terrorism. To him, Afghanistan and Pakistan constituted two theatres of the same war being waged to combat international terrorism by al-Qaeda and its terrorist allies. Therefore, the war in Afghanistan could not be won without tackling the threat of terrorism from Pakistan. It was no surprise, therefore, that soon after assuming office on January 20, 2009, President Obama appointed Richard Holbrooke, who had skilfully negotiated the Dayton Peace Accords on Bosnia in 1995, as his Representative for Afghanistan and Pakistan. Within three weeks, on February 10, 2009, he ordered a review of the US strategy towards the two countries by an Inter-Agency Policy Group chaired by Bruce Riedel, his advisor on Afghanistan and Pakistan during the election campaign, and co-chaired by Mr. Holbrooke and Michele Flournoy, the US Under-Secretary of Defense for Policy. Upon the completion of the said review, President Obama unveiled the new US strategy towards Afghanistan and Pakistan in a major speech on March 27, 2009.[1] A White Paper of the Inter-Agency Policy Group's Report outlining the basic elements of this strategy was also issued the same day.[2]

The Af-Pak strategy, as it is generally abbreviated, constitutes the essential framework for the Obama Administration's subsequent policy initiatives towards Afghanistan and Pakistan and review of the Afghan war strategy. It offers a more focused US approach to combat against al-Qaeda-led international terrorism, treading "a middle path between a narrow counter-terror mission and a much more ambitious nation-building agenda."[3] In this section of the study, we shall first discuss salient features of the Af-Pak strategy as it was unveiled in March 2009 and then analyze the main components of the Obama administration's review of the Afghan war strategy in December 2009.

First, the Af-Pak strategy shifts the focus of war from Iraq to Afghanistan and Pakistan and treats them as two countries but one challenge. The reason Pakistan is bracketed with Afghanistan is because its tribal areas alongside the Afghan border are perceived by the Obama Administration to be a safe haven for al-Qaeda and its terrorist allies, fuelling Afghan insurgency and threatening international terrorism. Under this perception, the threat the two countries face and the enemies they confront are common. As long as these enemies survive and the threat exists, the safety and security of the rest of the world from international terrorism cannot be guaranteed. The Inter-Agency Policy Group's Report stated that "the ability of extremists in Pakistan to undermine Afghanistan is proven, while insurgency in Afghanistan feeds instability in Pakistan. The threat that al-Qaeda poses to the US and our allies in Pakistan — including the possibility of extremists obtaining fissile material — is all too real. Without more effective action against these groups in Pakistan, Afghanistan will face continuing instability."[4] The Af-Pak strategy, therefore, focuses more intensively on Pakistan than in the past, calling for more significant increases in US and international support, both economic and military, linked to Pakistan's performance against terror. Additionally, it aims to engage Afghanistan and Pakistan in a new trilateral framework at the highest levels. Together in this trilateral format, the US aims to enhance intelligence sharing and military cooperation along the border and address common issues like trade, energy and economic development.

Second, the Af-Pak strategy is based on a "clear and focused" US strategic goal for Afghanistan and Pakistan: "To disrupt, dismantle and defeat al-Qaeda in Pakistan and Afghanistan, and to prevent their return to either country in the future."[5] The Bush Administration's policy towards the region emanated largely from the fact that its overall goal was based on the abstract phrase of the "War on Terror," which could mean anything: installing Western-style democracy in Afghanistan, defeating the Taliban, fighting Afghans, or waging a war against Muslims. Categorically stating the core US goal in the region is important for clarifying a widely held regional perception that the US and NATO have a long-term strategic ambition to use their presence in Afghanistan to exploit Central Asia's vast oil and natural gas resources. The clear identification of the terrorist enemy implies that the US and NATO forces will leave the region as soon as the terrorist threat is eliminated. Another indicator of the US/NATO intention not to stay longer in the region than it is necessary is the Af-Pak strategy's emphasis on involving regional players in the Afghan peace effort. Together with the United Nations, the Obama Administration aims to forge a new Contact Group for Afghanistan and Pakistan that brings together all who should have a stake in the security of the region, including "Central Asian states, the Gulf nations and Iran; Russia, India and China."[6]

Third, the Af-Pak strategy supports reconciliation with those local Taliban and insurgents who are ready to surrender arms and dissociate from al-Qaeda and its hardcore allies. In President Obama's words, "There is an uncompromising core of the Taliban. They must be met with force, and they must be defeated. But there are also those who've taken up arms because of coercion, or simply for a price. These Afghans must have the option to choose a different course."[7] The Bush Administration's strategy of treating al-Qaeda and the Taliban as synonymous brought these two diverse entities closer together, both ideologically and practically. Al-Qaeda got access to Taliban safe havens in Waziristan, and the Taliban learned lethal insurgency techniques such as suicide bombings from al-Qaeda. The idea of negotiating with less extremist elements among the Taliban is based on the experience of US and British forces in Iraq, where Sunni militias were paid and trained to fight their former al-Qaeda allies.[8] While implementing this component of the Af-Pak strategy, President Obama signed the Defense Bill on October 28, 2009, which contained a new provision under which the US was to pay Taliban fighters who renounced the insurgency for "mainly protection of their towns and villages."[9]

Fourth, the Af-Pak strategy shows a long-term US commitment to Afghanistan and Pakistan through significantly enhanced resource allocation for civilian development projects in the two countries. In his Af-Pak strategy speech on March 27, 2009, President Obama announced "to advance security, opportunity and justice — not just in Kabul, but from the bottom up in the provinces" through "ordering a substantial increase in our civilians on the ground" as well as with the help of "civilian support from our partners and allies, from the United Nations and international aid organizations."[10] In subsequent months, the Obama Administration has continued to dispatch US civilian experts to Afghanistan. It had originally set March 2010 as the deadline for filling in nearly 1,000 civilian positions in Afghanistan — including lawyers, agriculture and development experts and diplomats — but later moved it to the end of 2009. In November 2009, despite a worsening security situation in Afghanistan, the US State Department claimed it was "on track" in meeting this deadline.[11] During the Bush Administration, Afghanistan obtained billions of dollars in civilian assistance from the US and the international community, but it did not make much of an impact on the ground, in developing the countryside or dissuading the farmers from poppy cultivation. That is why the Obama Administration has decided to dispatch hundreds of US civilian experts to Afghanistan and set stringent accountability criteria for the utilization of US and international civilian assistance by the Afghan government.

In the case of Pakistan, assisting the country's capability to fight extremists is identified as an important objective of the Af-Pak strategy, including the provision of "increased U.S. military assistance for helicopters to provide air mobility, night vision equipment, and training and equipment specifically for Pakistani Special Operation Forces and their Frontier Corps."[12] The US Department of Defense has already allocated roughly $400 million to train and equip the Frontier Corps, and recently proposed a Pakistani

Counterinsurgency Capability Fund, which would allocate $3 billion over the next five years to train and equip Pakistan's army and paramilitary forces for a counterinsurgency mission. All of these efforts are likely to be accelerated and expanded within several years, provided Washington can supply more trainers, build new training facilities, and work closely with Pakistani and Afghan counterparts.[13]

However, the thrust of the Af-Pak strategy is on providing substantial US civilian assistance to Pakistan for "long-term capacity building, agricultural sector job creation, education and training, and on infrastructure requirements,"[14] as well as to support its efforts to "hold and build" in insurgency-ridden areas as soon as they are cleared of terrorist-insurgents. Strengthening US-Pakistan bilateral ties, implementing Reconstruction Opportunity Zones in Federally Administered Tribal Areas, encouraging foreign investment in key sectors, such as energy, assisting Pakistan with developing a concrete strategy for utilizing donor aid, and garnering additional support for the country from international institutions, including the UN, the World Bank, the Asian Development Bank as well as from the international forum Friends of Democratic Pakistan, are identified in the Af-Pak strategy as other objectives to help Pakistan make a long-term economic recovery.[15] The Kerry-Lugar-Berman Act,[16] under which the US will provide $7.5 billion civilian assistance to Pakistan in the next five years, including $1.5 billion each year, is the most obvious example of the US resolve to help build Pakistan's civilian sector — an objective that was never a priority for the Bush Administration, which preferred individual leadership over democratic institutions and military aid over civilian assistance.

The final important feature of the Af-Pak strategy is its support for the deployment of additional US troops in Afghanistan. This is the only area where the Obama Administration shares its approach to the Afghan war with that of the Bush Administration in its concluding months. Reconciliation with moderate insurgents and deployment of additional troops were two options exercised simultaneously in Iraq, resulting in considerable improvement in Iraqi security. The Af-Pak strategy incorporates such useful lessons of the Iraq war in Afghanistan. In fact, weeks before unveiling this strategy, on February 17, 2009, President Obama ordered the dispatch of 17,000 more US combat troops to Afghanistan.[17] Even though the Af-Pak strategy seeks to employ "all elements of international power — diplomatic, informational, military and economic,"[18] exercising military force is considered to be absolutely essential to realize the core goal of disrupting, dismantling and defeating al-Qaeda and its hardcore allies in Afghanistan and Pakistan. The fact that adding 17,000 more US combat troops to the Afghan war theatre meant taking the battle to the enemy became aptly clear when 4,000 US troops, along with 600 Afghan forces, launched Operation Khanjar (sword strike) on July 2, 2009 in Helmand Province where, over the past two years, the Taliban had been regrouping and regaining power from the British forces.[19] Likewise, the Obama Administration intensified drone attacks in Pakistan's tribal regions, perceiving them as having become a safe haven for al-Qaeda and its terrorist allies to fuel Afghan insurgency and conduct international terrorism. As of late October 2009, half of the 82 drone attacks since 2006 were carried out during the Obama Administration[20] — a trend that sufficiently indicates how seriously it takes the terrorist threat from Pakistan.

Unlike the Bush Administration, whose priority was to deploy more US and NATO troops for combat missions in Afghanistan, the Obama Administration seeks to build the Afghan security capacity through "a more rapid build-up of the Afghan Army and police up to 134,000 and 82,000 over the next two years."[21] On March 27, 2009, President Obama announced plans to send 4,000 more US troops for training Afghan security forces. However, in an assessment of the Afghan war submitted to President Obama in late August 2009, General Stanely McChrystal, the commander of US and NATO/ISAF forces in Afghanistan, said the Afghan mission was significantly "under-resourced" and, therefore, 40,000 additional US troops would be required to protect the Afghan people, shore up the government and counter Taliban militants. The assessment suggested a much faster assumption of security of Afghanistan by the Afghans themselves through much quicker expansion of Afghan security forces and a more radical increase in their number — up to 240,000 for the Afghan army and 160,000 for the Afghan police[22] — than the numbers sought originally by the Af-Pak strategy. That the Obama Administration wanted to quickly hand over the responsibility of Afghanistan's security to the Afghans themselves as part of its exit strategy was clear from US Secretary of Defense Robert Gates" September 2009 remarks about "the Afghan national security forces assuming a greater and greater role in controlling and protecting their own territory as we recede into an advisory capacity and ultimately withdraw."[23]

The Obama Administration had postponed its announcement on the issue of US troops' reinforcement in Afghanistan until the country's presidential elections were over. However, the controversial elections did not produce an outcome that President Obama desired: an Afghan government with a more popular base. The re-election of President Hamid Karzai certainly limited the Af-Pak options for overcoming problems of governance and development in Afghanistan. Yet the immediate nature of the insurgent terrorist threat required a decisive military campaign, for which 68,000 US troops and 42,000 NATO troops were not enough.[24] President Obama had already added 21,000 troops since assuming office. One of the important dilemmas facing him was that additional US troops' reinforcement could lead to a corresponding surge in US troops' casualty rate, thereby further eroding the public support to US engagement in the Afghan war. The Helmand operation, for instance, resulted in the largest ever US and British troop casualties. 2009 proved the bloodiest year for US, British and NATO forces, killing close to 300 US soldiers and over 100 British troops. In July and August 2009 alone, 153 US soldiers died in Afghanistan.[25] However, the major shift in US counter-insurgency strategy of "clear, hold and build" that Gen McChrystal proposed could tackle this dilemma. His assessment of the Afghan war suggested a focus on the volatile south and east of the country, emphasizing the protection of civilians even if it meant allowing individual militants to escape. The shift in strategy that Gen McChrystal recommended accepted that some territory would be ceded to the Taliban, but calculated that these would be remoter areas of limited value. The payoff would be a much denser concentration of Western troops around areas of higher population, including cities, major towns and key infrastructure. It was with saturating numbers of troops that US forces produced dramatic improvements in security during the 2007 "surge" in Baghdad. And it was in the cities and towns that the message that Western troops could deliver security and economic benefit stood the best chance of finding a receptive audience.[26]

As soon as Gen McChrystal submitted his assessment of the Afghan war in August 2009, President Obama began an extensive review of the Af-Pak strategy. However, even while this review was under way, some elements of the counter-insurgency strategy proposed by Gen McChrystal in his assessment were already operational in the war theatre. For instance, one of the first decisions he took when taking over the command of US and NATO/ISAF forces in Afghanistan was to restrict the use of airstrikes, arguing that the US risked losing the war if it did not reduce civilian causalities.[27] In November 2009, when it appeared that British public support for the war was declining fast due to growing British troop casualties, Gen McChrystal sought a radical alignment of British forces away from the frontlines of Helmand. The reason his Afghan war assessment and a new strategy for winning it won unanimous approval from NATO Defence ministers[28] in October 2009 was because it not only aimed to win the hearts and minds of the Afghan people but also sought to reduce troop casualties by making the defense of major population centers the primary goal of counter-insurgency as against the previous objective of fighting the Taliban in remote areas.

The fact that US strategic outlook on the Afghan war and Pakistan's counter-terrorism role in the region has undergone a qualitative shift during the Obama Administration is amply clear from the salient features of Af-Pak strategy discussed above. It is important to understand that the Af-Pak strategy as it was originally announced in March 2009 was meant to be a "work in progress . . . intended to provide a framework, not a strait-jacket, for US policy. Questions such as the correct prioritization of US objectives; the level of and manner in which US diplomatic, military, intelligence, and economic resources should be deployed; and the appropriate sequencing and duration of US efforts"[29] were left open for a review. These questions were addressed during the 92-day review that the Obama Administration conducted after receiving Gen McChrystal's assessment of the Afghan war. During this period, President Obama convened nine sessions of his war council in the White House situation room, where he pressed his advisers to provide exhaustive details on the policy options. A number of issues, such as eroding public support in the US and NATO countries for the Afghan war, the financial and human cost of the war and NATO's reluctance in recent years to send additional troops to Afghanistan were factored in.[30] As has been the case all along, the Obama Administration also consulted key US allies in the Afghan war effort, including leaders of NATO, Afghanistan and Pakistan. It was only then that President Obama announced the review of the

Af-Pak strategy in a major speech at the US Military Academy at West Point in New York on December 1, 2009, which was titled "A New Way Forward in Afghanistan and Pakistan."[31]

Given the wavering public support for the Afghan war due to rising troop casualties and financial cost, especially in times of economic hardship, President Obama began his speech by underlying the justification for the war in the shape of a worsening threat from al-Qaeda and its hardcore allies in Afghanistan. He underlined the progress that had been achieved in the war since the announcement of the Af-Pak strategy in March 2009, saying: "High-ranking al-Qaeda and Taliban leaders have been killed, and we've stepped up the pressure on al-Qaeda worldwide. In Pakistan, that nation's army has gone on its largest offensive in years. In Afghanistan, we and our allies prevented the Taliban from stopping a presidential election, and — although it was marred by fraud — that election produced a government that is consistent with Afghanistan's laws and constitution." However, he added that the grave terrorist challenge from al-Qaeda and its hardcore allies in the region to US and international security from the region had not yet disappeared. And then he announced the most important component of the long review of Afghan war strategy: the decision "to send an additional 30,000 U.S. troops to Afghanistan. After 18 months, our troops will begin to come home. These are the resources that we need to seize the initiative, while building the Afghan capacity that can allow for a responsible transition of our forces out of Afghanistan."

While reiterating the previously-declared "narrowed down" core goal of the Af-Pak strategy — "to disrupt, dismantle, and defeat al-Qaeda in Afghanistan and Pakistan, and to prevent its capacity to threaten America and our allies in the future," President Obama laid down its three core elements: "A military effort to create the conditions for a transition; a civilian surge that reinforces positive action; and an effective partnership with Pakistan." The objectives underpinning these core elements were to be achieved in three ways: First, by pursuing "a military strategy that will break the Taliban's momentum and increase Afghanistan's capacity over the next 18 months." For the purpose, 30,000 troops were to be deployed at "the fastest possible pace in the first part of 2010 to "target the insurgency and secure key population centers." They will be joined by additional troops from NATO. "Taken together, these additional

American and international troops will allow us to accelerate handing over responsibility to Afghan forces, and allow us to begin the transfer of our forces out of Afghanistan in July of 2011," President Obama said.

Second, building upon the previously-stated Af-Pak strategy' principle of civilizing the Afghan war effort, President Obama declared that the US would "work with our partners, the United Nations, and the Afghan people to pursue a more effective civilian strategy, so that the government can take advantage of improved security." However, he once again made clear that this "effort must be based on performance," meaning that US civilian help to Afghanistan would be linked to its performance to "combat corruption and deliver for the people." He assured the Afghan people that his country was interested in ending the war and their consequent suffering and not "in occupying your country." He reiterated the US support to "efforts by the Afghan government to open the door to those Taliban who abandon violence and respect the human rights of their fellow citizens." Finally, President Obama reinforced the aim that his administration has stated all along, that of treating Afghanistan and Pakistan as part of the same challenge: "We're in Afghanistan to prevent a cancer from once again spreading through that country. But this same cancer has also taken root in the border region of Pakistan. That's why we need a strategy that works on both sides of the border."

He said, "In the past, there have been those in Pakistan who've argued that the struggle against extremism is not their fight, and that Pakistan is better off doing little or seeking accommodation with those who use violence. But in recent years, as innocents have been killed from Karachi to Islamabad, it has become clear that it is the Pakistani people who are the most endangered by extremism. Public opinion has turned. The Pakistani army has waged an offensive in Swat and South Waziristan. And there is no doubt that the United States US and Pakistan share a common enemy." President Obama continued by highlighting why his administration perceives Pakistan as a strategic partner:

"In the past, we too often defined our relationship with Pakistan narrowly. Those days are over. Moving forward, we are committed to a partnership with Pakistan that is built on a foundation of mutual interest, mutual respect, and mutual trust. We will strengthen Pakistan's capacity to target those groups that threaten our countries, and have made it clear that we cannot tolerate a safe haven for terrorists whose location is known and whose intentions are clear. America is also providing substantial resources to support Pakistan's democracy and development. We are the largest international supporter for those Pakistanis displaced by the fighting. And going forward, the Pakistan people must know America will remain a strong supporter of Pakistan's security and prosperity long after the guns have fallen silent, so that the great potential of its people can be unleashed."

If, as a result of this escalation, Afghan security capacity-building activity gains momentum, the Afghans living in major cities feel more secure, the casualty rate of Afghan civilians and foreign troops is significantly decreased, and a credible process of reconciling with moderate insurgents gets underway, then President Obama's wish to "finish the job" in Afghanistan has a realistic chance of success. Obviously, all of these are big "ifs." Implementing an exit strategy at the same time as ordering an escalation of the military campaign may seem contradictory. However, as already pointed out, the troops" surge option is predicated on exercising a qualitatively different counter-insurgency campaign aimed at reducing Afghan civilian and foreign troop casualties, reconciling moderate insurgent forces and co-opting them in Afghanistan's political and security structure, and transferring the country's security responsibility to the Afghans themselves. Given the inherently evolutionary nature of the Af-Pak strategy, even if some elements of the revised war strategy did not produce the intended outcomes, they can always be modified or reformulated by the Obama Administration in consultation with NATO and the governments of Afghanistan and Pakistan, as has been the case before. Given that, it can be safely argued that the Af-Pak strategy as it evolves further will have greater scope for adapting to new political and security realities of the two countries, besides reinforcing and reshaping their respective counter-insurgency campaigns through a variety of cooperative mechanisms.

Pakistan's Response

It is an interesting coincidence that Pakistan's proactive counter-terrorism campaign against al-Qaeda-linked Tehreek-e-Taliban Pakistan (TTP) and other pro-Taliban groups in the Frontier and tribal regions of the country has evolved in synchronicity with the adoption of the Af-Pak strategy by the Obama Administration and its subsequent implementation and review. The Af-Pak strategy treated al-Qaeda-inspired Taliban insurgency-ridden areas of Afghanistan and Pakistan as one and expected Pakistan to complement US troops' surge in Afghanistan with a security operation in its own tribal areas. Within a month, Pakistan followed suit, with an air and ground assault on the Swat Valley. The period since then has seen intensified counter-insurgency campaigns on both sides of the border between Afghanistan and Pakistan, including the US-British military offensive in Helmand Province and the Pakistan Army's operation in South Waziristan. The Af-Pak strategy aims to defeat al-Qaeda and its terrorist allies among Taliban and other insurgent groups. Pakistan's consequent counter-terrorism response also confirms that the country's civil-military leadership shares the US objective in defeating al-Qaeda-inspired Taliban, and other local and foreign terrorists in their north-western tribal strongholds.

Given that, the main argument in this section of study is that Pakistan's perception of the enormity of threat from largely homegrown terrorism and its recent successes against the Taliban have enhanced the level of compatibility between the country's counter-terrorism policy and new US counter-terrorism interests in the region. Consequently, it can be argued that the areas of friction between Pakistan's counter-terrorism offensive in the frontier and tribal regions, and the US-led counter-insurgency campaign in southern and eastern Afghanistan may have considerably narrowed. Before analyzing Pakistan's counter-terrorism campaign and how it is compatible with US counter-terrorism goals in the region as stated in the Af-Pak strategy, it makes sense to discuss the implications of each of the five salient features of the strategy, including its December 2009 review, for Pakistan — since the conclusions drawn from the following discussion will also suggest that the US and Pakistan have more in common than is generally believed when it comes to combating terrorism in the region.

First, insofar as the question of hyphenating Afghanistan and Pakistan is concerned, Pakistan's security establishment did express its reservation about it, while arguing "that there was a large difference between the situation in Afghanistan and that in Pakistan, and if the US tried to implement the same policy in Pakistan than it would not only yield negative results but it will also affect Pak-US relations."[32] Such reservation is understandable, since Pakistan, as a fully functional nuclear-equipped state with a powerful army cannot be equated with the dysfunctional, war-ravaged state of Afghanistan, which is sustained through international security, political and economic support. Pakistan's security establishment also sees a paradox in the Obama Administration's approach to linking the country with Afghanistan while, at the same time, refusing to re-hyphenate Pakistan with its archrival India, as was the case throughout the Cold War period.

However, over time, the benefits of linking Pakistan with Afghanistan seem to outweigh the Pakistani establishment's concerns about this linkage. One, it has facilitated cooperation between Afghanistan and Pakistani on combating terrorism. Instead of trading accusations against each other on cross-border terrorism, as was the norm before, the leaders of the two countries have regularly interacted with each other to address the common threat from terrorism and attended trilateral and multilateral forums. The Bush Administration had not established this linkage, and, therefore, it could neither persuade Pakistan to "do more" in the "War on Terror," nor could it facilitate a cooperative relationship between Afghanistan and Pakistan. Two, like Afghanistan, Pakistan has started to receive international financial commitments, such as the US civilian aid package under the Kerry-Lugar-Berman Act and through the creation of a special multi-billion dollar fund by an international grouping called the Friends of Democratic Pakistan. Three, unlike the Bush Administration, which only pressured Pakistan to "do more" to prevent its tribal areas from fuelling Afghan insurgency, the Obama Administration has focused on facilitating Pakistan's counter-insurgency efforts in the area through greater intelligence sharing and building Pakistan's counter-insurgency capacity as well as through bilateral and trilateral cooperative mechanisms with Afghanistan.

Second, the Obama Administration's core goal of disrupting, dismantling and defeating al-Qaeda and its hardcore allies in Afghanistan and Pakistan is the same goal that Pakistan's civilian government and security establishment also wish to realize. Recent years have seen al-Qaeda-inspired insurgent-terrorist organizations, especially TTP, play havoc with the lives of Pakistani civilians and security personnel. The country already has the distinction of arresting the largest number of al-Qaeda leaders and activists following the fall of the Taliban regime in Afghanistan in late 2001. The objective behind its military offensive in South Waziristan has also been to disrupt, dismantle and defeat the al-Qaeda-linked TTP and other hardcore allies of the terror network, including terrorists belonging to the Islamic Movement of Uzbekistan (IMU). Since the start of 2009, Pakistan's security establishment seems to have realized the enormity of the threat posed to state apparatus and societal fabric by homegrown terrorist groups linked to al-Qaeda. Even before, its reluctance to go all out against the forces of religiously-motivated insurgency and terrorism was only with reference to insurgent groups who were perceived to be operating without any linkage with al-Qaeda. That is why Taliban groups such as that of Mullah Nazir Ahmad in South Waziristan were used by Pakistan's security establishment to fight against al-Qaeda-linked Uzbek terrorists in 2007.[33]

Third, reconciling with moderate insurgents — those who renounce violence, dissociate from al-Qaeda and are willing to participate in the political process — is another important component of the Af-Pak strategy that is largely compatible with Pakistan's own counter-terrorism interests in the region. In Pakistan's perception — shared equally by the security establishment, civilian government and informed public opinion — the marginalization of the Pashtun majority in the political, economic and security structure of post-Taliban Afghanistan is one of the main reasons for the growth of Taliban-led insurgency in the war-torn country. This implies that a credible process of reconciliation with the local forces of insurgency is the only viable option for a lasting resolution of the Afghan conflict. Since the Taliban and other Afghan insurgents are essentially Pashtun, and the Pashtun ethnicity straddling the long porous border between Afghanistan and Pakistan is an inescapable ground reality for both the countries, Pakistan cannot but support a process of reconciliation in Afghanistan that aims to address legitimate grievances of the Afghan Pashtun population. If and when such a reconciliation process begins in Afghanistan, it will provide Pakistan an opportunity to seek a negotiated outcome of its own counter-insurgency campaign in the tribal areas. The security and economic cost of successive rounds of warfare in Afghanistan since 1979 has been the most severe compared to all other countries bordering Afghanistan. That is why Pakistan perceives the continuing conflict in Afghanistan as a major source of domestic insecurity and negative social and economic consequences. Anything that brings an end to the war in Afghanistan is, therefore, in Pakistan's interests.

Fourth, the Af-Pak y'focus on civilizing the war effort is also an area where Pakistan's counter-terrorism interest is compatible with that of the US. If this helps stabilize the situation in Afghanistan, then this is a goal that Pakistan also aspires to, largely due to its own domestic security concerns. Afghanistan and Pakistan share the bitter experience of being abandoned by the US in the aftermath of the 1980s jihad against the Soviets. The public opinion in Pakistan, as a relatively functioning state unlike Afghanistan, would naturally have been apprehensive about whether the country's post-9/11 relationship with the US to fight international terrorism would be strategic and long-term, or the US would once again abandon it after the achievement of its relatively short-term strategic interests in the region. The Af-Pak strategy recognizes this "trust deficit," while stating that the US government "must engage the Pakistani people based on our long-term commitment to helping them build a stable economy, a stronger democracy, and a vibrant civil society."[34] Pakistan may have obtained billions of dollars of counter-terrorism military assistance from the US in the years following the fall of the Taliban in Afghanistan in late 2001, but the civilian assistance it received during the period pales in comparison to what the US and the international community have pledged for Afghanistan at successive international donor conferences since then. This was despite the enormity of the terrorist backlash the country experienced during the period.

While recognizing Pakistan's legitimate grievances in this regard, the Obama Administration has declared that it will engage the country on the basis of a strategic partnership "grounded in support for Pakistan's democratic institutions and the Pakistani people." The Kerry-Lugar-Berman Act, which formalizes this partnership, is a tangible manifestation of the broad support for Pakistan in the US, as evidenced by its bipartisan, bicameral, unanimous passage in the Congress. And the reading of this Act also makes it pivotally clear that after decades of coddling military dictators in Pakistan, Washington wants a different relationship with Islamabad, as the $7.5 billion in non-military aid for the next five years, with a pledge of another such package afterwards, is essentially meant to help Pakistan's civilian government deliver essential services to its population and develop the country's civilian institutions and infrastructure. The previous major US aid packages that Pakistan received were when the country was under military rule, which somehow coincided with an increase in its regional strategic significance for Washington. For the first time in the history of US-Pakistan relations, the Obama Administration is attempting to transform a traditionally state-to-state/military-to-military relationship into a genuinely people-to-people one.

Yet the response from Pakistan to this unprecedented shift in US aid priority has not been as encouraging as the Obama Administration may have expected. When President Obama announced the Af-Pak strategy in March 2009, two different versions of what eventually became the Kerry-Lugar-Berman Act were before the US Senate and the House of Representatives. In his Af-Pak strategy speech, the President strongly urged Congress to move quickly on the said bipartisan legislation, as well as pass another bill "that creates opportunity zones in the border regions to develop the economy and bring hope to places plagued with violence." On June 12, 2009, the House passed the Pakistan Enduring Assistance and Cooperation Enhancement (PEACE) Act of 2009, which was sponsored by Democratic Congressman Howard Berman, Chairman of the House Committee on Foreign Affairs. On September 24, 2009, the Senate passed the Kerry-Lugar Bill, which was co-sponsored by Democratic Senator John Kerry, who heads the Senate Foreign Relations Committee, and Republican Senator Richard Lugar. The PEACE Act had set more stringent conditions for Pakistan to qualify for US military assistance, which were a matter of concern for both the Pakistani government and the Obama Administration. These conditions were softened through a joint Congressional effort, following which the new changes were incorporated in the Kerry-Lugar Bill, before the Senate passed it. On September 30, 2009, the House of Representatives also passed this Bill, which became the Kerry-Lugar-Berman Act.[35]

The Kerry-Lugar-Berman Act does not impose any conditionality on Pakistan for benefiting from $71.5 billion US civilian assistance each year from 2009 to 2013, with a pledge for a similar package for another five years. The aid is meant for improving the country's education and health sectors, reforming its police service, expanding infrastructure, strengthening judiciary and democracy and developing other civilian sectors. However, the

Act does impose conditions on "security-related assistance" to the country, which is what led the Pakistan army to openly express its reservations about the US intention behind it. This generated a huge controversy in Pakistan's political sphere and media, with widespread anger at the Pakistan Peoples Party (PPP)-led government for its diplomatic failure to allow the passage of a Congressional aid bill for Pakistan that compromises the country's national sovereignty.

As for the conditions, for Pakistan to acquire security-related assistance from the US in the future, the US Secretary of State will have to first certify before appropriate congressional committees that:

> (1) the Government of Pakistan is continuing to cooperate with the United States US in efforts to dismantle supplier networks relating to the acquisition of nuclear weapons-related materials, such as providing relevant information from or direct access to Pakistani nationals associated with such networks; (2) the Government of Pakistan during the preceding fiscal year has demonstrated a sustained commitment to and is making significant efforts towards combating terrorist groups . . . including taking into account the extent to which the Government of Pakistan has made progress on matters such as — (A) ceasing support, including by any elements within the Pakistan military or its intelligence agency, to extremist and terrorist groups, particularly to any group that has conducted attacks against United States US or coalition forces in Afghanistan, or against the territory or people of neighbouring countries; (B) preventing al-Qaeda, the Taliban and associated terrorist groups, such as Lashker-e-Tayyiba and Jaish-e-Mohammed, from operating in the territory of Pakistan, including carrying out cross-border attacks into neighbouring countries, closing terrorist camps in the FATA, dismantling terrorist bases of operations in other parts of the country, including Quetta and Muridke, and taking action when provided with intelligence about high-level terrorist targets; and (C) strengthening counterterrorism and anti-money laundering laws; and (3) the security forces of Pakistan are not materially and substantially subverting the political or judicial processes of Pakistan.[36]

Almost all of the conditions mentioned above correspond with Pakistan's publicly pronounced foreign policy objectives and domestic political priorities.

It is not that the Pakistan army's national or regional agenda is any way in conflict with any of the issues included in the above conditions. Since the unearthing of the A.Q. Khan nuclear smuggling network in 2003, the army, which essentially guards the country's nuclear assets, has consistently assured the international community not to worry about the risks of nuclear proliferation in Pakistan. Pakistan's civilian government and security establishment are likewise committed to combat terrorism in all its forms and manifestations, and not to let terrorist groups use Pakistani territory to conduct terrorism abroad. Unlike his predecessor, Army Chief Gen Ashfaq Pervez Kayani also does not seem to have any intention of subverting the country's civilian rule, since the army is yet to recover from the considerable loss of its societal image during the Musharraf regime and it is fully engaged in a military campaign against Taliban insurgents in the tribal areas. The army's regional strategic concerns may be indicative of a dual counter-terrorism approach on its part — one that draws a distinction between domestic insurgent-terrorist groups linked to insurgencies in Afghanistan and Kashmir and those committing terrorism inside Pakistan. However, the recent wave of terrorism across Pakistan has been so deadly that it has become difficult to make such a distinction anymore, especially when a number of spectacular terrorist incidents in 2008 and 2009 allegedly involved the very Afghan- and Kashmir-specific militant groups, such as Lashkar-e-Jhangvi and Jaish-e-Mohammed, about which the security establishment is believed to have had a softness in the past. Insofar as al-Qaeda and affiliated groups such as TTP are concerned, the army has shown no hesitation in taking them on directly, or doing it through its Taliban protégés such as Mullah Nazir in South Waziristan and Hafiz Gul Bahadur in North Waziristan.

Given that, the reason the Pakistan army has expressed its reservations about conditions in the Kerry-Lugar Bill is not because the issues they raise contradict its regional security agenda; rather, the real explanation for its reaction lies in Pakistan's peculiar political context. In a country where the army has dominated politics for most of its history and benefited from US assistance, the imposition of such conditions was likely to upset the army leadership. That the inflow of US civilian assistance to the country was free of any conditionality meant that Washington was taking sides in Pakistan's civil-military divide and preferring its new partner in the counter-terrorism effort in the region, the civilian government, over its traditional partner for the purpose, the military establishment. Political stability in Pakistan depends largely on a relatively smooth working civil-military relationship; and without political stability, the country cannot be expected to effectively combat terrorism. The security assistance-specific conditions in the Kerry-Lugar Bill threatened to upset the precarious civil-military relationship and that is why the PPP leadership engaged in hectic diplomacy with its US counterparts, and, on October 14, 2009, secured a joint explanatory statement of the US Congress attached to the Kerry-Lugar-Berman Bill, as it was called after the House of Representatives passed it on September 30. On October 15, President Obama signed the Bill, making it an Act. The Congressional statement said, "There is no intent to, and nothing in this act in any way suggests that there should be, any US role in micromanaging internal Pakistani affairs, including the promotion of Pakistani military officers or the internal operations of the Pakistani military."[37]

The explanatory note, which was issued jointly by the US House of Representatives and the Senate, also diluted the requirement that needed Pakistan to interrogate any Pakistani national involved in nuclear proliferation and to allow US officials access to such a person. A new clause included in the explanatory talked about "our understanding that cooperative effort currently being undertaken by the governments of Pakistan and the United States US to combat proliferation will continue." As for civilian control over military affairs, an issue that caused much of the controversy over the Kerry-Lugar Bill, the explanatory note did not include words like "civilian executive leaders and parliament" exercising the power of "oversight and approval," and the requirement that the military will not get involved in civil administration. It also stated that even the remaining requirement can be "waived if the determination is made by the Secretary of State in the interest of (US) national security that this was necessary to continue" military assistance to Pakistan. The Congressional statement clarified that the legislation "does not seek in any way to compromise Pakistan's sovereignty, impinge on Pakistan's national security interests, or micromanage any aspect of Pakistani military or civilian operations."[38]

In late October 2009, US Secretary of State Hillary Clinton visited Pakistan. In her several public appearances, she acknowledged the existence of a "serious trust deficit" in US-Pakistan relations. She confessed that the US made a mistake by abandoning strategic partnership with Pakistan after the Soviet defeat in Afghanistan, thereby contributing to Pakistan's current terrorist quagmire. She assured Pakistanis that the US was not pursuing yet another traditional state-to-state or government-to-government relationship guided by short-term, real-politick ambitions; rather, for the first time in the history of its relations with Islamabad, Washington was truly interested in long-term strategic ties, whose primary focus would be on strengthening people-to-people relations between the two countries. It was not merely a statement of intent on Clinton's part, as she announced over $243 million US civilian aid, which will be in addition to $7.5 billion under the Kerry-Lugar-Berman Act, to help improve Pakistan's energy generation and efficiency, raise the level of its higher education and meet some other urgent socio-economic needs.[39]

It is still unclear how far the incorporation of the said explanatory note in the Kerry-Lugar-Berman Act and the US Secretary of State's visit has allevi-ated the army's concern over the issue of conditions. However, since Pakistan's civilian and military leaders know the crucial value of US and international financial and security assistance in fighting a protracted war against terrorists which has no early end in sight, they can be expected to cooperate with each other as well as with the US as the country's pivotal partner in this. The issue of conditions will become irrelevant if the army's counter-terrorism campaign in the tribal areas continues to make headway, and its scope expands further in response to the terrorist backlash from TTP and other insurgent-terrorist groups operating in tribal areas and parts of the frontier and Punjab prov-inces. Moreover, top US military commanders regularly interact with the Pakistan army's high command, and this sustained interaction provides a framework within which the security-related grievances of each side are addressed in a mutually satisfactory manner.

A final implication of the Af-Pak strategy for Pakistan pertains to the deployment of additional troops by the US and NATO in Afghanistan in 2010 as part of the review of Afghan war strategy that President Obama announced in December 2009. However, as stated before, the troops' surge is only a short-term military means to facilitate a qualitatively different counter-insurgency campaign that places greater emphasis on expanding Afghan security capacity, reinforcing the civilian development campaign and reconciling with moderate insurgent forces in Afghanistan. It is a military escalation that is essentially meant to prepare the ground for the eventual withdrawal of the US and NATO forces from Afghanistan and a political resolution of the Afghan conflict. Pakistan hopes for the same. Even if the deployment of additional US and NATO troops in Afghanistan leads to intensification in the counter-insurgency campaign in its southern and eastern areas, the only worry for Pakistan is the infiltration of Afghan insurgents into the country's tribal regions bordering southern and eastern Afghanistan. However, since Pakistan's security forces are themselves engaged in a resolute military offensive against Taliban in tribal areas, the runaway insurgents from Afghanistan may not find these areas as hospitable as was the case before. Heightened security campaigns across the Durand Line by Pakistan and US-NATO, respectively, would have a shared objective: to weaken the resolve of the terrorist-insurgent forces and, consequently, create moderate constituencies among them who are willing to renounce violence, dissociate from al-Qaeda and its hardcore allies and participate in the political process largely on the terms of respective state parties and international forces.

Unlike its predecessor, the Obama Administration has preferred to take Pakistan on board on the issue of combating terrorism through regular high-level consultations with its civilian and military leaders; rather than engaging in coercive diplomacy to force Pakistan to "do more" in the fight against terrorism in the region — as was the case with the Bush Administration, especially during its second term. For instance, President Obama sent his National Security Advisor James Jones to Pakistan in November 2009 to consult its leadership about the US-revised Afghan war strategy. He personally called President Asif Ali Zardari and took him in confidence before announcing the revised Af-Pak strategy in December 2009, while Jones spoke to Prime Minister Yousuf Raza Gilani, who was at the time visiting Germany. Holbrooke's frequent visits to Pakistan as a special envoy of the US President helped to sustain cooperative spirit in US-Pakistan ties over the issue of terrorism, as does the regular interaction of top US commanders — including Gen McChrystal, Central Command Chief Gen David Petraeus, Chairman of the Joint Chiefs of Staff Adm Michael Mullen and Army Chief of Staff Gen George Casey — with Pakistani military leadership. Whatever issues and concerns each side has on combating terrorism are mutually shared in these meetings. The intelligence chiefs of the two countries likewise meet regularly to coordinate their organizational activities. There are regular diplomatic and political leadership-level contacts between the two countries. All of this is a public display of a proactive cooperation between the Obama Administration and the civilian regime in Pakistan. However, there are sensitive issues, such as the US drone attacks in tribal areas and the safety and security of Pakistan's nuclear assets, over which some tacit understanding or cooperative arrangement may exist between the two countries" civilian and security establishments, but they are not made public for fear of public backlash in Pakistan.[40]

The Obama Administration does sometimes pressure Pakistan to deliver on terrorism according to US expectations. For instance, Secretary of State Hillary Clinton concluded her October 2009 visit to Pakistan by suspecting Pakistan's proclaimed ignorance about the whereabouts of top al-Qaeda leaders. She found "it hard to believe that nobody in your government knows where they are and couldn't get them if they really wanted to." "So far as we know," she said, "they're in Pakistan."[41] Then, just a couple of days before President Obama announced the new US strategy for the Afghan war, British Prime Minister Gordon Brown toed the US line by questioning "why, eight years after September 11, nobody has been able to spot or detain or get close to Osama bin Laden, nobody has been able to get close to Zawahiri . . . We have got to ask the Pakistani security forces, army and politicians to join us in the major effort that the world is committing resources to, not only to isolate al-Qaeda but to break them in Pakistan."[42] Since the fall of the Taliban in late 2001, Pakistan has killed or captured over 700 suspected al-Qaeda leaders and activists, extraditing most of them to the US, yet al-Qaeda's two top leaders, Osama bin Laden and Ayman Al-Zawahiri, continue to survive, allegedly somewhere along the Pakistan-Afghan border. If the US suspects they are hiding on the Pakistani side of the border, then obviously Islamabad will remain under US pressure to hunt them down. But, then, in the absence of credible intelligence information — which is relatively hard to come by in an inaccessible rugged and mountainous area known for tribal Pashtun hospitality for the erstwhile Arab Mujahideen leaders — mystery will continue to shroud the actual whereabouts of the two al-Qaeda leaders.

The only possibility for tackling this dilemma is through undertaking a final showdown against the forces of insurgency on both sides of the Durand Line. During the course of 2009, Pakistan in Swat and South Waziristan and the US in the Helmand province of Afghanistan did engage in such a showdown, which could over time increase the chances of al-Qaeda leaders of being captured or killed by the security forces. Until then, however, Pakistan's failure to capture bin Laden and Al-Zawahiri will remain a major irritant in US-Pakistan relations. However, insofar as the country's fight against Taliban and other al-Qaeda-linked groups is concerned, it has created more compatibility between the two countries on the issue of combating terrorism in the region than was the case during the second term of the Bush Administration. This is because Pakistan, in recent years, has seen terrorism becoming a pivotal danger to state apparatus and societal fabric and responded in kind by launching major military offensives against terrorist insurgent forces in the frontier and tribal regions. The rapidity with which the terrorist events have occurred in the country from the summer of 2007 onwards has brought about a qualitative shift in the security situation and the security establishment's subsequent response to it. The resolute counter-terrorism military offensive that the Pakistan army has waged against the al-Qaeda-linked TTP and other terrorist-insurgent groups since the start of 2009 are indicative of this shift.

It is important to understand the domestic, political and security context and recent historical background within which this shift has occurred. In March 2008, Pakistan's present civilian regime inherited a country beset by terrorism. Prior to the Red Mosque operation in July 2007, the country had never experienced a wave of terrorism as it did from the summer of that year onwards, targeting both security personnel and innocent civilians. In December 2007, former Prime Minister Benazir Bhutto also became a casualty of terrorism. There was some respite in terrorism on the eve of February 2008 election and, for some months, in its aftermath. During this period, the government, being an elected one, attempted to build political consensus for finding an amicable solution to the problem of terrorism, since the first task before the newly elected leadership was to win over public support for what Prime Minister Yousuf Raza Gilani said on March 29, 2008, was "Pakistan's own war."[43] He also declared he would make combating terrorism his government's "No. 1 priority" and adopt a "comprehensive approach" for combating terrorism. The Musharraf regime did cooperate with the US in the "War on Terror," but mostly under pressure and in a lacklustre manner. It did deploy close to 80,000 troops in the tribal areas in spring 2004, but, subsequently, instead of undertaking sustained armed campaign against the Taliban, preferred to cut deals with their leaders. In a statement on March 25, 2008, former Prime Minister Nawaz Sharif, whose Pakistan Muslim League (PML) entered into a power-sharing arrangement with the PPP in the Centre and the Punjab province, explained why Pakistanis perceived their country was fighting "America's war:" "Pervaiz Musharraf used the war on terrorism to perpetuate his rule. No cabinet, no parliament was taken into confidence in any of his decisions. That is why it did not have popular support."[44] A sea change was visible in the country's approach to counter-terrorism as soon as the elected government took over. Declaring an intention to make the "War on Terror" Pakistan's own war implied that this war had to be fought indigenously, since its repercussions were indigenous. Given that, the issue was referred to a parliamentary committee set up for the purpose.[45]

In May 2008, the Awami National Government in the Frontier province signed an agreement with the pro-Taliban Tehrik-e-Nifaz-e-Shariat-e-Muhammadi (TNSM) in Swat. Earlier, Prime Minister Gilani had also offered an olive branch to the Taliban, provided they agreed to renounce violence and join the political process. That deal collapsed, as the PPP-led government in the Centre refused to accept it. In fact, the same month the deal was concluded, the federal government decided to intensify the security operation against the Taliban in tribal areas. After that, hell broke loose across Pakistan, as the TTP undertook scores of devastating suicide bombings in cities, including the August 2008 attack outside the Wah Ordnance Factory and the September 2008 attack on the Marriott Hotel in Islamabad. TNSM also intensified its terror campaign against security personnel and common people in Swat. Consequently, in October 2008, a gathering of the Muttahida Ulema Council at Jamia Naeemia, presided over by Dr. Maulana Sarfraz Naeemi, a renowned Alim of the country's majority Sunni Barelvi sect, issued a unanimous fatwa declaring suicide attacks in Pakistan as haram (unlawful) and najaez (unjustified) under Islam. In a country with a religiously conservative population traditionally known for sympathizing with the Taliban, this was a crucial and unprecedented development.[46] Yet, the same month saw the country's parliament unanimously passing a vague resolution, saying the militants posed a "grave danger" to the integrity of the state and pursuing dialogue with them should be "the highest priority."[47] This meant that politicians had still not abandoned hope for tackling terrorism peacefully, even though TTP and TNSM had shown no inclination for renouncing violence. Investigation into the Marriott attack revealed another bitter reality: that a Punjab-based Sunni sectarian group, Lashkar-e-Jhangvi, had joined ranks with the Taliban in the terror campaign.[48] In November 2008, Jamaat-ud-Dawa, the front organization of the banned Lashker-e-Tayyiba, known for its role in Kashmir militancy, introduced another irritant in the country's fight against terrorism by launching a devastating terrorist attack in Mumbai, and thereby jeopardizing the peace process between India and Pakistan.[49]

While the Mumbai attack threatened to create a serious standoff in relations between the two traditionally hostile neighbours, the TTP and the TNSM continued their terrorist campaigns. The government could not sustain the mounting internal and external pressure, and caved in before the TNSM in February 2009, by agreeing to introduce Nizam-e-Adl, a Sharia-based system in Swat, as demanded by the pro-Taliban group. This was despite all the death and destruction that the TNSM had caused in the region in the preceding months. This capitulation on the part of the government only encouraged the TTP and its south Punjab affiliates to orchestrate the most lethal terrorist campaign in the country in subsequent months, beginning with attacks on the Sri Lankan cricket team and Manawan Police Academy in Lahore in March 2009. In June 2009, Dr. Sarfraz Naeemi was killed in a suicide attack in Lahore. The attack received nationwide condemnation and helped build a much-needed political consensus in the country against terrorism, as the Provincial Assembly of the Punjab, governed by Nawaz Sharif's PML, unanimously condemned the incident and voiced its support for a military operation against Taliban. For its part, TNSM declared to expand its Sharia cause to the rest of the country, while engaging in a beheading spree and publicly lashing a 17-year-old girl. The video footage of the latter incident was broadcast through national media in March 2009, leading to public outrage against the Taliban. TNSM militants also started to expand their activities beyond Swat, capturing parts of Dir and Bajaur region, located just 60 miles from Islamabad.[50]

It was to this backdrop that the country's security establishment decided to act firmly against the TNSM and the TTP and launched Operation Rah-e-Rast in Swat in late April 2009. In early May, in a national address Prime Minister Gilani announced his government's full support for this operation. Within months, the army had routed the TNSM, killing or capturing many of its key leaders. The army operation did generate a massive humanitarian crisis, displacing over a million people from the Swat valley and its adjoining regions, which was also successfully managed by the government and civil society with help from the UN World Food Programme (WFP). While TNSM was being wiped out in Swat, TTP continued its terror campaign from its base in South Waziristan, including a major one attack against the Pearl Continental Hotel in Peshawar in June 2009. However, on August 3, the terrorist group suffered a mortal blow, as its leader Baitullah Mehsud, declared by the government as Pakistan's "Public Enemy No. 1," was killed in a US drone attack. He was succeeded by Hakimullah Mehsud, Baitullah's cousin and a relatively younger TTP leader. Under his leadership, TTP and its south Punjabi affiliates began to avenge the death of their leader by launching lethal suicidal missions in Bannu, Kohat and Peshawar and against WFP headquarters in Islamabad, until early October 2009. Then, on October 10, the TTP, with the help of Lashkar-e-Jhangvi terrorist leader Muhammad Aqil, alias Dr. Usman, launched a deadly terrorist operation on the army's General Headquarters in Rawalpindi. By attacking the nerve centre of Pakistani military, TTP paved the way for a resolute military offensive against it — just as its affiliate TNSM had invited the wrath of the military by expanding its terrorist reach beyond Swat in early 2009. Soon after this attack, Prime Minister Gilani convened a national security conference, where government leaders, opposition politicians and military commanders unanimously decided to eliminate the terrorist threat from Taliban once and for all. It was in this backdrop that the army launched Operation Rah-e-Nijat in South Waziristan on October 17, 2009.[51]

In over two years of sustained terrorist activity until the start of this operation, the TTP and its affiliates had claimed the lives of over 2,000 Pakistanis, including both security personnel and unarmed civilians. The terror campaign had ruined the country's economy by scuttling domestic business activity and discouraging foreign investment. The Taliban and other terrorist-insurgent groups had damaged Pakistan's international reputation, and distorted the image of Islam. So, when the army's two divisions advanced from three directions against the TTP stronghold in South Waziristan, the military mission they were assigned to was meant to physically exterminate the enemy. In the initial weeks, as the TTP started to suffer considerable losses, its backlash was expressed in several suicidal acts of terrorism with multiple targets, including the International Islamic University (October 20) and a busy market in Peshawar (October 28). The latter attack, which took place on the day Secretary of State Clinton arrived in Pakistan, killed well over 100 civilians, including women and children.[52] However, by November, as the federal and provincial governments tightened security in and around major cities and the army operation claimed more successes, the terrorist campaign waged by TTP and its affiliates had considerably waned. However, given the enormity of Taliban terrorism in recent years, there did not appear to be any short end in sight to the army's protracted counter-insurgency campaign in tribal and Frontier regions — and so seemed to be the case with the consequent terrorist backlash for Pakistanis at large.

The above description about the evolution of terrorism in Pakistan and the factors underpinning the country's response to it seem to prove that a number of "firsts" have occurred insofar as how the security establishment, the civilian government and the society as a whole perceives the threat from terrorism and desires to combat it. There exists broader political consensus to eliminate terrorism. The public opinion is heavily against Taliban and supportive of army operations. The security establishment is engaged in a resolute counter-insurgency campaign against terrorists. And the civilian government fully owns this campaign. Throughout the Musharraf era, and at least during the first year of the present government, this was not the case. The army remained reluctant to launch credible counter-insurgency operations, and whenever it did, they were limited in scope and conducted largely under external pressure. The public opinion was confused and, in fact, often supportive of the Taliban cause. Political consensus to tackle terrorism was lacking. The Musharraf regime did conduct a successful security operation at the Red Mosque, but without clear-cut support from its political allies.[53] Thus, by the time President Obama announced a review of the Afghan war strategy in December 2009, Pakistan's counter-terrorism approach had already undergone a qualitative shift. On the eve of the announcement of the Af-Pak strategy in March 2009, the country's civilian government and security establishment were still indecisive about managing the terrorist-insurgent problem posed by TNSM in Swat and TTP in South Waziristan. By December 2009, they could claim to have achieved one major counter-insurgency victory in Swat and an increasingly impressive counter-insurgency campaign in South Waziristan.

Promising Future?

In terms of achievement, the US and NATO troops' eight-year-long counter-insurgency campaign in Afghanistan paled in comparison with the Pakistan army's eight-month-long military offensive in the country's Frontier and tribal regions, by the time President Obama announced to shore up US forces in Afghanistan in December 2009. Since the Pakistan' army's offensive against TTP and its foreign terrorist allies in South Waziristan was still not fully over, it was but natural on the part of the country's civilian leadership and security establishment to express its concerns over the expected infiltration of Afghan insurgents across the Durand Line into the border regions in Balochistan and tribal areas. Still combating with the leftover TNSM insurgents in Swat and fully engaged in the fight against the TTP and its allies in South Waziristan, Pakistani security forces could hardly afford to simultaneously tackle other fronts that the insurgent infiltration threatened. The "fastest possible pace" of US troops" deployment that President Obama indicated meant that all of the major hotspots of insurgency in Afghanistan's southern and eastern regions bordering Pakistan, including the provinces of Helmand, Kandahar, Paktia and Paktika, were to experience a heightened security campaign, especially in the spring of 2010. 30,000 additional US troops, plus several thousands NATO troop reinforcements, were to increase the total number of foreign troops in Afghanistan to approximately 150,000, from the December 2009 level of 68,000 US troops and 42,000 troops from 42 nations under NATO command. The ripple effect of the intensified military campaign in Afghanistan's border regions with Pakistan in the shape of insurgent infiltration and refugee influx from Afghanistan was, indeed, a justified concern of the country's civilian rulers and security establishment.

But then, in the wake of worsening insurgency in Afghanistan, the US and NATO were left with no choice but to undertake a resolute counter-insurgency campaign. Despite the reservations of its civil-military leadership, Pakistan was, therefore, left with no choice but to continue to build upon its hitherto successful military missions in Swat and South Waziristan, and expand the counter-insurgency campaign to other areas of the tribal belt, particularly North Waziristan, and border regions of Balochistan, if and when the terrorist-insurgent danger surfaced there. This was because Pakistan's inaction to fight the runaway Afghan insurgents and their local protectorates could threaten renewed pressure from the US and its allies in Afghanistan as well as jeopardize its internal security situation. As we have seen in the preceding discussion about the major components of the Obama Administration's originally pronounced Af-Pak strategy and its subsequent review as well as policies grounded in them, the level of compatibility between Pakistan's counter-terrorism interests and those of the US and its allies in the region has significantly increased over time. The only area of friction in terms of the priorities of the two sides in tackling terrorism pertains to Pakistan's traditional policy of showing no leniency towards those insurgents groups that commit terrorism inside the country and a softer approach for those who do not commit domestic terrorism but undertake or facilitate insurgency in Afghanistan.

Pakistan, for instance, has cut deals with two Taliban groups, one led by Mullah Nazir Ahmad in South Waziristan and another led by Hafiz Gul Bahadur in North Waziristan, both of which allegedly provide safe havens to the Afghan insurgent group of Jalaluddin Haqqani, a former Afghan Mujahideen leader, besides directly participating in Afghan insurgency. These deals have helped to isolate the TTP in South Waziristan, thereby facilitating the army's counter-insurgency campaign there. However, for its part, the US expects Pakistan to go after these groups as well as the Afghan Taliban hiding in tribal areas and Balochistan with as much interest as it has displayed in fighting the TNSM, TTP and al-Qaeda-linked Uzbek warriors, and the US has concerns about al-Qaeda leaders and other terrorist groups such as Lashker-e-Tayyiba, Lashkar-e-Jhangvi and the country's failure to bring them to task. All of these concerns were expressed by President Obama in a letter delivered by his National Security Advisor to President Zardari when he visited Pakistan in November 2009. In the letter, the US President warned Pakistan that its use of insurgent groups to pursue policy goals "cannot continue," while calling for "closer collaboration against all extremist groups," including al-Qaeda, the Afghan Taliban, the Haqqani network, Lashker-e-Tayyiba, and the TTP."[54] However, simultaneously, to encourage the country into action against these groups, President Obama in the same communication guaranteed Pakistan "an expanded strategic partnership," including "an effort to help reduce tensions between Pakistan and India."[55]

As part of this expanded strategic partnership, proffered US carrots for Pakistan, outlined during Secretary of State Clinton's October visit to Islamabad, center on a far more comprehensive and long-term bilateral relationship. It would feature enhanced development and trade assistance, improved intelligence collaboration and an upgraded military equipment pipeline, more public praise and less public criticism of Pakistan and an initiative to build greater regional cooperation among Pakistan, India and Afghanistan.[56] One of the main reasons for the Pakistani security establishment's relative leniency towards Afghanistan or Kashmir-specific insurgent groups is the perceived fear about the US once again doing what it did in the aftermath of the Soviet troops' withdrawal from Afghanistan: simply leave the region after the fulfilment of its strategic interest, leaving Pakistan alone to deal with the messy consequences of the Afghan jihad. Pakistan may have contributed to the current terrorist quagmire by sponsoring or overlooking the forces of insurgency in the disputed region of Kashmir and backing the Taliban in Afghanistan prior to the events of 9/11, but its fears regarding US abandonment are, nonetheless, justified.

However, the fact that future US-Pakistan relations may have a radically different, positivist context is amply clear from repeated assurances by President Obama and Secretary of State Clinton that the US's relationship with the country is long term and strategic in orientation as well as from concrete pledges of billions of dollars of US civilian and security assistance to the country, especially under the Kerry-Lugar-Berman Act. Obviously, nothing could be said with certainty regarding whether the US and NATO troops' surge would make the expected difference in the insurgency-ridden ground-reality of Afghanistan to pave the way for the eventual withdrawal of foreign troops. But, given the inherently evolutionary nature of the Af-Pak strategy, it can be argued that the targets of counter-insurgency, including the option of reconciling moderate insurgents, much faster security capacity-building and enhanced civilian development in Afghanistan it has set in its original shape or reviewed form, can always be modified.

In the context of US-Pakistan relations pertaining to tackling terrorism, perhaps the most important development is the grand transformation that is under way in this relationship, from the traditional state-to-state towards people-to-people. If such a guarantee is there, then Pakistan's civilian and military leadership can also be expected to start making no distinction between who conducts terrorism inside the country and who is involved in insurgency beyond the country's frontiers. Already, as is clear from the preceding discussion about how terrorism has evolved in recent years in Pakistan, some of the most spectacular acts of terrorism, including the October 2009 attack on the army's General Headquarters; have been orchestrated by south Punjabi Jihadi groups like Lashkar-e-Jhangvi, traditionally identified with sectarian terrorism. If the Obama Administration is indeed willing to play a role in helping India and Pakistan to resolve Kashmir amicably, then the Pakistani security establishment can also be expected to change its current course against Kashmir-specific banned militant outfits like Jaish-e-Muhammad and Lashker-e-Tayyiba.

And if Washington is guaranteeing Pakistan a strategic partnership and is willing to co-opt moderate insurgents in Afghanistan's political and security structure, then this will surely encourage Pakistani security establishment to re-think its strategic depth strategy. Co-opting moderate insurgents, meaning Pashtun majority, amid an intensified security campaign, will be an option that cannot be exercised successfully without Pakistan's cooperation, because of the most crucial ground reality of the Durand Line: the Pashtun ethnicity straddling across this frontier, which is a major source of current insurgent trouble in the region, but can be a potential factor in overcoming the terrorist quagmire in Afghanistan and Pakistan. Being Afghanistan's principal neighbour, Pakistan seeks an Afghan solution that credibly incorporates the security, political and economic grievances of its majority Pashtun population, simply because, without that, its own Pashtun population inhabiting tribal areas east of the Durand Line remains aggrieved. A military campaign that crushes terrorist-insurgents to the extent that moderate constituencies are created among the forces of insurgency — be they in Afghanistan or Pakistan — which are willing to renounce violence, dissociate their links from al-Qaeda and participate in the political process largely on the basis of the interests of the state parties does have a scope of success. However uncertain its outcome, it must be given a chance.

Notes

1   See the transcript of President Obama's speech (hereafter cited as Obama's Speech March 27, 2009) at http://www.whitehouse.gov/the_press_office/Remarks-by-the-President-on-a-New-Strategy-for-Afghanistan-and-Pakistan/ (accessed March 22, 2010).

2   Report of the Inter-Agency Group (Hereafter cited as Inter-Agency Group Report) available at: http://www.whitehouse.gov/assets/documents/afghanistan_pakistan_white_paper_final.pdf (accessed March 22, 2010).

3   Daniel Markey, *From Af-Pak to Pak-Af: A Response to the New US Strategy for South Asia.* Washington, DC: Council on Foreign Relations, April 2009, p. 2.

4   Inter-Agency Group Report, p. 1.

5   Obama's Speech, March 27, 2009.

6   Inter-Agency Group Report, p. 1.

7   Obama's Speech, March 27, 2009.

8   Ibid. For Iraq strategy and its lessons for Afghanistan, see Mustafa Qadri, "Obama's New 'AfPak' Strategy — The View from Pakistan," *Common Ground News Service*, April 28, 2009, available at http://www.commongroundnews.org/article.php?id=25394&lan=en&sid=1&sp=0 accessed on March 22, 2010; and George Friedman, "Petraeus, Afghanistan and the Lessons of Iraq," in *Stratfor*, May 6, 2008, available at: www.stratfor.com/weekly/petraeus_afghanistan_and_lessons_iraq (accessed March 22, 2010).

9   Susan Cornwell, "U.S Defense Bill Would Pay Taliban to Switch Sides," *Reuters*, October 27, 2009.

10   Obama's Speech, March 27, 2009.

11   "Civilian Deployments to Afghanistan 'on Track': Obama Administration," *Agence France-Presse*, November 6, 2009.

12   Jeremy Scahill, "The Expanding US War in Pakistan," *The Nation*, February 4, 2010. Available at: http://www.thenation.com/doc/20100222/scahill2 (accessed March 22, 2010).

13   Markey, op. cit., p. 2.

14   Inter-Agency Group Report, p. 1.

15   Ibid.

16   See full text of the Kerry-Lugar-Berman Act (Hereafter cited as Kerry-Lugar-Berman Act) at http://thomas.loc.gov/home/gpoxmlc111/s1707_enr.xml (accessed December 2, 2009).

17   Joe Klein, "Can Obama Avoid a Quagmire in Afghanistan?" *Time*, March 5, 2009.

18   Inter-Agency Group Report, p. 1.

19   The aim of Operation Khanjar was to retake the initiative in Helmand, and make it safer for the elections due the next month. The US-led operation was preceded and complemented by a British airborne assault north of Lashkar Gah, the provincial capital of Helmand, just over a week before, code-named Panther's Claw and intended to wrest control of river crossings from the Taliban and expand the area under British control, also with the aim of preparing the ground for elections. For details, see Julian Borger, "New American tactics and resolve undergo test in Helmand," *The Guardian*, July 2, 2009.

20   Peter Bergen and Katherine Tiedemann, *Revenge of the Drones: An Analysis of Drone Strikes in Pakistan*. Washington, DC: New America Foundation, October 19, 2009.

21   Inter-Agency Group Report, p. 3.

22   Bob Woodward, "McChrystal: More Forces or 'Mission Failure,'" *The Washington Post*, September 21, 2009.

23   Access Secretary of Defense Robert Gates' interview with *Al-Jazeera* on September 8, 2009 at http://english.aljazeera.net/news/americas/2009/09/200995202939732522.html (accessed March 22, 2010).

24   Julian E. Barnes, "NATO Members Support US Troop Hike in Afghanistan," *Los Angeles Times*, October 24, 2009.

25   Latest accounts of yearly and monthly casualties of US and NATO troops in the Afghan war can be accessed at www.icasualties.org/OEF/index.aspx (accessed March 22, 2010).

26   For details, see Anne Gearan and Matthew Lee, "Obama Eyes Smaller Afghan Troop Option," *The Associated Press*, October 28, 2009; and Tom Coghlan, "Stanley McChrystal's Strategy Faces an Old Problem — Convincing the Locals," *The Times*, November 9, 2009.

27   Dexter Filkins, "U.S. Tightens Air strike Policy in Afghanistan," *The New York Times*, June 21, 2009.

28   Barnes, op. cit.

29   Markey, op. cit., p. 1.

30   For details, see Con Coughlin, "Afghanistan: Can Barack Obama Destroy the Enemy, Get the Troops out and Save Himself?" *The Daily Telegraph*, November 27, 2009; and "US Scrambles to Gain Support of Allies in Afghanistan," *Press TV*, November 27, 2009.

31   See the full transcript of President Obama's speech at the official website of The White

House at www.whitehouse.gov/the-press-office/remarks-president-address-nation-way-forward-afghanistan-and-pakistan (accessed March 22, 2010).

32   "Army Expresses Reservation over Af-Pak Policy," *Online*, September 16, 2009.

33   M Ilyas Khan, "Pakistan's Tribals — Who Is Killing Whom?" *BBC*, April 5, 2009.

34   Inter-Agency Group Report, p. 6.

35   Anwar Iqbal, "Obama Signs Kerry-Lugar Bill into Law," *Dawn*, October 16, 2009.

36   Kerry-Lugar-Berman Act, op. cit.

37   Anwar Iqbal, "Note Dilutes Some Conditions in Kerry-Lugar Bill," *Dawn*, October 14, 2009.

38   Ibid.

39   "Clinton Pledges More Than 243 Million Dollars as Additional Aid for Pakistan," *ANI*, October 29, 2009.

40   See, for instance, Karen De Young and Joby Warrick, "Don't-ask-don't-tell Policy: Pakistan and U.S. Have Tacit Deal on Air Sstrikes," *The Washington Post*, November 16, 2008; and David E Sanger and William J Broad, "U.S. Secretly Aids Pakistan in Guarding Nuclear Arms," *The Washington Post*, November 16, 2009.

41   Karen de Young, "Clinton Presses Pakistan on Al-Qaeda," *The Washington Post*, October 30, 2009.

42   Nicholas Watt and Ed Pilkington, "Gordon Brown to Announce 500 More British Troops for Afghanistan," *The Guardian*, November 29, 2009.

43   Raja Asghar, "Gilani Wins Unanimous Trust Vote," *Dawn*, March 30, 2008.

44   "PML-N Asks Pak Govt to Review Policy on the War against Terror," *Times of India*, March 12, 2010.

45   For details, see Ishtiaq Ahmad, "Making War on Terror Pakistan's 'Own War'" *Weekly Pulse*, April 4–10, 2008. Available at: www.ishtiaqahmad.com/item_display. aspx?listing_id=145&listing_type=1 (accessed March 22, 2010).

46   See Ishtiaq Ahmad, "The Battle for Pakistan," *Weekly Pulse*, October 23, 2008. Available at: www.ishtiaqahmad.com/item_display.aspx?listing_id=396&listing_type=1 (accessed March 22, 2010).

47   "Pakistan Parliament Passes Vague Terrorism Resolution," *VOA News*, October 17–23, 2009.

48   "Lashkar-e-Jhangvi," *The New York Times*, October 10, 2009. Available at: http://topics. nytimes.com/topics/reference/timestopics/organizations/l/lashkarejhangvi/index. html (accessed March 22, 2010).

49   Ishtiaq Ahmad, "Aftermath of Mumbai Attacks," *Weekly Pulse*, December 19–25, 2008. Available at: http://www.ishtiaqahmad.com/item_display.aspx?listing_id=417&listing_type=1 (accessed March 22, 2010).

50   For details, see Ishtiaq Ahmad, "Climax of Terror," *Weekly Pulse*, March 16–12, 2009. Available at: http://www.ishtiaqahmad.com/item_display.aspx?listing_id=435&listing_type=1 (accessed March 22, 2010); and Ishtiaq Ahmad, "Pakistan Army's Offensive to

'Eliminate' Taliban," *Weekly Pulse*, May 1–7, 2009. Available at: http://www.ishtiaqah mad.com/commentaries.aspx?listing_year=2008 (accessed March 22, 2010).

51   See Ishtiaq Ahmad, "Final Showdown: Security Operation in South Waziristan," *Weekly Pulse*, October 9–15, 2009. Available at: www.ishtiaqahmad.com/item_display. aspx?listing_id=622&listing_type=1; and Ishtiaq Ahmad, "Course of Action after the Terrorist Attack on GHQ," *Weekly Pulse*, October 16–22, 2009. Available at: www. ishtiaqahmad.com/item_display.aspx?listing_id=627&listing_type=1 (accessed March 22, 2010).

52   Ishtiaq Ahmad, "Taliban on the Warpath," *Weekly Pulse*, October 23–29, 2009. Available at: www.ishtiaqahmad.com/item_display.aspx?listing_id=630&listing_ type=1 (accessed March 22, 2010).

53   Ishtiaq Ahmad, "In Pakistan, the Tide Finally Turns against Taliban," *Weekly Pulse*, July 10–16, 2009. Available at: www.ishtiaqahmad.com/item_display.aspx?listing_ id=513&listing_type=1 (accessed March 22, 2010).

54   Karen de Young, "Obama Wants New Role for Pakistan," *The Washington Post*, November 30, 2009.

55   Ibid.

56   Ibid.

CHAPTER THREE

The Economic Cost of Extremism

Sartaj Aziz

Abstract

The "war on terror" has left Pakistan's economy in tatters. The author of this chapter, an ex-finance and foreign minister of Pakistan, discusses the "initial benefits" of the "war on terror" during its early years and analyzes the genesis of the "war" economy leading to its current trend and future discourses. Whilst explaining the "typology" of costs of the "war on terror," the author analyzes the impacts of previous, existent and future international particularly US economic aid to Pakistan. The overall argument of the chapter is that Pakistan and its economy is paying too high price for the "war on terror" and the international, particularly the US economic aid, is not even near sufficient against the incurred costs and unless this crisis is averted, the future of Pakistan's economy may be even more gloomier.

Introduction

Economic deprivation and lack of education in the tribal areas are two factors that have contributed to the growth of extremism in Pakistan. The Federally Administered Tribal Area (FATA), with an estimated population of about 4.0 million (2.4 percent of Pakistan's population of 170 million), is the least developed part of Pakistan, with a literacy rate of only 18 percent. Its mountainous terrain, combined with the primitive structure of governance that FATA inherited from the British-control era, has physically isolated the tribal communities from the economic and social progress that the rest of Pakistan has experienced in the past six decades.

The Russian invasion of Afghanistan in December 1979 and the US-supported counter offensive by the Afghan "Mujahideen" to end the foreign occupation of their country added to the misery of the tribal population due to the influx of 3.5 million refugees and a large volume of weapons and narcotic drugs.

When the Russians, having failed in their objective of occupying Afghanistan, left in 1990, a civil war broke out among the seven warlords and their supporters for the control of Afghanistan. If the US and its allies had stayed on and provided substantial assistance for rehabilitation and reconstruction, the Mujahideen, who had fought the Russians throughout the 1980s, would have found alternative employment. But the world simply abandoned Afghanistan, leaving the people to suffer the prolonged consequences of an intensified civil war.

The Taliban emerged as a new force in Afghanistan in August 1994, when Mullah Omar led a small revolt against a local commander in Kandahar. The students of his Madrassah, called Taliban after they captured Kandahar, were welcomed by the people in other provinces because they promised peace. By August 1998, the Taliban had taken over 90 percent of Afghanistan.

But then came 9/11. Since many foreign Mujahideen, including Osama bin Laden, who, after winning the Jihad against the Soviet Union in the 1980s, had helped the Taliban to gain control of Afghanistan in the 1990s, had established their network (later labelled the al-Qaeda network), they became the target of the 9/11 revenge. In October 2001, the US and allies captured Afghanistan and pushed out many of the Taliban fighters and their foreign supporters into the Tribal areas of Pakistan. US President George W. Bush declared a global "war on terror" and Pakistan readily agreed to join this campaign. In retaliation, the Taliban and their foreign supporters established facilities and safe havens in the tribal areas and began to expand their influence and terrorist activities to other parts of Pakistan.

Initial Benefits

The decision to participate in the "war on terror" did lead to a major outpouring of international support for Pakistan. In 2001, Pakistan was emerging from a tough stabilization program with the IMF, which, in the process of reducing macroeconomic imbalances had, more or less, "suffocated" the process of growth. Per-capita income was stagnant and there had been a substantial increase in unemployment and poverty. Foreign exchange resources were scarce and at the beginning of the 2001–02 financial year, foreign reserves stood at $3,231 million, only enough to finance three months of imports of goods and services.

Participation in the war effort led to a substantial increase in the inflow of concessional assistance, especially in the form of grants from the US. As shown in Table 3.1, since 2001–02 Pakistan has cumulatively received $12.2 billion in funding from the US. This has consisted primarily (almost 70 percent) of reimbursement for the costs incurred by the military in counter-terrorism operations in the north of the country. Development and economic assistance has totalled $3.2 billion during the period. Therefore, the direct contribution to the growth process in the country has been limited. However, the overall assistance, including the funding of military operations (mostly incurred in local currency) contributed to a rapid build-up in the foreign exchange reserves of the country. These reserves increased to $12,389 million by the end of 2003–04.

The consequence was not only the alleviation of the foreign exchange constraint to growth but also the associated rapid expansion in money supply this led to a precipitous fall in interest rates and stimulated aggregate demand in the economy. The economy went back, after a long time, on to the path of rapid growth from 2003–04 onwards, averaging a GDP growth rate of almost 7 percent.

Table 3.1 US Funding to Pakistan Since 2001 ($ million)

Purpose	FY 2002	FY 2003	FY 2004	FY 2005	FY 2006	FY 2007	FY 2008	Cumulative
Military	1465	1473	782	1273	1218	1095	1387	8694
Law enforcement	100	32	36	40	46	31	31	318
Development and economic	665	258	304	405	677	442	445	3194
Diplomacy	3	4	7	6	9	9	1	39
Total	2232	1767	1129	1724	1951	1578	1866	12245

Source: US Government Accountability Office, Securing, Stabilizing and Developing Pakistan's Border with Afghanistan, February 2009.

But the large inflows of aid, along with higher remittances and, more recently, foreign direct investment, led to symptoms of "Dutch Disease" in the Pakistani economy. The currency appreciated in real terms, which promoted import-based consumption-led growth. By 2006–07, the process of rapid growth was beginning to look increasingly unsustainable, with the current account deficit in the balance of payments reaching 5 percent of the GDP. Following the sharp increase in oil prices, Pakistan found itself confronted with a full-blown financial crisis in 2007–08. This led to the plummeting of the growth rate to 2 percent in 2008–09. Increasingly, the benefits of participation in the "war on terror" were not only declining but were also frittered away in rising consumption levels, especially in the richer sections of Pakistani society.

The Pakistan Security Report prepared by the Pakistan Institute of Peace Studies (PIPS) quantifies carefully the incidence of terrorism in the country on the basis of day-to-day monitoring of the national and local print and electronic media. The estimated number of attacks in 2008 along with the numbers killed and injured is given in Table 3.2. The bulk of the incidents were terrorist attacks. An estimated 2,267 people were killed in these attacks and 4,558 were injured. In addition, "operational attacks" (security force's operations against terrorists) have led to 3,182 deaths and 2,267 injured (mostly "collateral" damage). According to some estimates, missile attacks by US drones have killed almost 1,000 innocent civilians in 2008.

The highest number of attacks were reported in NWFP at 1,009, followed by Balochistan at 682 and the tribal areas at 385. As many as 35 attacks took

Table 3.2 Nature and Incidence of Attacks in 2008

Attacks/Clashes	Number of Incidents	Killed	Injured
Terrorist attacks	2148	2267	4558
Operational attacks	—	3182	2267
Clashes between security forces and militants	95	655	557
Political violence	88	162	419
Inter-tribe sectarian clashes	55	395	207
Total		**6661**	**8008**

Source: PIPS (2008) "Pakistan Security Report," Pakistan Institute for Peace Studies, 4th Chapter.

Table 3.3 Terrorist and Other Attacks from 2005 to 2008

Years	Total Attacks	% increase	Number Killed	% increase	Number Injured	% increase
2005	254		216		571	
2006	675	159	907	320	1543	170
2007	1503	129	3448	280	5353	247
2008	2386	59	6661	93	8008	50

Source: PIPS (2008) "Pakistan Security Report," Pakistan Institute for Peace Studies, 4th Chapter.

place in Punjab, 25 in Sindh, seven in Islamabad and four in Azad Kashmir. The major attacks in 2008 involving the death of 25 people or more are listed in Table 3.3. The striking conclusion is that these "mega-attacks" have occurred throughout the country, including in high-security locations like the capital city, Islamabad. Such major acts of terrorism disproportionately magnify general perceptions of risk throughout the country and demonstrate the difficulties encountered by counter-terrorism efforts.

The inescapable conclusion from Table 3.3 is that the incidence of terrorism is increasing exponentially in Pakistan. These estimates indicate that the costs of terrorism are rising very rapidly in the country, due not only to the increasing number but also because of the rising intensity and widespread nature of this activity. The first half of 2009, in fact, saw a big jump in the number of suicide attacks against security forces and foreigners, especially after the military operation in Swat, launched in the first week of May.

Government Estimates of the Costs of Terrorism

The Ministry of Finance has prepared estimates of the cost of the "war on terror" to Pakistan in the Poverty Reduction Strategy Paper (PRSP-II document).[1] The following indirect costs have been identified in addition to the direct costs:

  i. delay in implementation of development projects in affected areas, like NWFP and FATA, leading to cost overruns
 ii. increasing uncertainty leading to capital flight and affecting FDI
iii. slowing down of domestic economic activity

iv. excessive increase in the country's credit risk, making borrowing very expensive

v. increased unemployment in affected regions

vi. costs of displacement of local population.

According to Table 3.4, the costs of the "war on terror" are expected to approach Rs. 678 billion (approximately $8.4 billion) in 2008–09, equivalent to over 5 percent of the projected GDP. Indirect costs on account of loss of exports, foreign investment, and industrial output represent the bulk of the costs, with a share of over 83 percent. According to government estimates, the cumulative cost of the "war on terror" since 2004–05 is $31.4 billion, substantially in excess of the flow of concessional assistance, estimated at about $1.7 billion annually. The government estimates reveal very rapid growth in these costs of over 27 percent per annum since 2004–05. This is consistent with the sharply rising incidence of attacks highlighted in the previous section.

The literature is replete with attempts at quantification of the costs of the 9/11 terrorist attacks on the US economy.[2] According to the Institute for the Analysis of Global Security 2003 the total cost was $244 billion, with the share of direct and indirect costs being 44 percent and 56 percent respectively. This is equivalent to about 2.5 percent of the US GDP in 2001. If the loss in stock-market wealth is included, then the costs rise substantially. A recent book

Table 3.4 Costs of "War on Terror" to Pakistan (Rs. billion)

	2004–05	2005–06	2006–07	2007–08	2008–09*	Growth Rate (%)
Direct cost (Rs. billion)	67.1	78.1	82.5	108.5	114.0	14.1
Indirect cost** (Rs. billion)	192.0	222.7	278.4	375.8	563.8	30.9
Total (Rs. billion)	259.1	300.8	360.9	484.4	677.8	27.2
Total ($ billion)	4365	5025	5752	7744	8368	17.7
% of GDP	4.0	3.9	4.1	4.6	5.1	

*   Assumed exchange rate $1–81.00 Rs.

** On account of loss of exports, foreign investment, privatization, industrial output, tax collection, etc.

Source: Finance Division, Government of Pakistan, September 2008, PRSP II.

by Bruce Reidel puts the cost of 9/11 for the US economy at over \$1 trillion. According to the Milken Institute, if losses to the global stock markets are included, the costs approach \$2 trillion.

Typology of Costs

The costs of terrorism, as highlighted above, are both direct and indirect as well as of a short-term and more long-term nature.[3]

Direct costs include the following:

   i. value of human lives lost or of injuries
  ii. value of property or infrastructure destroyed or damaged
 iii. costs of enhanced spending on security

Here, the major conceptual issue relates to the valuation of the human cost, either in terms of loss of life or of injuries. In order to avoid controversy over any assumed value, we can simply compute the financial cost as the (potential or actual) compensation due to affected families as per a prescribed government formula.

Indirect costs are diverse in nature and include the following:

Costs to local economies

Areas that are severely impacted by terrorism, like NWFP and FATA, are likely to experience dislocation of economic activity resulting in loss of output and employment. In addition, due to the heightened sense of insecurity, loss of livelihood, and damage to shelter, terrorism may lead to internally displaced persons (IDPs) on whom costs will need to be incurred in the form of relief and rehabilitation.

Costs of greater uncertainty and risk perceptions

The first cost incurred is in terms of lost investment, both foreign and domestic, due to heightened risk perceptions, especially arising from "mega-attacks" like the assassination of Benazir Bhutto in December 2007 and the bombing of the Marriott Hotel in September 2008. The enhanced uncertainty may also be reflected in the decline in share-market capitalization. In addition, travel and tourism to the country is likely to be adversely affected, leading to a decline in associated services by hotels, restaurants, tourist guides and transport operators. Finally, an important category of costs relates to the higher costs of insurance premiums for coverage against acts of terrorism.

Higher transaction costs

These costs are associated with delays in the movement of goods and consignments. Firms may also incur costs of higher inventories to avoid the possibility of disruption in supplies. In addition there are enhanced time costs, arising, for example, at airports, due to greater security checks, and immigration restrictions.

Psychological costs

These are very difficult to measure, and include added anxiety, stress and even mental disorders.

In attempting a quantification of the costs, deliberate effort has been made to keep the estimates on the conservative side for the latest year, 2007–08. For this year, the counter-factual in the case of direct costs is the projection of the trend observed in 2000–01 while in the case of indirect costs the counter-factual assumed is the projection of trend estimated in 2006–07.

Direct Costs

Starting with the damage to human lives and property, as mentioned above, we focus only on the cost of compensation for loss of life or injury. The Prime Minister had announced a compensation formula to affected families following the Wali Bagh suicide attack on October 3, 2008 of Rs. 300,000 per deceased and Rs. 100,000 per injured person. Given the number killed and injured in 2008, shown in Table 3.2, the total potential compensation cost is estimated at about Rs. 3 billion. This is, of course, a low estimate compared to the present value of the lifetime income stream lost due to either death or injury.

As far as the damage to property and infrastructure is concerned, no systematic data is available except for "mega-attacks" like the bombing of the Marriott Hotel, in which case the renovation cost is estimated at over Rs. 500 million. Also, an inventory has been made of the damage caused by the riots following the assassination of Benazir Bhutto. A notional estimate of loss of property due to terrorist attacks can be made as about Rs. 1 million per person killed. This is equivalent to about one sixth of the damage per person killed in a high-value property bombing like the Marriott Hotel. Accordingly, the loss of property and infrastructure due to attacks in 2008 is approximately Rs. 8 billion.

Turning next to expenditure on security, defence expenditure has been higher because of the need to place the armed forces at the Western borders and for undertaking counter-terrorism operations, especially in the North. This is demonstrated by the numbers in Table 3.5. Between 1993–94 and 1999–2000 there was a gradual drop in real current defense expenditure (at 1999–2000 prices) of about 2 percent per annum. From 2001–02 onwards, at the time of the onset of the "war on terror," the trend in real defense expenditure is one of positive growth of over 5.5 percent per annum. It appears that defence expenditure is about 62 percent higher than what it would have been in the absence of the "war on terror." This implies that at current prices the cost of engaging in the war in 2007–08 is Rs. 109 billion. This, of course, does not include the cost of acquisition of specialized military equipment for the war, on which no information is available. As such, the overall cost is understated. The upward pressure on defense expenditure is highlighted by the fact that in recent years actual expenditure has consistently exceeded budget estimates.

Turning to expenditure on law and order and public safety by provincial governments, primarily on police, we also observe a distinct change in the trend after 2001–02, as shown in Table 3.5.

Prior to 2001–02, the trend growth rate in real law and order expenditure was 7 percent, which doubled to 14 percent after 2001–02. It thus appears that law and order expenditure is higher by about 48 percent in the presence of the "war on terror" than it would have been without the war. This implies a higher cost of Rs. 21 billion in 2007–08. Here again, no provision is made for higher expenditure on special equipment for police.

Table 3.5 Defence Expenditure* and Expenditure on Law and Order**
(Rs. billion)

Years	Defence Expenditure			Expenditure on Law and Order		
	at current prices	at constant prices+	Growth Rate (%)	at current prices	at constant prices	Growth Rate (%)
1993–94	91.8	171.3		5.6	10.4	
1994–95	104.5	161.8	–5.5	7.4	11.5	10.0
1995–96	119.7	156.9	–3.0	9.5	12.5	8.8
1996–97	127.4	158.7	1.1	11.0	13.7	9.5
1997–98	136.2	161.4	1.7	11.9	14.1	3.1
1998–99	143.5	159.8	–1.0	13.2	14.7	4.2
1999–2000	150.4	150.4	–5.9	15.6	15.6	6.1
2000–01	131.2	125.7	–16.4	17.5	16.8	7.7
2001–02	149.3	138.1	9.9	19.5	18.0	7.1
2002–03	159.7	144.8	4.9	23.7	21.5	19.4
2003–04	184.9	158.3	9.3	32.1	27.5	27.9
2004–05	211.7	165.8	4.7	35.5	27.8	1.1
2005–06	241.1	176.4	6.4	46.7	34.2	23.0
2006–07	277.3	188.3	6.7	57.1	38.8	13.4
2007–08	297.0	184.1	–2.2	65.0b	40.3	3.9

*   By federal government.
** By provincial governments.
+ Of 1999–2000.
b Budget estimate.
Source: MoF, Pakistan Economic Survey, FBS, Statistical Year Book.

Another aspect of enhanced security is the development of private security arrangements in the country. There has, in fact, been a mushroom growth in this service in recent years. According to an informal survey carried out by the Pakistani *Daily Times* newspaper, the number of men employed by private security companies in Lahore is about 50 percent more than the number of policemen stationed in the city. The enactment of the Private Security Companies (Regulation and Control) Ordinance by the Punjab government in 2002 has facilitated the establishment of such companies, of which there are over 200 in Lahore alone. Currently it is estimated that there are over 30,000 security guards in Lahore and probably over 200,000

Table 3.6 Direct Costs of Terrorism (Rs. billion)

(Potential) costs of compensation to victims	3
Costs of damage to property and infrastructure	8
Higher costs of defence	109
Higher costs of policing	21
Higher cost of private security	8
Total Direct Cost	**149**
(SAY)	**Rs. 150 Billion**

in the country. With the total cost (wages plus overheads) per guard about Rs. 7,000 per month, the total cost of private security services is estimated at Rs. 16.8 billion. We assume that about half, or Rs. 8 billion, is attributable to the "war on terror."

Overall, a summary of the direct costs of terrorism presented in Table 3.6, add up to Rs. 150 billion. Despite the conservative and incomplete nature of these estimates, they work out to be significantly greater than the government's estimate of direct costs in 2007–08 of about Rs. 109 billion.

Indirect Costs

We first take up the impact of the "war on terror" on local economies.

Costs to Local Economies

The local economies in the Pakistani context are NWFP and FATA, where the bulk of the terrorist attacks have occurred and where military operations (including the drone attacks) are concentrated. The shares of the two regions in the national population, according to the 1998 Census, are 13.4 percent and 2.4 percent respectively. Estimates of the Gross Regional Product of NWFP have been made by the World Bank (2006) up to 2004–05. No such estimates are available for FATA. Table 3.7 gives a comparison of the growth trends in the regional and national economies. Some interesting conclusions emerge from the table. It appears that in the immediate aftermath of the war, there was actually greater buoyancy in the NWFP economy due to the "war multiplier" of an enlarged military presence and the stimulus provided to services like transport in the process of supplies to the NATO forces in

Table 3.7 GDP and Sectoral Growth Trends In NWFP and Pakistan (Percentage)

	1995–96 to 2000–01	2001–02 to 2003–04	2004–05
GDP			
NWFP**	2.8	6.8	6.2
Pakistan	3.5	4.8	8.6
NWFP Sectoral Growth			
Agriculture	3.5	3.4	2.9
Industry	1.8	7.5	10.2
Services	3.0	7.9*	5.7

*   Fast growth in transport and communications, public administration, wholesale and retail trade.

** Share of NWFP in national GDP is 9.6% in 2004–05.

Source: The World Bank (2006) "Pakistan Growth and Competitiveness"

Afghanistan. Consequently, between 2001–02 and 2003–04, the regional growth rate approached 7 percent. However, as the incidence of acts of terrorism increased, especially in Peshawar, and military operations became more intense and widespread, there was much greater dislocation of economic activity. In 2004–05, the differential in the growth rates of Pakistan as a whole and NWFP in particular was almost 2.5 percentage points. By 2008, it has probably exceeded 3 percentage points.

The estimated growth rate of the NWFP economy has been about 3 percentage points less than the national economy in recent years. This implies that in 2007–08, the growth rate of NWFP was less than 3 percent and, in 2008–09, the regional economy is likely to exhibit little or no growth. Given that NWFP accounts for about 10 percent of the national GDP, the implication is that the cost of lower growth in the local economy due to the "war on terror" is about 0.3 percent of Pakistan's GDP, equivalent to Rs. 31 billion in 2007–08. We notionally add about 30 percent to this cost to incorporate the impact on the economy of FATA. Therefore, the indirect cost on local economies of the "war on terror" is estimated at about Rs. 40 billion.

There is need also for inclusion of costs of internally displaced persons (IDPs) in terms of the potential relief and rehabilitation costs. In 2008, 337,772 people left their homes because of the security situation in parts of

NWFP and FATA, but in 2009, following military operations in Malakand, over 3 million persons were displaced.

The annual cost of relief efforts is estimated at about Rs. 50 billion for the IDP population, but the cost of resettlement and reconstruction would be many times higher.

Cost of Greater Uncertainty and Risk Perception

These costs are reflected primarily in falling investment by both domestic and foreign investors. Between 2003–04 and 2006–07, as the economy exhibited high growth, private investment was, in fact, quite dynamic. It increased from 10.9 percent of the GDP in 2003–04 to reach a peak of 15.7 percent in 2005–06. Since then, however, there has been a declining trend and it was estimated at 14.2 percent in 2007–08. A larger decline of 25.7 percent is observed in foreign private investment in 2007–08, equivalent to Rs. 52 billion.

Beyond this, the enhanced level of risk has affected the stock market capitalization. In fact, the Karachi Stock Exchange had shown remarkable buoyancy since 2003 and had emerged as one of the best performers in emerging markets. But in 2007–08 a process of decline set in, not only due to local factors but also because of the incipient global financial crisis which led to a fall in most markets in share values. Between July 1, 2007 and June 30, 2008 the share price index in the Karachi Stock Exchange (KSE) fell by 10.8 percent.

The extreme sensitivity of stock prices to mega-terrorist attacks is demonstrated by the consequences of the assassination of Benazir Bhutto. Prior to the December 27, 2007, the day she was killed by a terrorist, the stock market had been showing an upward trend. The first day after the event the market collapsed by 696 points, or almost 5 percent. Market capitalization of Rs. 213 billion was wiped out overnight.

Given the fact that global factors are responsible for the fall in stock values in most markets, we estimate the differential between the fall of the market in Pakistan and elsewhere in Asia. It is assumed that local factors are responsible for this differential. Within the local factors, terrorism is assumed once again to have contributed one-third to the incremental fall. The composite regional index (S&P ASIA 50 INDEX) fell by 1.8 percent between the end of June 2007 and the end of June 2008. Therefore, the differential in rate of decline of the

KSE was 9 percent. With a market capitalization at the beginning of 2007–08 of Rs. 4019 billion, this implies that the loss of value was about Rs. 362 billion, of which one-third can be attributed as the cost of terrorism, amounting to about Rs. 120 billion.

The next cost of higher risk and uncertainty arising from acts of terrorism is the negative impact on tourism and associated services performed by hotels, restaurants, etc. This is particularly relevant as some of the most attractive tourist locations are in the north of the country. There had, in fact, been buoyancy in travel expenditures to Pakistan, as indicated by the balance of payments statistics maintained by the SBP. Between 2000–01 and 2006–07, income from travel to Pakistan had increased at the annual rate of almost 22 percent. But there was a significant drop in 2007–08. We estimate that in relation to the level projected on the basis of the past trend of growth, there was a fall of $71 million. This is primarily attributable to the greater reluctance to travel to Pakistan because of higher risk associated with acts of terrorism. Therefore, the indirect cost of less travel to Pakistan is Rs. 4 billion. This, of course, does not factor in the decline in domestic tourism. It is not surprising that losses of the national carrier, PIA, have been rising from Rs. 4.4 billion in 2005 to Rs. 13.4 billion in 2007, due to loss of market and higher fuel prices.

Combined with the fall in tourism is the negative impact on the hotel industry and other linked service activities. During 2008, the Pakistan Hotels Association indicated a sharp drop in hotel occupancy rates, especially after the bombing of the Marriott Hotel. In addition, there are less hotel events like conventions and marriages, due to excessive security arrangements. A conservative estimate is that occupancy rates in 2007–08 have declined from 60 percent to about 40 percent.

The Tourism Division of the Government of Pakistan estimates that there are about 38,000 let-able rooms in hotels in Pakistan. The average tariff per room is estimated at Rs. 2000 per day. A fall in occupancy of 20 percentage points implies a loss in income of over Rs. 5 billion. We double this estimate to allow for the loss in other hotel income and in the income of associated services like restaurants, tour operators, transport, etc. Therefore, the indirect cost of loss of travel and tourism and downstream activities due to terrorism is about Rs. 10 billion.

Table 3.8 Indirect Costs of Terrorism (Rs. billion)

Costs to Local Economies	
Loss of economic growth in NWFP and FATA	40
Cost of IDPs	50
Costs of Higher Risk Perception and Uncertainty	
Fall in private investment	52
Fall in stock market capitalization	120
Decline in travel and tourism	4
Fall in hotel occupancy and income from associated services	10
Total Indirect Costs	279

Finally, in the area of indirect costs, we have to factor in the higher costs of insurance. With the rise in terror-related acts, premiums for providing insurance cover on such acts has skyrocketed. Following the destruction of property during the riots in the aftermath of the assassination of Benazir Bhutto, general insurance companies had to honour claims of over Rs. 3 billion, which wiped out the premium income for more than a year. There has, in fact, been a big increase in demand for terrorism insurance following the Marriott bombing. However, domestic insurance companies are limited by the reluctance of foreign companies to provide reinsurance to Pakistani companies. Some companies have started to provide cover of up to Rs. 100 million against acts of terror but the premium rate has gone up to a high of 4 percent, as compared to the past rate of about 1 percent. We estimate that the cost of higher insurance premiums is about Rs. 3 billion on an annual basis.

Overall, the indirect costs of terrorism can be totaled to Rs. 280 billion (see Table 3.8). The implications of higher transaction costs due to terrorism in the form of delays in the movement of consignments, costs of maintaining higher inventories and larger time costs at airports have not been quantified due to lack of data. These represent areas for further research.

Conclusion

The total costs of terrorism in Pakistan are high, estimated at Rs. 430 billion at the 2007–08 bases. The distributional consequences of these costs on the "war on terror" need to be highlighted. Higher security expenditures run the risk of "crowding out" other expenditures related to the provision of basic social and economic services and thereby having an adverse impact, especially on the lower income groups. This is mitigated partly by the reimbursement from the US of the additional military expenses, but remains a real threat in the context of higher expenditures on law and order (especially police) by the provincial governments.

Beyond this, the negative implications for the relatively poor include the loss of property and livelihoods in affected areas, which are among the most backward regions of the country, primarily as a consequence of dislocation of economic activity, including in the labor-intensive sector of tourism. The human dimension is manifested most acutely not only in the loss of life but also in the emergence of large numbers of IDPs.

A number of important conclusions emerge from the analysis of the costs of terrorism. First, as the incidence of terrorist acts and counter-terrorism operations has increased rapidly, the benefits of participation in the "war on terror" are falling, while the costs are rising sharply. In 2007–08, the inflow of concessional assistance from the US was about $1.9 billion, whereas the cost is three times higher, at $6 billion. There has, therefore, been substantial under-compensation for Pakistan's participation in the "war on terror," which has been limited largely to reimbursement only for the costs of military operations. This, at least, partly explains the lack of some ownership of the war effort. The recent authorization of a bill in Congress to authorize economic aid to Pakistan of $1.5 billion per year for the next five years, will raise the quantum of concessional assistance from the US to Pakistan but the level of support will still remain at less than half the costs of the "war on terror."

Second, past experience with utilization of the concessional support is not very positive. From the viewpoint of achieving sustainable higher growth and promoting employment, especially for alleviating poverty, it will be better if Pakistan is also given preferential access to markets, especially for textiles, in the US, EU and Japan. While the proposal for Reconstruction Opportunity Zones (ROZs) in the affected areas, enjoying preferential access, is worthy of consideration, it is unlikely that in the short run much investment will be diverted to these areas, despite the incentive given the prevailing situation. It is important that as an alternative, fast-track concessional assistance is provided for public investment in infrastructure and basic services and employment-intensive public works in affected areas, which are cleared up either through military operations or peace agreements in order to provide an early "peace dividend." At the national as well as local level, the problem of militancy can be tackled effectively by fast implementation of a Youth Skill Development and Employment Program, which aims to absorb the over 1.5 million unemployed youth in the country.

Finally, the higher direct costs being incurred by the military and police operations against counter-terrorism of almost Rs. 130 billion per annum and the concomitant increase in acts of terrorism, highlight the ineffectiveness of the current strategy being followed in the "war on terror." There is a need for a comprehensive review of the strategy and the development of a stronger political consensus and broad-based public commitment to participation in this war.

To conclude, this analysis demonstrates that the country is paying a heavy price for growing extremism in the tribal and adjoining areas following the US occupation of Afghanistan after 9/11. Potentially, GDP could have been higher by almost Rs. 590 billion if the problems of security were not adversely impacting on the economy. The concomitant repercussions for exports, employment and poverty are also sizable. Any further inaction or inadequate policy action on adequate assistance and market access could further frustrate the country's growth potential, which it can ill afford in these times of increasingly unfavorable global developments.

Notes

1 Poverty Reduction Strategy Paper II, Finance Division, Government of Pakistan, September 2008.
2 See, for instance, The Milken Institute (2004), J. Brauer (2002), Warshawsky (2001) and Chan 2002.
3 See "9/11 Terrorism: Global Economic Costs," the Saxton Report of US Congress (2002). Looney (2002), Frey, Luchinger and Stutzer (2007), Paul Krugman (2002).

CHAPTER FOUR

Insurrection, Terrorism and the Pakistan Army

Brian Cloughley

Abstract

Few armies in the world are terror-centric, because their main role is the defense of their country from external threats. But many have had to develop the ability to counter terrorism and acquire the expertise necessary to defeat internal threats. The Pakistani army had little experience in counter-insurgency warfare (COIN), and its first operations against militant bases were unsuccessful to the point of being disastrous. The army trained for conventional warfare: the fast-moving, armour-centric, high-tech manoeuvres that would be necessary to first counter and then defeat a massive attack by a similarly skilled enemy. Soldiers of the Pakistan army acquired their COIN expertise while concurrently having to defend their fellow citizens against the barbarity of the insurgents. It took time, but eventually they succeeded, as was evident in the operations in Swat in 2009. South Waziristan is an even more difficult region, in both terrain and type of insurgent, and the army could not act until it was certain that it had enough units appropriately trained. The challenge was accepted, but more challenges lie ahead. This chapter deals in detail with the problems, failures and successes of the army in tackling Pakistan's most serious threat to its existence and analyzes the army's current and future capabilities of fighting guerrilla warfare.

Introduction

There are two main domestic challenges facing the Pakistan army: the insurgency in the Federally Administered Tribal Areas (FATA), and other extremist violence throughout the country. The two eruptions are promoted by criminally fanatical groups who have been cooperating to extend terrorism with the aim of destroying Pakistan's limping democracy. They base their justification for havoc and slaughter on wilfully misrepresented tenets of Islam and claim that they wish to create a caliphate, but should they ever attain supremacy, their rule would be one of unrestrained bigotry and ferocity. These obnoxious characteristics were amply demonstrated during the brief but horrific reign of the Taliban in the Swat region of Pakistan, before the army operation to overcome the fanatics and restore a degree of normality.

The army, as directed by the government, has the constitutional duty "to defend Pakistan against external aggression or threat of war, and, subject to law, to act in aid of the civil power when called upon to do so."[1] Its military operations within Pakistan, in FATA, North-West Frontier Province (NWFP) and Balochistan are therefore lawful providing they continue to be under the control of the "civil power," just as was the army's drive against insurgents in Balochistan that was ordered by Zulfikar Ali Bhutto in 1973.[2]

The difference between the 1970s campaign against Baloch dissidents (which was ended by General Zia ul Haq after he took over Pakistan in a coup in 1977) and the present conflict in NWFP/FATA is that the Baloch insurrection had little resonance in most of Pakistan, while the conflict in the west that began in 2003 has had grave consequences throughout the country. In both cases, the scale of operations required many more troops than were in place in the affected regions.

Complications of Redeployment and Training

The army did not have enough troops in NWFP to combat the growing insurgency (and had none at all based in FATA; all army units were withdrawn in the period from November 1947 to January 1948[3]). It was not possible for the 11 Corps and the paramilitary Frontier Corps, both with their headquarters in Peshawar, to conduct operations without considerable reinforcement. 11 Corps has only two infantry divisions to cover the entire region, and little in the way of dedicated armour and artillery support, while the role of the lightly-armed, locally-recruited Frontier Corps has always been more akin to policing than to engaging in conventional military operations. Dealing with inter-tribe skirmishes and cross-border smugglers is very different to combating organized bands of fanatics whose objective is destruction of the state.

In 2007 it was therefore decided to redeploy some units and formations[4] from the eastern frontier to the west, but the main problem with the decision, no matter its appropriateness, was that troops facing India along the border and Line of Control are skilled in conventional warfare tactics but not trained in counter insurgency. Along the border the emphasis is on armour-centric mobility, with the aim of countering a major Indian advance aimed at deeply penetrating Pakistan (the "Cold Start" doctrine) and even pushing east to take territory (Pakistan's "Riposte"). Formations along the Line of Control are essentially static and defensive in posture and are not required to have expertise in guerrilla warfare. Retraining was essential if there was to be a properly conducted campaign against militants in the west of the country. The process requires much time and effort. But there is another important factor in the equation of committing troops to tasks: the stance of India.

The Indian government and people reacted strongly to the terrorist attacks in Mumbai in November 2008, and blamed Pakistan for fostering those who carried them out. Of even more significance, many in India considered that Pakistan actually had some formal and official role in assisting the attackers, and most Indians — spurred by an active media — now firmly believe that Pakistan was involved. In this atmosphere it was tempting for politicians, especially those of ultra-nationalist persuasion, to beat war drums and threaten Pakistan with dire consequences if there were another terrorist outrage — which there is likely to be.

Although there was no reinforcement or movement of troops on the Indian side of the border after the Mumbai atrocities, Pakistan could not forget the major deployment, Operation Parakram, which took place in 2001–2002 following a terrorist assault on the Indian Parliament. There was grounds for complacency concerning Indian intentions, given the similarity of the Mumbai and Delhi attacks and the ensuing rhetoric, and Pakistan's armed forces were required to remain vigilant. There could be no question of lowering guard on the eastern border unless there were assurances from India that it would not engage in military action. This was not given.

Even after the initial outburst of anti-Pakistan bellicosity had died down, there came carefully composed but aggressive and confrontational statements by highly placed Indian officials that gave cause for concern in Islamabad and Rawalpindi. These were measured threats made by prominent national figures that could not be ignored, and they came in a period of especial concern to Pakistan — the very time at which it was necessary to continue relocating troops from the eastern frontier area in order to combat the menace of terror and insurrection in the west.

On June 4, 2009 the Air Officer Commanding-in-Chief of India's South-Western Air Command, Air Marshal K. D. Singh, said in a public lecture that, "In case of a misadventure by Pakistan in shape of major terrorist attack or the attack like the one we had on the Parliament, attack on our leader, a major city, public or hijacking an aircraft, can obviously lead to a reaction from India, which could be a short intense war."[5]

Then on November 1, 2009 the Indian Home Minister, Palaniappan Chidambaram, was reported as saying, "I've been warning Pakistan not to play any more games. Let Mumbai be the last such game. If they carry out any more attacks on India, they will not only be defeated, but we will also retaliate with the force of a sledgehammer."[6]

The threat from Delhi, which many observers[7] had considered to have been negligible, given the apparent pragmatism of the government of Manmohan Singh, was spelled out in blunt and menacing terms. Given the stature and appointments of those who warned so clearly of conflict, the prospect of an attack could not and cannot be treated lightly. For this reason many senior military officers in Pakistan argued that denuding formations along the border could have serious consequences if India decided to engage in a "short, intense conventional war," as a result of another terrorist attack. Were there then to be widespread clamorous allegations in India that the culprits had been trained in Pakistan, then there could be war — and although it might be "short and intense" it almost certainly would escalate from conventional to nuclear if Indian troops penetrated Pakistan's territory as far as, say, to encircle Lahore. The army, the senior officers felt, would be failing in its duty if it dropped its guard along the frontier; so there had to be compromise, which, in military affairs as in most others, usually results in a less-than-desirable solution.

The army was presented with the problem of retraining large numbers of troops and re-equipping for counter-insurgency and anti-terrorist operations concurrently with assessing India's posture along the eastern border and deciding how many units might be moved to the west. The threat in the west was growing, and casualties were being taken, mainly because units were not experienced in anti-guerrilla warfare. Many units had not been trained in how to react when ambushed in vehicle convoy, for example, the incident of August 30, 2007, when over 200 soldiers surrendered to an initially small force of tribesmen, was a distinct embarrassment to the army as a whole.

They were released on November 4, following the reciprocal freeing of some 25 convicted tribal terrorists. The affair was disturbing for the army and the country, especially as the rebels had murdered three soldiers, but President Musharraf reacted in an unexpectedly laid-back fashion and permitted the drama to run its course, and it ended in the usual tribal way, with concessions on both sides. In almost all Western eyes this compromise was seen as craven submission to the dictates of criminals, and in the tenets of Western-style law there is indeed no admission of such an advanced style of plea-bargaining. It cannot be expected that the practise of negotiation will be endorsed by Pakistan's critics, or even by those many Pakistanis who consider the tribal regions to be as foreign as any South Sea island. But it is the way of the region, and although it may stoke up trouble for the future, it is wise to consider what might have happened otherwise in this and other instances of tribal lawlessness.

There has been domestic and foreign criticism of the Pakistan army for having few units trained in counter-insurgency operations, but given its externally imposed priorities on the eastern border it is unsurprising that such specialized training had not been given precedence over conventional warfare.

As was found by the British in Northern Ireland, and then by the US in Iraq and Afghanistan, it is costly in casualties and can be gravely counter-productive in terms of community acceptance and achievement of the strategic objective to commit a unit to COIN if it is not trained in such skills. The British, for example, had to design a comprehensive training programme in which a conventionally-focused unit would take up to eight months to prepare for deployment to Northern Ireland during the conflict with the Irish Republican Army and other terrorist groups. Similar instruction and other preparation were — eventually — realized to be necessary for US troops before deployment to Iraq and Afghanistan, and it was essential that such training be imparted to Pakistan's soldiers, as operations in the tribal areas during 2003–07 had demonstrated weaknesses in procedures. But then another and more pressing threat presented itself, not in FATA but in one of the "settled areas," the beautiful Swat region. Unfortunately, when the army had to turn its attention to Swat the problems in the tribal areas did not go away: they grew in intensity and in importance to Pakistan as a whole.

The Tribal Areas and Beyond

No Man who has ever read a page of Indian history will prophesy about the Frontier.

— Lord Curzon, Viceroy of India, July 20, 1904

There are seven Federally Administered Tribal Agencies: from north to south, Bajaur, Mohmand, Khyber, Orakzai, Kurram, North Waziristan and South Waziristan. Orakzai is the only one not abutting Afghanistan. FATA is represented in Pakistan's Senate and National Assembly, but their laws do not apply unless ordered by the President, who has executive authority over the region.

Agencies are administered by political agents whose authority has been eroded over the past eight years and who are now largely ineffective. There are compelling arguments for terminating the system, but this would be dependent on bringing the tribal areas into mainstream life in Pakistan, and would meet varying degrees of resistance.[8]

Their area is 27,220 km^2, about the size of Albania or West Virginia, with a population estimated at 3.35 million,[9] 80 percent of whom are illiterate (at a generous estimate, only 5 percent of females are literate).

The main economic activity is smuggling, although there are some tracts of good agricultural land and sizeable mineral deposits. Kidnapping for ransom is common and poppies are grown for heroin manufacture. The region is almost totally undeveloped, with little healthcare, education or access to clean water. Roads are mainly unmetalled tracks and there are no airports

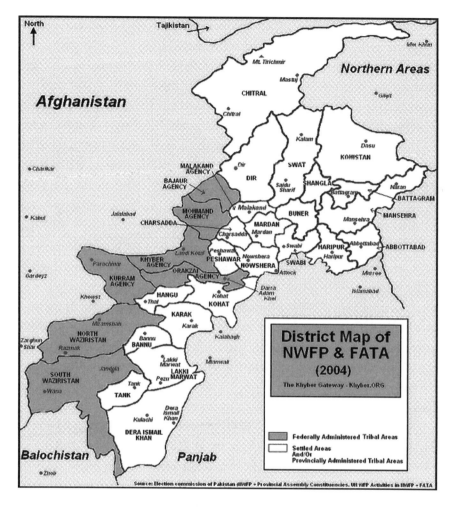

Map 2 District map of North-Western Frontier Province (NWFP) and FATA
Source: Election commission of Pakistan NWFP — Provincial Assembly
Constituencies.

(although there are some landing strips). Weapons of all types, including
mortars, heavy machine guns and rocket launchers are in plentiful supply.
Almost all tribesmen carry a rifle as a matter of course. There are some
60 main tribes and scores of sub-tribes, and all are notoriously quarrelsome
and aggressive towards each other and especially antagonistic towards foreigners, in whose number they include citizens, and especially the authorities,
of Pakistan.

Adjacent to FATA lies the "settled areas" of North-West Frontier Province, in which, in the north, lies the former Malakand Division, which comprised the Districts of Chitral, Dir, Swat, Malakand and Buner. For the sake of convenience the region is often still referred to by this name.[10]

Before the US invasion of Afghanistan in 2001 there were undoubtedly zealots with quasi-religious agendas in Pakistani tribal areas, but the region had been spared the excesses of ignorant and savage Taliban bigots, who had confined themselves to establishing a so-called Islamic State in Afghanistan. After the invasion, however, increasing numbers of Taliban and freelance mercenaries of many nationalities sought refuge in Pakistan, mainly in the tribal areas, where they sought to take over the regions in which they had settled, and from where they mounted attacks across the border. Their presence was welcomed by homegrown extremists, some of whom had been in Afghanistan, who seized on the opportunity to spread their own brand of religious intolerance. There was increasing emphasis on gathering young men into Madrassah's, ostensibly religious-oriented schools, in many of which they were not only taught to memorize the Qur'an but were encouraged to adopt the mindless bigotry of their mentors. NWFP Madrassahs, and most others, do not encourage the imparting of a general education, with emphasis on open-mindedness, the humanities and employment-oriented skills.

Given the nature of Pakistan's unsought confrontation with India on the eastern border, there was no possibility in 2001 of mounting blocking or search and destroy operations against militants driven out of Afghanistan by the US/British operations at Tora Bora in the east of the country, although the Commander US Central Command, General Tommy Franks, wrote in 2004 in the *New York Times* (being described as "a member of Veterans for Bush"[11]) that "Pakistani troops also provided significant help [during the Tora Bora operation] — as many as 100,000 sealed the border and rounded up hundreds of Qaeda and Taliban fighters."

His claims are fallacious, because the border was not "sealed" and there were not "hundreds" of fighters rounded up. The figure of 100,000 is unsubstantiated.[12] And his statement is at variance with what Secretary of Defence Donald Rumsfeld said in December 2001: "They [Pakistan] must have seven or eight, nine battalions along the Pakistan-Afghan border, which is clearly a deterrent to people trying to come across — trying to escape from

Afghanistan," and "we took custody of about 20 people turned over to us by Pakistani authorities. These detainees are now being held in facilities at Kandahar. And that brings us to 45 . . . Taliban and Al Qaeda personnel in custody."[13] The pronouncement about "nine battalions" was erroneous, but was not queried by the media.

The facts are that on December 8, 2001 the then Director General of Military Operations, Major General Ashfaq Kayani,[14] spoke with senior commanders and, according to one of them, in discussion with the writer, "discussed the implications of [the] coalition forces operation in Tora Bora and the possibility of deploying our troops in the areas opposite the Tora Bora Mountains. *Interestingly, our coalition friends had not informed us about their operation in Tora Bora and we came to know about it through the press.*" [Emphasis added.] And on December 18, 11 Corps received orders to move from NWFP to its emergency deployment positions along the Indian frontier in consequence of the massive Indian build-up to over half a million troops. (12 Corps in Balochistan was similarly redeployed.) There was thus no possibility that the western border could have been blocked or even effectively patrolled, as so few troops were left in the Province. The planners in the Pentagon did not take into account the fact that their operations would first fail and then backfire catastrophically. The United States Special Operations Command *History 1987–2007* states that: "Given the commitment of fewer than 100 American personnel, U.S. forces proved unable to block egress routes from Tora Bora south into Pakistan, the route that UBL [Osama bin Laden] most likely took. Regardless, the defeat for AQ [Al Qaeda] at Tora Bora, coupled with the later defeat during Operation ANACONDA, ensured that neither AQ, nor the Taliban would mass forces to challenge American troops in the field until 2006."[15] There is no mention of Pakistan being requested or expected to take action before or during the Tora Bora operation. Later in the *History* it is observed that "the Soviets could not seal the border [with Pakistan] two decades previously with over 100,000 troops in Afghanistan."[16]

US and "coalition" forces have conducted many operations in the east of Afghanistan, most of which failed to eradicate extremists but resulted in large numbers of Pashtuns and foreign militants seeking sanctuary in Western Pakistan. They then destabilized not only FATA and much of the North-West

Frontier Province, but have given impetus to primitive zealots elsewhere in the country.

With considerable reluctance the Pakistan army began low-key operations in the tribal areas in 2002–03, generally in support of the Frontier Corps. They entered the "no go" areas, in which no non-tribal had set foot for decades, and tried to bring development to a sadly backward region. But as time passed it became apparent that not only was the insurgency expanding, with more determination being displayed by well-equipped militants, but the influence of Taliban leaders was becoming dangerously predominant. The tribal system itself, while far from a perfect societal arrangement, was under threat from influential, charismatic leaders who cared nothing for time-tested tribal traditions and sought to use the tribes as a base from which to destabilize the entire country. The entire structure of tribal life, based on a fusion of family and clan allegiances, religion and custom, appeared near to collapse. It seemed that the hierarchal stability, involving tribal leaders and the jirga system that enabled the government to conduct negotiations, could disappear entirely.

In 2007 Waziristan, especially South Waziristan Agency (SWA), was causing concern to the government of then President Musharraf, who had ordered the signing of a peace agreement with the local Taliban the previous September. The policy of restricting the army's presence had not worked, and foreign militants had not been ejected, as had been agreed. Extremists operated with impunity, and the writ of the state, never strong at the best of times, had broken down entirely.

Waziristan — Recent Chronology

March/April 2004: Army and Frontier Corps operations ended in negotiations and agreement with the rebel leader, Nek Mohammad.

June 2004: Nek Mohammad killed by US drone-fired missile. Agreement collapses.

January–Feb 2005: Peace deal with new rebel leader Baitullah Mehsud brings calm, and army withdraws.

June 2006: Rebel leader Sirajuddin Haqqani decrees that the army is not to be engaged militarily. Suicide bomber kills six soldiers in NWA.

5 September 2006: Waziristan Accord signed.

July 2007 onwards: Attacks by insurgents and army retaliation; army operation against fanatics in Islamabad's Lal Masjid (July 10–11); 60 soldiers and 250 rebels killed in July–August.

December 2007–January 2008: Army operation in Mehsud area partially successful but ends in peace deal with Baitullah Mehsud.

January 2008: Rebels capture paramilitary-held forts. 14 Division begins Operation Zalzala (Earthquake).

7 February 2008: Baitullah Mehsud offers truce.

21 May 2008: Agreement signed between rebels and government.

June 2009: Army begins troop build-up in SWA.

6 August 2009: US drone strike kills Baitullah Mehsud. Replaced by Hakimullah Mehsud.

October 2009: Many suicide attacks across the country.

16 October 2009: Government orders the army to begin its offensive in South Waziristan the next day.

The landscape of SWA is well described in the century-old but still relevant, *Imperial Gazetteer of India*: "The Mehsud country is a tangled mess of mountains and hills of every size, shape and bearing, and is intersected in all directions by ravines generally flanked through their course by high hills. At first sight the country appears to be occupied by hills and mountains running irregularly in all directions, but there are well-defined ranges which protect the interior of the country by double barriers, and make penetration into it a matter of extreme difficulty." It is a major challenge to mount operations against an agile, well-armed, locally protected enemy with bases in country that is so suitable for guerrilla-style resistance. The breakdown of the so-called Waziristan Accord was caused in the main by reaction to the army's operation against revolutionaries who had taken over the Lal Masjid, the Red Mosque, in central Islamabad. The complex was the fiefdom of two brothers, Abdul Aziz and Abdul Rashid Ghazi, both fanatics whose equally crazy father, the founder, was killed by unknown gunmen at the mosque in 1998. Abdul Aziz had tested the waters by announcing in 2004 that Pakistan army soldiers killed in Balochistan (the family is Baloch) and Waziristan should not be buried according to Islamic custom, and his challenge went unmet.

His uncompromising confrontation continued, but in the interests of not rocking the boat the government declined to arrest him. It was considered that direct military action to eject the militants would result in wider violence. As it transpired, this is exactly what happened.

On March 31, 2007 Aziz gave an ultimatum concerning Sharia law. As the Pakistani *Daily Times* reported, "Maulana Abdul Aziz, the prayer leader at Lal Masjid and principal of Jamia Hafsa, on Friday gave the government a week's deadline to 'enforce Sharia' in the country, otherwise 'clerics will Islamise society themselves.' 'If the government does not impose Sharia within a week, we will do it,' Aziz told a gathering after Friday prayers. Similarly, he gave the Islamabad administration a week to shut down 'brothels,' otherwise 'seminary students will take action themselves.' 'If we find a woman with loose morals, we will prosecute her in Lal Masjid,' he said."[17] Obviously the government could not permit a parallel system of quasi-legal prosecution, but nothing was done until on May 18, Aziz threatened suicide attacks throughout the country and then openly encouraged desertion from the police, paramilitary forces and the army. It became obvious that action had to be taken against direct threats to the stability of Pakistan.

The crisis began to come to a head on July 3, 2007 when "students" in the complex fired on police and paramilitary Pakistan Rangers who were attempting to maintain order outside the mosque, and took prisoner four policemen, whom they tortured. When it appeared that government reaction would almost certainly involve force, Abdul Aziz decided to flee the premises, which he did dressed in a burqa. After being unveiled, as it were, by a police-woman, he was shown to be a coward and a joke, and most of the young male and female student activists remaining in the mosque — some 1,100 in all — decided they would also leave, which they did without incident. His brother, Abdul Ghazi, remained in the complex and tried to negotiate his freedom, but his demands were both minatory and excessive, involving pensions for family members, pardon for all involved in the siege, and his own safe passage to an unspecified country. He was killed in a well-conducted operation by members of the Special Services Group seven days later, on July 10.

Thus, yet another rift was created between military (and patriotic, con-stitutional) duty as exemplified by what the SSG achieved at the Lal Masjid, and the normal loyalty any Muslim owes to his or her religion. On the one hand there was a group of fanatics determined to subvert and destroy the laws of the land, and on the other the majority of the people of Pakistan who wish only to be able to get on with their lives unhindered by self-righteous thugs whose highly personal and supremely selective interpretations of the word of God can be accepted in neither intellectually analytical terms nor in practical, common sense, day-to-day living. The citizens of Pakistan were (and are) confused about their religious leaders, whom they have been taught to respect, because some of these figures take advantage of ignorance — the facilitator of religious bigots through the centuries — to purvey their own self-serving explanations of the Koran and the Hadith.[18] The army is in the middle, being assailed by wild-eyed, raving pulpit-bashers while attempting to abide by "enlightened moderation" in religious matters, as espoused by their Chief. (General Kayani's views are similar to those of former President Musharraf, who first used that phrase.) And a major consequence appears to have been the steep rise in suicide attacks specifically directed against military targets.

When it became apparent that the peace agreement in South Waziristan had broken down and that negotiations were no longer feasible, Musharraf ordered the commander of 1st Armoured Division, Major General Tariq Khan, to assume command of 14 Infantry Division, with its headquarters at Okara, near the border with India, and restore order in the area. The division moved there in early 2007, in operation al-Mizan, and encountered strong resistance, initially taking casualties because of lack of expertise in counter-insurgency warfare. The formation was experienced in fast-moving tactics of conventional war, but understandably, and, as noted above, in common with all formations in the east, had little training in COIN, which Khan rectified. This took time, and had to be done concurrently with establishing military dominance over a region occupied by a well-trained and highly-motivated enemy who had constructed trench systems, bunkers and arms caches, and planted mines and improvised explosive devices (IEDs) on most main routes and some village-linking tracks.

Air strikes and artillery bombardments were conducted in many areas in which militants were either based or had concentrated in sufficient numbers to make targeting advisable; mostly in the west of South Waziristan where in late 2007 there were several attacks, some in support of tribesmen who had engaged militants. There were notable successes, but also a large number of civilian casualties. In October 2007, for example, some 165 wounded civilians from western regions were treated in Bannu Hospital.

The insurgents preferred to attack lightly armed paramilitaries rather than the army, and, in one demonstration of their capability, on January 15–16, 2008 some 200 attacked the fort in Sararogha in South Waziristan, manned by a platoon of Frontier Corps soldiers, using mortars and rocket launchers. According to official sources seven soldiers were killed, 15 escaped and the remaining 16 were "missing." (It appears that some of them were captured and killed.) In attempts to propagandize Baitullah Mehsud as a hero, the Taliban announced that he had personally led the attack, although this is considered most unlikely.

But operations then had to be placed on hold because of the deteriorating situation in Swat District, where an agreement with the Taliban had broken down in similar fashion to that in SWA. At the end of the year there was fierce fighting between paramilitary forces and the followers of Maulana, Fazlullah who were behaving barbarically by burning down girls' schools, destroying shops selling "un-Islamic" items such as DVDs, banning women from the women's market in the main town, Mingora, murdering moderate Muslims who sought only to live normal lives free of intolerance and violence and in general demonstrating the cruelty and savage persecution that is their trademark. This was a warning of what life would be like in Pakistan and the so-called Caliphate if such extremists managed to defeat the government.[19] What happened in Swat was an alarm signal, and the army had to act.

Swat

In 1995 an extremist cleric, Maulana Sufi Mohammad Khan, the leader of the now-banned Tehreek-e-Nifaz-e-Shariat-e-Muhammadi (TNSM: Movement for Enforcement of Islamic Law) demanded that Sharia law be imposed in Swat. Fighting took place between the Frontier Constabulary and his support-ers, and the province government first agreed to negotiate and then gave in to the extremists and permitted Sharia in the District. The valley's main income generator, tourism, collapsed. It was an economic and social catastrophe.

In 2002 Sufi Mohammad encouraged thousands of tribesmen to cross into

Afghanistan to fight against foreign forces who had displaced the Taliban government. He was imprisoned on his return (and released in a deal in April 2008, then again detained on June 4, 2009), and his place was taken by his son-in-law, Maulana Fazlullah, who began a reign of intimidation and terror in Swat District and beyond. The police were rendered powerless, most of them taking off their uniforms and fleeing or seeking alternative employment — or joining the insurgents — and the army's single under-strength brigade could not establish security.

Eventually, as recorded by the Pakistani *Daily Times*, "President Asif Ali Zardari signed the Nizam-e-Adl (Order of Justice) Regulation for Swat on Monday 13 April [2009] after the National Assembly passed a resolution in favour of the draft regulation . . . in accordance with a peace agreement between the NWFP government and Sufi Muhammad, the chief of [the TNSM] and father-in-law of Taliban chief Mullah Fazlullah."[20] The "Order of Justice" recognized Sharia Law in the region and was condemned by many as surrendering to the extremists, prompting US Secretary of State Clinton to comment about "abdicating to the Taliban," but it bought time for the army to redeploy and retrain troops from the eastern border. Concurrently, however, the militants built bunker and cave systems of considerable sophistication, through which the army eventually had to fight.

In the period between August 2008 and mid-2009, the army redeployed formations and units to deal with the emergency in Swat. The campaign eventually involved over 20,000 troops and extensive air support by Army Aviation attack helicopters and Pakistan Air Force fixed-wing ground-attack aircraft. The Army Chief, General Kayani, stated that "We are conducting this operation to bring misguided people back on the *right path*"[21] [emphasis added], which in Urdu is *Rah-e-Rast*, the name given to the army's mission. The army announcement concerning its orders from the government was that: "After the complete breakdown of law and order and the non-adherence of the militants to the peace deal in Swat Valley, the Army was called out in aid of the civil power to eliminate the militants and restore the writ of the Government. The operation will continue until such time as we have liberated the people of Swat from the clutches of the militants. The military will not leave unless it is taken over by the civil administration and the writ of the Government is restored."[22]

Prior operations included the placement of roadblocks to prevent movement of the Taliban, and it appears the plan was to deploy into the region in strength, defeat the insurgents in outlying areas, making use of maximum air support, and end the main thrust by taking the town of Mingora (population 300,000), where the Taliban had a major presence.

In March and early April units of the Frontier Corps moved into southern Malakand Division, mainly in the Lower Dir and Buner Districts, and set up roadblocks, to provide reserves in the event of there being significant opposition, which did not transpire, although there were some minor contacts.

In mid-April brigades of 11 Corps (HQ Peshawar) took positions in Lower Dir, Buner and along the Barikot-Mingora axis, securing ground for further northern movement by two brigades of 19 Division (of 10 Corps, based in the Mangla area), commanded by Major General Sajjad Ghani; two brigades of 37 Division (of 1 Corps, from Rahwali Cantonment, Gujranwala, commanded by Major General Ijaz Awan); two brigades of 23 Division (of 10 Corps, usually responsible for depth and reinforcement along the Line of Control and probably placed under command HQ 19 Division); and 54 Independent Infantry Brigade (of 30 Corps, HQ Gujranwala, based at Sialkot). Overall command was exercised from GHQ Rawalpindi, with HQ 10 Corps (Rawalpindi) participation. Two armoured units and 2–3 artillery regiments were also deployed, together with logistic elements. Small parties of the Special Services Group were inserted into the north and tasked with securing ground for helicopter landings by more SSG troops.

Preparatory air strikes were conducted on Taliban/Jihadi positions identified by army intelligence (whose detachments have cover names and cooperate at all levels with the Directorate of Inter-Services Intelligence), and appeared successful until it became apparent that many insurgents had taken refuge in well-protected caves or in civilian-occupied buildings. Curfews were imposed and the inhabitants began to leave in rapidly increasing numbers, jamming some roads and hindering movement by military vehicles.

The offensive proper began in Lower Dir on April 26, in Buner two days later (by the Frontier Corps) and Swat itself on May 8. Despite the roadblocks it proved impossible to prevent the exit of Taliban among the hundreds of thousands of refugees streaming out of the region, although Afghans, Uzbeks and Arabs were among those reported to have been detained. Concurrently, to the north of Mingora, sub-units of the Special Services Group were inserted by helicopter in the Peochar area where it was thought that Fazlullah may have been based.[23] Nothing was announced officially about their operations, although they may have been involved in the taking of a cave complex on May 20 at Banani Baba Ziarat, which, according to Major General Ghani, was a Taliban "training, communication and operational base"[24] of considerable sophistication, having electric lighting, air conditioning and stores of weapons and explosives. (The electricity must have been supplied by generators, because the insurgents had destroyed power lines in the region.)

The 19 Division units moved north and struck sizeable resistance, fighting through until taking the centres of Peochar and Bahrain. The 37 Division units cleared the region around Mingora and began to fight through the city on May 22, establishing control on May 31. In the course of northern fighting an Al-Zarrar tank (modified Type 59) was damaged in an ambush that was said to involve IED suicide attacks, but the crew escaped without injury. Army and Frontier Corps casualties are estimated at 85 killed, including seven officers, and over 200 wounded.

The army is thinly spread in the tribal areas, and neither it nor the Frontier Corps (nor the many thousand foreign troops in Afghanistan) has been capable of stemming the flow of Afghan and foreign Jihadist into Pakistan.[25] On June 3, 2009 Pakistan army intelligence became aware that some 200 foreigners, said to be mainly Uzbeks and Chechens, had crossed into the Suran Valley of the Mohmand Agency, opposite Afghanistan's Kunar province, a main area of resistance to Afghan and foreign forces. It was assessed that they were en route to Dir and Swat to assist insurgents, but there were no reports of any subsequent activities.

The Swat operation was an overall success, although resistance continued after the capture of Mingora, and the displacement of some 2 million inhabitants was unforeseen to the point of administrative incapacity in dealing with them. But operations had to continue in Malakand, Swat, Buner and Lower Dir, with the aim of eradicating remaining Taliban outposts.

The challenge for the government was and continues to be to restore civilian governance and overall administration as speedily as possible, with the army taking a low public profile. It is intended to enlist former soldiers in the police force and have as many as 2,500 police in the area.[26] Safe return of refugees was the highest priority. But then the government had to turn its attention once more to South Waziristan.

Operations in Bajaur and South Waziristan Agencies

While progressively withdrawing troops from the still-threatened eastern border region, and conducting lengthy and demanding counter-insurgency training, the army, assisted by the Frontier Corps, blocked routes and carried out preliminary operations in SWA in the spring and summer of 2009. These included targeting of known commanders and bases by soldiers of the Special Services Group, and, as in Swat, strikes by armed helicopters of the Army Aviation Corps, and ground attack sorties by the Pakistan Air Force. Additionally, and most controversially, the US continued its program of drone-fired missile attacks within Pakistan, concentrating on SWA. These dozens of attacks had proved counter-productive by killing many innocent people in the tribal areas, although they killed extremists as well. But there is no doubt that these strikes are illegal in international law, as they do not have the formal acceptance of the government of Pakistan.[27] They have contributed greatly to anti-US sentiment in the country.[28]

In November 2009, former President Musharraf was quoted as observing that "he had been concerned about the US-controlled drone attacks against targets inside Pakistan, which began in 2005. 'I told the Americans, give us the Predators. It was refused. I told the Americans; then just say publicly that you're giving them to us. You keep on firing, but put the marks of the Pakistan Air Force on them. That was also denied.'"[29] (The US has created a dangerous example in embracing such cross-border illegality, and although the world is undoubtedly better off without some of the people who have been killed by US missiles, it is a more dangerous place for the fact that other countries may claim legitimacy by precedent for such operations. The fact that the UN Security Council has not condemned the sovereignty violations is endorsement enough for China, for example, to take similar action vis-à-vis India, or India with Bangladesh. The implications for Russia's strategy concerning its former satellites, and for inter-state squabbles in South America, are disturbing.)

Concurrently with the build-up for the projected operation in South Waziristan it was necessary not only to continue to dominate Swat but to clear Bajaur, the northernmost Agency, which borders Afghanistan's Kunar Province.

The Agency had become a haven for foreign insurgents, most of whom had crossed the Afghan border despite the large US military presence in Kunar. The commander of Operation Sherdil, aimed at ejecting or otherwise neutralizing the insurrectionists, Major General Tariq Khan,[30] estimated their strength at some 2,000, including homegrown Taliban, and stated that in spite of many casualties the strength remained high because of reinforcements from Afghanistan. The operation began in August 2008, and General Khan described the Agency as being the "centre of gravity" for the Taliban. "If they lose here," he said, "they've lost almost everything . . . Why we are calling this a test case? If we dismantle the training camps here, the headquarters, the communication centres, the roots which come in, stop the inter-agency movement and destroy the leadership . . . we feel that about 65 percent or so of militancy [in the five northern Agencies] will have been controlled."[31]

By March 2009 his forces controlled Bajaur and its surrounds, if at considerable cost in soldiers' lives and disruption to the inhabitants. Over 80 soldiers were killed, and there was much damage to property, which of course had begun during the militants' reign of terror, when there was large-scale destruction of schools, health clinics, and houses and shops of those suspected of resenting their domination or behaving in an "un-Islamic" fashion.

Pakistan's legislators were kept informed about military operations. In addition to regular updating of senior government representatives, a secret session of the Senate and National Assembly in October 2008 was given a comprehensive briefing on the counter-terrorist and counter-insurgency campaign.[32] The operation's success resulted in an agreement with the tribes. As recorded by Pakistan's *Dawn* newspaper on March 9, 2009, "[the] Mamoond, the largest and most strategically placed tribe in Bajaur, signed a comprehensive 28-point undertaking to surrender key figures of the Tehreek-e-Taliban Pakistan in Bajaur, lay down arms, disband militant groups and stop militant training camps." While this accord seemed to stand the test of time, some of the militants who were driven out of the Agency appeared to have regrouped elsewhere, as evidenced by, for example, a Frontier Corps" convoy ambush in Mohmand on November 11, 2009, in which many soldiers were killed.

Little has changed in the Tribal Areas over the years . . . As *Dawn* reported on November 12, 2009: "Taliban militants ambushed a convoy of 52 paramilitary Frontier Corps troops early Wednesday morning in Ghanam Shah area of Mohmand tribal region . . . At least 32 security personnel went missing and two soldiers [were] found dead . . . they had been decapitated." The *Illustrated London News* had reported on October 23, 1937: "A large convoy was held up [at Shahur Tangi] and the leading lorry drivers were shot, while their vehicles slewed across the road. There was no room to turn the other Lorries around and thirty-four officers and men were killed and forty-eight wounded during the ambush and subsequent rescue operations."

The Frontier Corps came under great pressure throughout much of FATA, because the main commitment of the army was in South Waziristan, where

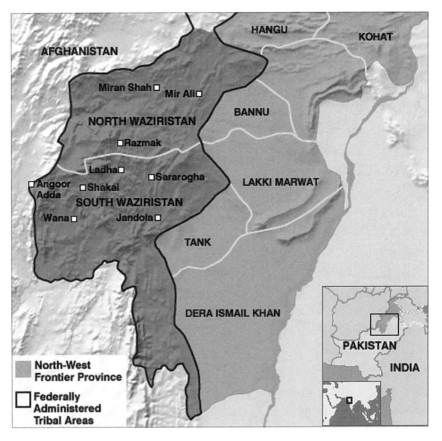

Map 3 Map of the NWFP (renamed Khyber-Pakhtoonkhwa)

Operation Rah-e-Nijat (Path to Deliverance) began on October 17, 2009.

The army was being stretched thin over the region, but the open threat by India's Home Minister of a "sledgehammer" blow, just after the operation began, could not be ignored. Threatened internally and externally, Pakistan was placed in a most difficult situation as regards troop redeployment. It would be comparatively simple in military terms to deploy 100,000 or even more troops to Waziristan — but they would have to come from the eastern border, and this could not be done, given the seriousness of the warning delivered by one of India's highest (and, with reason, most highly regarded) government ministers. The army and the Frontier Corps were going to have to take on the militants with what they already had in both numbers and equipment.

Before operations began in South Waziristan, however, the army per-suaded a powerful Waziri figure, Maulvi Nazir Ahmad, a Taliban devotee, to be at least neutral concerning operations, and have the Wazirs refrain from engaging the army or interfering in its campaign against the mutually dis-trusted Mehsuds. Maulvi Nazir is at best an unreliable semi-ally, as his beliefs are entirely antithetical to the purposes and objectives of Pakistan as a state, but it was essential that even the most risky tactics be at least explored and, if considered viable, pursued at the cost of appearing to validate a self-declared revolutionary Jihadi. As recorded by the Jamestown Foundation, "When asked why the Mujahideen fight the democratic and Islamic government of Pakistan, Maulvi Nazir said Pakistan is run by an infidel government equiva-lent to Christian and Jewish governments, corroborating his claim by quoting a verse from the Qur'an that forbids Muslims from allying themselves with Christians and Jews. In typical Salafist [usually interpreted as 'fundamental-ist'] fashion, Maulvi Nazir considers democracy a defective and mundane system devised by Western infidels."[33]

Nazir and his adherents had concentrated on crossing the border to attack Afghan, US and other foreign forces in Afghanistan, and although he indi-cated that he considered this his priority, it appeared he was willing to deal with the army — until the operation in SWA actually began, when he and another leader, Hafiz Gul Bahadur, said they were "abandoning the peace deal because of continued US missile strikes and Pakistan's widening anti-Taliban offensive in the north-west."[34] In the event, however, neither Bahadur nor

Nazir seemed to encourage or be involved in attacks on the army during the operation in SWA, but as access to the region is limited it is difficult to state without qualification that they and their supporters have remained neutral or will continue that stance. What is likely is that the Wazirs will continue to sit on the fence and present a potential problem to the authorities.

Concurrent with operations in Waziristan and Bajaur it was necessary to maintain a strong presence in Swat, while combating militants in Orakzai, Mohmand and Khyber. The tribals thought they detected weakness, and, as ever, throughout the centuries, sought to take advantage of what they considered a golden opportunity to wreak havoc. The Pakistan Air Force's F-16s and the Army Aviation Corps's Cobra attack helicopters to an extent made up for lack of numbers on the ground, although, as foreign armies found in Iraq and Afghanistan while fighting a similar war, there is never any satisfactory alternative to occupying and dominating an operational area with ground troops.

Casualties in SWA were high among both rebels and the army, and in the period between October 17 and November 4, 42 soldiers and officers were killed and 123 wounded[35] — more than any casualty list in a comparable period of foreign contingents in Afghanistan, some of whose national politicians, military officers and media complained that "Pakistan isn't doing enough" about combating the threat to the existence of the country.

It was announced in November 2009 that South Waziristan would be divided into two separate Agencies, based as far as practicable on tribal locations. The Mehsud, the largest tribe in SWA, are mainly in the centre and south-west, and the Wazirs, the other main tribe, are generally in the west and north, abutting Afghanistan and North Waziristan.

Propaganda and Psychological Operations

On November 16, 2009 it was reported from Islamabad that the visiting US National Security Adviser, General James L. Jones, "praised the Pakistani operation in South Waziristan but urged Pakistani officials to combat extremists who fled to North Waziristan."[36] This is not only impertinent, in terms of a foreign general prescribing the tactics of a supposed ally, but absurd in the sense of being at variance with reason. Plans had already been made concerning North Waziristan, but in the light of Jones" statement an operation in the Agency could be propagandized by the Mullah Nazir as evidence of endorsement by the Pakistan army of an infidel general's instructions. The fact that such guidance was made public was regarded by many in Pakistan as being part of a pattern of condescension and arrogance. Whether or not this attitude is intentional is irrelevant: it is a perception held by many in the army as well as in government and the population at large that the US is at best patronizing and at worst an actual enemy.[37]

Of equal significance, such statements can provide warning to insurgents concerning possible future operations while being valuable to the surprisingly effective propaganda machinery of the rebels. The Taliban use the internet, FM radio stations, DVDs and CDs and printed material to spread their message.[38] The tribes themselves have always had a most effective system of passing information by word of mouth, unofficially — it is amazing how quickly news can be passed over hundreds of miles — and by messenger if formal matters are concerned. The latter method is now in extensive use, given the insurgents' belated wariness of the vulnerability of electronic transmissions, which are intercepted by US and other agencies.[39]

In combating Taliban propaganda, the Pakistan army has made use of psychological operations, and in 2008 leaflets were air-dropped in South Waziristan, notably around Miranshah and Mir Ali townships, in both of which the presence of foreign militants had been detected by military intelligence. The leaflets purported to come from religious authorities and local tribes and some quoted the Saudi cleric, Mufti-e-Azam Sheikh Abdul Aziz, warning Muslim youths against "false jihad." Others were more directly aimed at non-tribals; one of them titled "You Were My Guests," reading "Because of you [foreign militants], I am in trouble. My house is under attack and family members are dying and wounded because of you . . . You are using my soil and you are spreading unrest in my area and country."

As the leaflets were in Urdu, which is not spoken by many residents of FATA and unlikely to be familiar to Uzbeks and other guest Jihadis, and the level of literacy is so low, it is unlikely that this PSYOPS effort had much effect, but it is understood that there have been later and more sophisticated campaigns in concert with ground operations. The fact remains that the best weapon against propaganda is truth — but the truth must be palatable.

The army and government agencies can present the facts in refutation of Taliban claims, but it is almost impossible to deflect highly effective statements that may be presented emotionally but are nonetheless unquestionably factual. Much publicity has been given, for example, to US drone-fired missile attacks within the territory of Pakistan. It is impossible to deny that "the real total of civilian deaths since 2006 appears to be in the range of 250 to 320, or between 31 and 33 percent [of the total number of people killed],"[40] and even if in some Western eyes "only" some 300 Pakistani civilians killed may appear a negligible price to pay for the elimination of militants, the propaganda dividend to the Taliban, while unquantifiable in numerical terms, has undoubtedly been massive.[41] It cannot be judged what effect such well-based propaganda may have on the army, but, whatever this may be, the unpalatable fact is that the army's tasks are made much more difficult by inferred linkage to US missile attacks.

According to sources in Pakistan, PSYOPS leaflets distributed in the border region by foreign forces in Afghanistan have proved to be at best amateur and in general counter-productive.

Conclusion

Although the army has been stretched thin and has had to make many alterations to its war-fighting posture and training, it has succeeded in effectively conducting counter-insurgency operations in difficult terrain in FATA/NWFP. The stability that has been restored thus far, however, depends for its continuation on a blend of military ascendancy and energetic social and economic development aimed at bringing the tribal areas into the twentieth century and providing reasonable employment opportunities for youth. The requirement for education is paramount, followed by concentration on healthcare, communications and political representation. The list of "to do" imperatives is depressingly long, but cannot be ignored. While the army can continue to secure the region, it has to be recognized that this is not its primary function, and that civilian structures for policing and legal process are essential if the tribes are to be drawn into the mainstream of national life.

Terrorism has thrived in Pakistan largely because the education system has failed throughout the country, thus allowing quasi-religious fanaticism to thrive more than it might otherwise have done. The essentiality of education and employment for potentially disaffected young people cannot be over-emphasized. The army can play its part by ensuring that schools can operate without interference, but it is the responsibility of the civil power to build, staff and maintain the schools and to create a societal organization that supports their operation. Without this realization, the army's efforts will have been in vain.

The situation in Balochistan is also disquieting because rebels, in the name of nationalism, have attempted to disrupt the province, which is said to be a base for insurgents engaged in conflict in Afghanistan. In November 2009 the central government offered a major package of development and social improvements, including withdrawal of troops, in return for cessation of violence, but the rebels rejected the offer.[42] The need to maintain or even reinforce the army presence in the province is an important factor in the army's overall planning.

The overall picture in Pakistan is somber. The army is regarded as a bastion of reliability by most of the population, but it is disturbing that a survey in late 2009 found that "An overwhelming majority of young Pakistanis say their country is headed in the wrong direction . . . and only 1 in 10 has confidence in the government . . . The despair among the young generation is rooted in the condition of their lives, the report found. Only a fifth of those interviewed had permanent full-time jobs. Half said they did not have sufficient skills to enter the workplace. And one in four could not read or write a legacy of the country's abysmal public education system, in which less than 40 percent of children are enrolled in school, far below the South Asian average of 58 percent."

The report included the disquieting findings that "The highest-ranking institution was [considered to be] Pakistan's military. Sixty percent of those interviewed said that they trusted it. Second highest was religious educational institutions, trusted by about 50 percent of respondents. The national government came last at 10 percent."[43]

No matter how supportive the public may be of the army as an institution, the military leaders of Pakistan are determined not to again have an army takeover. General Kayani, the army's chief, who has indicated he will not seek an extension of his tenure beyond November 2010, is resolute in supporting democratic governance.

But if civilian government continues to perform as dismally as it appears to have done in 2008–2009, and terrorism becomes rampant to the degree that there is a total breakdown of the rule of law, then there may be no alternative. It is entirely up to civil power to lead the country, and the world had hopes that restoration of democracy would lead to economic and social development — the best countermeasure to domestic terrorism — but the citizens of Pakistan have been sadly disappointed.

It is probable that the large increase in US troop strength in Afghanistan will result in larger numbers of extremists crossing the border into Pakistan,[44] in which case the army will be presented with an even greater challenge than in 2007–2009. If there is to be maintenance of stability in the west of the country the army will require more troops to be moved from the eastern border and can be expected to take more casualties.

It is thought that the army will abide by its duty under the Constitution "to defend Pakistan against external aggression or threat of war, and, subject to law, to act in aid of the civil power when called upon to do so"[45] for so long as the civil power is itself legitimate. And it will continue to commit its soldiers to countering insurgency and terrorism as directed by government. It is the duty and most important priority of government, however, to create social conditions in which insurgents and terrorists cannot thrive.

Notes

1   *The Constitution of the Islamic Republic of Pakistan*, Chapter 2, Paragraph 245 (1).

2   Lawrence Ziring, *Pakistan in the Twentieth Century*, Oxford University Press, 1997, pp. 392–3. It is notable that the Iranian Air Force assisted in the military campaign against Baloch insurrectionists.

3   "Pakistan's New Frontier Policy: the Withdrawal from Tribal Territory," *Illustrated London News*, January 24, 1948.

4   Fighting units are battalions of infantry and, for example, regiments of armour and artillery, respectively of some 800 and 500 in strength; formations are brigades (usually 4–5,000 in infantry brigades) and divisions (approximately 12–17,000, according to role).

5   "Can have short war against Pak, says South West air chief, slams China," *Indian*

Express, June 4, 2009. Available at: www.indianexpress.com/news/can-have-short-war-against-pak-says-south-w/470870/(); also *Zee news*, June 4, 2009. Available at: www.zeenews.com/news536804.html (accessed April 9, 2010).

6 "Enough is enough, say Army chief," *Tribune*, Chandigarh, November 4, 2009. Available at: www.tribuneindia.com/2009/20091105/nation.htm#12 (accessed April 9, 2010); also "Any more terror attacks from Pak will be retaliated: Chidambaram," *Times of India*, November 1, 2009. Available at: http://timesofindia.indiatimes.com/india/Any-more-terror-attacks-from-Pak-will-be-retaliated-Chidambaram/articleshow/5185506.cms (accessed April 9, 2010).

7 Including this writer.

8 See *Tribal Areas of Pakistan: Challenges and Responses*, Pervaiz Iqbal Cheema and Maqsudul Hasan Nuri (eds), for the Islamabad Policy Research Institute, 2005. An excellent series of analyses by distinguished experts.

9 Based on the 1998 census, which the government indicates "is likely to have been distorted by problems in gathering data, since tribal custom forbids the disclosure of information about women to outsiders." Available at: http://fata.gov.pk/subpages/population.php (accessed April 9, 2010). The decadal census is unlikely to be conducted in the foreseeable future.

10 In 2000 it was decided to dispense with the tier of government involved in administering Divisions.

11 Tommy Franks, "War of Words," The *New York Times*, October 19, 2004. Available at: www.nytimes.com/2004/10/19/opinion/19franks.html?_r=1 (accessed April 9, 2010).

12 100,000 would be more than the then total strength of the Frontier Corps (40,000) and XI Corps (30,000) in the province.

13 "Donald Rumsfeld holds Defence Briefing," *CNN* December 27, 2001. (General Myers, Chairman of the Joint Chiefs of Staff also answered questions). Available at: http://edition.cnn.com/TRANSCRIPTS/0112/27/se.02.html (accessed April 9, 2010).

14 Later Director General Inter-Services Intelligence, then, in October 2007, Vice Chief of Army Staff, and, on November 28, 2007, Chief of Army Staff.

15 USSOCOM History and Research Office. *United States Special Operations Command History: 20 (1987–2007) Proven in the Past, Vigilant Today, Prepared for the Future*. MacDill AFB, FL: US Special Operations Command, 2007.

16 Ibid.

17 The *Daily Times*, Pakistan, March 31, 2007.

18 There are two types of Hadith, or descriptions of the deeds and sayings of the Prophet: the Sacred Hadith, in which God speaks through the Prophet; and the Noble Hadith, the sayings of the Prophet as recounted by his followers. Arguments concerning relevance and degrees of validity can go on forever, but the opportunities for revisionist interpretation and plain manipulation are, unfortunately, limitless.

19 In early 2009 a video was taken of a 17-year-old girl being mercilessly beaten by a Taliban man while being held down by another, neither of which actions is in accordance with Islamic teaching. The video was shown widely on the internet and played an important part in convincing normal citizens that the fanatics had to be dealt with. Available at: www.timesonline.co.uk/tol/news/world/asia/article6022878.ece (accessed April 9, 2010).

20 *Daily Times*, Pakistan, April 14, 2009.

21 "Taliban head 'must be eliminated'," *BBC News Online*, June 15, 2009. Available at: http://news.bbc.co.uk/2/hi/south_asia/8100896.stm (accessed April 8, 2010).

22 "Pakistan Army strikes in Swat," *The Hindu Online*, May 9, 2009. Available at: http://www.thehindu.com/2009/05/09/stories/2009050957650100.htm (accessed April 9, 2010).

23 On November 17, 2009 the BBC reported Fazlullah as saying by telephone to a reporter that "I have reached Afghanistan safely," from where he intended to "launch full-fledged punitive raids against the army in Swat" (see http://news.bbc.co.uk/2/hi/south_asia/8364243.stm).

24 Brian Cloughley, "Insurrection, Terrorism, and the Pakistan Army." Pakistan Security Research Unit (PSRU), Brief Number 53, December 10, 2009. Available at: http://spaces.brad.ac.uk:8080/download/attachments/748/Brief+53Finalised.pdf (accessed April 9, 2010).

25 The US blames Pakistan for being unable to prevent border-crossings but ignores the fact that 60,000 US troops are deployed in Afghanistan, of whom half are in the east of the country and are incapable of securing the border on the Afghan side.

26 "Police return to former Taliban haven," *BBC*, November 15, 2009. Available at: http://news.bbc.co.uk/2/hi/south_asia/8302950.stm (accessed April 8, 2010).

27 *Reuters*, January 2009: ""There is no understanding between Pakistan and the United States on Predator attacks," [foreign ministry] spokesman Mohammad Sadiq said." Available at: www.reuters.com/article/idUSISL332751 (accessed t/c) Also the *New York Times*, November 4, 2008: "After the meeting with General Petraeus, President Asif Ali Zardari of Pakistan said in a statement: 'Continuing drone attacks on our territory, which result in loss of precious lives and property, are counterproductive and difficult to explain by a democratically elected government. It is creating a credibility gap.'" Available at: www.nytimes.com/2008/11/04/world/asia/04pstan.html (accessed ????).

28 "Pakistanis see US as biggest threat," *Al Jazeera*, August 13, 2009. Available at: http://english.aljazeera.net/news/asia/2009/08/20098910857878664.html (accessed April 9, 2010).

29 Quoted by Seymour Hersh in his analysis "Defending the Arsenal," *New Yorker*, November 9, 2009. Available at: www.newyorker.com/reporting/2009/11/16/091116fa_

fact_hersh?currentPage=all (accessed April 9, 2010). He quotes this writer in the piece, commenting on the unlikely possibility of mutiny in the army.

30   Who had commanded 14 Infantry Division in its early operations in South Waziristan, then was appointed Inspector General Frontier Corps, North-West Frontier Province. An outstandingly capable officer.

31   "The Battle for Bajaur," *Outlook India*, October 17, 2008. Available at: www.outlook-india.com/article.aspx?238667 (accessed April 9, 2010).

32   This was only the third joint sitting in the country's history, the others having been in 1974 when, shamefully, the Ahmadi community was deemed to be non-Muslim, and in Available at: http://news.bbc.co.uk/2/hi/7658325.stm (accessed April 9, 2010).

33   "Taliban Leader Mullah Nazir Defends Jihad in South Waziristan," Jamestown Foundation. *Terrorism Monitor*, May 8, 2009. Available at: www.jamestown.org/single/?no_cache=1&tx_ttnews[tt_news]=34959 (accessed April 9, 2010).

34   *BBC News*, June 30, 2009. Available at: http://news.bbc.co.uk/2/hi/8125725.stm (accessed April 9, 2010).

35   Major General Athar Abbas, interview on Pakistan television 4 November 2009. Available at: www.app.com.pk/en_/index.php?option=com_content&task=view&id=89336&Itemid=2 (accessed April 9, 2010). In some foreign media there is continuing comment about "half-hearted" operations by the army. Apart from the fact that such statements are absurd, the factual evidence of army casualties is evidence enough of commitment. The Pakistan army has lost over 1,200 soldiers killed in their offensives against Taliban and other insurgents. It is insulting and nonsensical to claim that its officers and soldiers are being "half-hearted" in its pursuit of extremists who seek to destroy their country.

36   "U.S. asks for more from Pakistan in Terror War" by Eric Schmitt and David Sanger, *New York Times*, November 16, 2009. Available at: www.nytimes.com/2009/11/16/world/asia/16policy.html?hp (accessed April 9, 2010).

37   Gallup Pakistan August 2009: "an overwhelming number, 59 percent of respondents, said the greatest threat to Pakistan right now is, in fact, the US." Available at: http://english.aljazeera.net/news/asia/2009/08/20098910857878664.html (accessed April 9, 2010).

38   For example, "Taliban slick propaganda confronts US," *BBC*, August 3, 2009. Available at: http://news.bbc.co.uk/2/hi/south_asia/8176259.stm (accessed April 9, 2010).

39   In 2007 the writer was informed by General Kayani, then Director General Inter-Services Intelligence, that his agency could intercept at most a hundred electronic conversations at any one time. While Pakistan's domestic intercept capability has improved considerably, the reluctance of US and British agencies to provide real-time information has detracted from efficacy in counter insurgency and anti-terrorist operations. The extent and precision of technological intelligence gathering in the region by the US, UK and Australia are awe-inspiring. Interpretation, however, in the

final essence, rests with individuals who appear to have little knowledge of or empathy with tribal proclivities or affairs.

40 "Revenge of the Drones," *New America Foundation*, October 19, 2009.

41 *World Public Opinion* mid-2009: "The US Predator drone attacks aimed at militant camps within the Pakistani border are rejected by 82 percent [of the population] as unjustified." Available at: www.worldpublicopinion.org/pipa/articles/brasiapacificra/ 619.php (accessed April 9, 2010).

42 *Reuters*, November 25, 2009. Available at: www.reuters.com/article/idUSISL542211 (accessed April 9, 2010). "Pakistan's reform package 'peanuts': Baloch leaders," *Dawn*, November 25, 2009. Available at: www.dawn.com/wps/wcm/connect/ dawn-content-library/dawn/news/pakistan/03-pakistans-reform-package-peanuts-baloch-leaders-ss-08 (accessed April 9, 2010).

43 "Survey of Pakistan's Young Predicts 'Disaster' if Their Needs Aren't Addressed," *New York Times*, November 22, 2009. Available at: www.nytimes.com/2009/11/22/world/ asia/22pstan.html (accessed April 9, 2010). Describes the results of a survey commissioned by the British Council and conducted by Nielsen.

44 *The News*, Pakistan, November 29, 2009: "Prime Minister, Yousuf Raza Gilani has said that the increase in US force in Afghanistan might lead to the spill over of militants in Pakistan and make the situation worse . . ." Available at: www.thenews.com.pk/ updates.asp?id=92431 (accessed April 9, 2010).

45 The Constitution of Pakistan, Chapter 2: Armed Forces. Avaliable at: http://www. pakistani.org/pakistan/constitution/part12.ch2.html (accessed April 9, 2010).

CHAPTER FIVE

The Existential Threat: Tehreek-e-Taliban Pakistan (TTP) and al-Qaeda in Pakistan?

N Ilahi

Abstract

Tehreek-e-Taliban Pakistan (TTP) and al-Qaeda, operating from the federally Administered Tribal Areas (FATA) of Pakistan, are considered a grave threat to Pakistan and the US. They emerged when a large number of Taliban and al-Qaeda fighters fled to FATA to escape the onslaught of the US forces in 2001. TTP is fighting with the Pakistan army in FATA and Swat and has carried out suicide bombings across Pakistan. Al-Qaeda has attracted US drone attacks into Pakistan territory which at times is predicted to be a prelude to the US invasion into FATA area. The situation is, therefore, alarming. The objective of this chapter is to ascertain the reasons, repercussions and especially the dangers of these elements' presence and activities in Pakistan.

Introduction

Rarely has an insurgency in any part of the world aroused so much international concern as the ongoing insurgency and terrorism carried out by the Pakistani Taliban, known as Tehreek-e-Taliban Pakistan (TTP), in the tribal areas of Pakistan and elsewhere. There are primarily three reasons for this concern. First, the US and the West have a fear that the al-Qaeda elements based in Pak-Afghan border, lurking behind the TTP, are planning another 9/11-like terrorist attack.[1] Second, their activities are detrimental to the operations of the US, NATO and international forces in Afghanistan where they have been battling with the Afghan Taliban for the last eight years. Third, internally, their activities are considered an existential threat to Pakistan.[2] These reasons have generated genuine international consternation over the presence and activities of TTP and al-Qaeda in the tribal belt of Pakistan.

The question is why Pakistan is unable to control and subdue this threat to its survival. And why the US and international forces, that are battling with the menace of the same genre in the neighbourhood, are incapable to resolve it?

A quick look at TTP structure and strength further puzzles the mind. They are small in number, equipped with small arms, living a medieval lifestyle and without access to air-power or artillery. They live in a remote corner of Pakistan that is 1/20 of the size of the country, away from the cities of significance. They lack the numerical and military strength to beat the Pakistani security forces to extend their writ to other areas of Pakistan outside their strongholds. Yet they are considered an ever-increasing threat to the existence of Pakistan.

On the other hand, al-Qaeda had sneaked into Pakistan after the 2001 US attack on their hideouts in Afghanistan and regrouped in the tribal areas of Pakistan. The US raised a call that FATA has turned it into "a key centre for planning and preparing operations to strike the United States as well as its allies and friends."[3] But now it is not in a comfortable position in FATA. Relentless US drone attacks have killed a number of its members and dispersed others. But the top objective of the current US strategy to defeat al-Qaeda remains unfulfilled.[4]

The fact is that TTP and al-Qaeda in Pakistan pose a real danger to Pakistan and the world at large, but they can be bridled, provided proper planned and sustained strategies are adopted to counter them. It needs to be understood that it is the TTP coupled with al-Qaeda that has produced a lethal combination attracting the worldwide attention. If al-Qaeda was not operating from this area, the TTP and its activities, however devastating within Pakistan, would not have bothered the US and the West, and vice versa — sans TTP, Pakistan would not have considered al-Qaeda a threat to Pakistan, at least in a direct manner.

It is imperative to look at the birth and growth of these groups and find out the factors that enabled them to couple together, gain strength and expand their areas of influence. In so doing, this chapter concentrates on understanding the genesis and phased growth of militancy and extremism in Pakistan; discusses the birth and growth of TTP and al-Qaeda in Pakistan and also the Afghan Taliban and the nature of their activities and their nexus; provides details of the counter-insurgency and terrorism strategies of Pakistan and the US; explores the irritants and impediments that hamper the strategies and their fallouts, including the role of the security agencies of Pakistan; and scrutinizes the socio-economic implications of the security situation, avenues of its expansion across Pakistan and fluctuation in public pulse regarding this scenario.

Extremism, Militancy and Terrorism in Pakistan

The Genesis

It was the vision of the founder of Pakistan, Muhammad Ali Jinnah, popularly known as Quaid-e-Azam (the great leader), earlier a harbinger of Muslim-Hindu unity, who came to realize in the 1940s that Muslims could not survive politically and thrive economically in Hindu-dominated India after freedom from the British rule. It was, therefore, the need, envisioned by him and endorsed by the followers, to safeguard the political and economic survival and wellbeing of the Muslims of India as a separate nation that necessitated the creation of Pakistan. It was not created to protect, profess or propel Islam. He clearly stated his "fundamental principle" to run the state on this basis:

> We are starting with this fundamental principle that we are all citizens and equal citizens of the state. We should keep that in front of us as our ideal and you will find that in the course of time Hindus will cease to be Hindus and Muslims will cease to be Muslims, not in the religious sense because that is the personal faith of each individual, but in the political sense, as citizens of the State.[5]

This spirit got a blow, however, 30 years after its creation when in 1977 the democratic government of Prime Minister Zulfikar Ali Bhutto was overthrown by General Zia-ul-Haq, who relied on religious parties to legitimize and perpetuate his rule. In return, these religious parties, seeking similar foothold in the society, propagated that Pakistan was created in the name of Islam and it was an ideological state. In this process the original history, concepts and visions were muddled and muted. Thus this marriage of convenience laid down the foundations of the beginning of Islamic extremism and radicalization in Pakistan.

The beginning of Islamic extremism and subsequently terrorism in Pakistan can be attributed to two eras of military dictatorships, that of General Zia-ul-Haq (1977–89) and that of General Pervez Musharraf (1999–2008). Both grabbed the opportunities arising from the crises in Afghanistan and secured the US blessing to rule with impunity and to keep democracy at bay in return for helping the US achieve its objectives in Afghanistan.

Seeds of Extremism and Militancy

The roots of the present-day security situation in the tribal areas of Pakistan, adjacent to Afghanistan, owe much to Pakistan's more than two decade-long support of the US-backed anti-Soviet jihad in Afghanistan, and later on to the Saudi Arabia-United Arab Emirates-backed Taliban regime. It made Pakistanis view the militancy in Afghanistan as a normal phenomenon that was not detrimental to them. They were made to feel that it was their religious and moral duty to be at least sympathetic towards them.

The Pakistanis who fought or supported those wars and conflicts at the behest of several states and their own government were left in the lurch and were not guided on what to do next. Post-operation care was non-existent. Psychological and physical rehabilitation of battle-hardened fighters, to refit them into society, was not considered necessary. The post-9/11 U-turn on Afghan policy not only plagued their ideological frame of mind but also rendered them useless and jobless. However, the regrouping of al-Qaeda, the resurgence of Afghan Taliban and the birth of local Taliban attracted a number of these elements. So their training, temperament and experience made them useful for these organizations, which welcomed them back to where they belonged.

Three Phases of Extremism/Terrorism

The mother of all phases and faces of religious extremism and later on insurgency and terrorism in Pakistan can be attributed to the Afghan Jihad, which gave birth to jihadi parties and jihad culture during and after the Afghan Jihad. The Jihadi organizations whose many members have turned into militants and extremists, siding with Taliban, TTP and al-Qaeda are: (i) Harkat-ul-Jihad-al-Islami (HJI), led by Qari Saifullah Akhtar; (ii) Jamiat-ul-Ansar (JA), led by Maulana Khalil; (iii) Jaish-e-Mohammad (JeM) or the Army of the Prophet Mohammad, a Sunni Deobandi organization, launched by Maulana Masood Azhar in Febuary 2000; (iv) Lashkar-e-Tayyiba (LeT), "Army of the Pure," an Ahle Hadith (Wahhabi) jihadi group founded in 1991 at the Kunar province of Afghanistan, which is an armed wing of Markaz Dawatul Irshad (MDI) or the Centre for Proselytisation and Preaching formed in 1988 by Hafiz Mohammad Saeed and now working as Falah-e-Insaniat Foundation; and (v) Hizb-ul Mujahideen (HM) or the Party of Freedom Fighters, led by a militant Yousuf Shaqh, alias Pir Syed Salahuddin.[6]

The end of Afghan Jihad was in fact the beginning of terrorism and then insurgency in Pakistan. The ten year-long Afghan Jihad had strengthened the milieu of mullah, military and Madrassah, which pervaded society, as did the "Kalashnikov culture." From it stemmed the next three phases and different faces of terrorism, which have snow-balled into the present security situation.

The first phase of terrorism and sabotage erupted in the 1980s, when a streak of Indian-sponsored bomb-blasts was experienced in various areas of Pakistan, especially in the province of Punjab, in retaliation for Pakistan's alleged support of the Khalistan movement of Sikhs of East Punjab in India and later, support for the Kashmiris' uprising in the Indian Administered Kashmir. Pakistan accused Indian intelligence agencies like the Research and Analysis Wing (RAW) of carrying out bomb blasts in Pakistan.

On January 29, 1999, an Indian saboteur, Subhash Chander, was apprehended by the security agencies of Pakistan for carrying out bomb blasts in Sialkot. The then Prime Minister of Pakistan, Nawaz Sharif, brought this Indian activity to the notice of the US Deputy Secretary of State, Strobe Talbot, who was on a visit to Pakistan. Sialkot, being a border town, was worst hit by Indian terrorism — from 1998 to 2000 it suffered 25 Indian-sponsored bomb blasts, resulting in many deaths of innocent civilians.[7]

Though General Musharraf banned jihadi organizations in January 2002, arrested its leaders, like Hafiz Saeed (LeT) and Maulana Masood Azhar (JeM) and curbed infiltration into Indian Administered Kashmir, the Indians considered it inadequate. Thus the RAW-sponsored terrorism continued. The threat of retaliation by these banned organizations posed problems for the internal security of Pakistan.[8]

The second phase, sectarian terrorism, started in late 1980s. Three organizations were responsible for this phase: (i) Sipah-e-Sahaba Pakistan (SSP), the Sunni Deobandi militant sectarian organization, formed in 1985; (ii) Sipah-e-Muhammad Pakistan (SMP), the militant Shia organization formed in 1990; and (iii) Lashkar-e-Jhangvi, an ultra-militant splinter group of SSP, formed in 1996.[9] These parties shed the blood of clerics, professionals, civil servants and innocent worshippers, until they were proscribed and their top-ranking militants were subdued. Hundreds were dispersed, of whom many have joined forces with the militants in FATA. During the same period the ethnic political party, Muhajir Qaumi Movement (MQM), resorted to urban insurgency and terrorism in Karachi. It was quelled during Benazir Bhutto's regime through operation "Clean-up" (July 1995–96).[10]

The third phase started at the end of 2001 when a large number of Taliban and al-Qaeda fighters, pressed by the US attack, sneaked into Pakistan through the porous Pak-Afghan border. Soon FATA became a fertile base for the al-Qaeda, Afghan Taliban and their local sympathizers, who were soon to become a formidable force titled Tehreek-e-Taliban Pakistan (TTP). These local militants rapidly gained enough strength not only to create mischief in FATA, NWFP and across Pakistan but also alarmed the US and the Western countries who saw a nexus between the al-Qaeda and the Pakistani Taliban that was considered a threat to them and to Pakistan's existence.

The Four Factors

In this outcry against al-Qaeda and its local allies, four aspects figured prominently as the basis of the new menace, sectarian/jihadi parties, FATA, madrassah and Inter-Services Intelligence (ISI). The perceptions and realities about these four factors are addressed below before discussing the actual threats, i.e. al-Qaeda, Taliban and TTP.

i. The Jihadi and sectarian parties that have been instrumental in different phases of violence and terrorism in Pakistan have been mentioned above. Many rudderless activists of these proscribed organizations, like LeJ, JeM, and HM have joined the militants in FATA and Swat and are participating in militancy and terrorism. In fact in character they are malleable, like al-Qaeda. They find one form or the other to demonstrate their extremist tactics.

ii. FATA: It was only after 2001 that FATA started earning the notoriety of a safe haven for all sorts of Islamist militants, local, regional and international. At the end of 2007 CIA Director Michael Hayden described al-Qaeda safe havens in FATA as a "clear and present danger" to the US. The FBI Director expressed similar sentiments. Chairman of the US Joint Chiefs of Staff Michael Mullen opined that "if I were going to pick the next attack to hit the United States, it would come out of the FATA."

The Pakistani courts and police have no jurisdiction in tribal areas. It is administered through political agents, the Maliks (tribal elders), Jirga and the Frontier Crime Regulation (FCR).[11] Why and how FATA has acquired the reputation of the epicenter of terror can be best explained by the complex inter-relation of the refugee influx from Afghanistan of the last 30 years, its rugged terrain that is ideal for guerrilla warfare, which the absence of state law makes more convenient, the US invasion of Afghanistan, which created a sympatric ground amongst tribal leaders, and the failure of security and intelligence agencies to fathom the severity of threat.

iii. Madaris: After 9/11, the madaris (plural of madrassah) in Pakistan were alleged to be incubators of terrorists in Pakistan.[12] The Taliban (students), who had emerged from the madaris established in Afghan refugee camps in tribal areas of Pakistan during the Afghan Jihad changed the Western perception about the thousand-year-old institution of Islamic teaching. Western journalists termed the Darul Uloom Haqqania, Akora Khattak, where Mullah Omar got his education, the "University of Jihad."[13] The International Crisis Group (ICG) issued a report in 2002 that "about a third of all students in Pakistan were enrolled in madaris."[14] This estimation is grossly overstated. As per a survey conducted between 1991 and 2001, the students of madaris were less than 1 percent of all students enrolled in Pakistan.[15] Moreover, Christine Fair's thorough research "found out little evidence to support popular assertions that *madaris* are the cradle of militancy."[16] However, she adds that "small numbers can have large consequences including sectarianism and connections to sectarian violence, the productions of suicide attacks in Pakistan and elsewhere."[17] Her assessment about Madrassah-sectarianism connection is correct because madaris are established on sectarian lines, however, the involvement of madaris students in suicide bombings is not confirmed.[18] The religious quarters in Pakistan assert that the West is wary of political Islam, which it thinks stems from the Qur'an, Masjid and Madrassah. Hence Madrassah is being targeted. Moreover, many Pakistanis are suspicious that the US seeks to de-Islamize Pakistan's educational system. Christine Fair met high-level officials in the US State Department who confirmed that it was one of their goals.[19] The recruitment patterns of TTP and al-Qaeda in Pakistan show that their recruits do not come from madaris. Moreover, as per intelligence sources, none of the suicide bombers who have carried out suicide attacks in Pakistan has been identified to be a student of any Madrassah. But this consolation can be short-lived, as the Madrassah students are most vulnerable to be influenced by prolonged militancy and extremism in Pakistan. Some research data indicates that Madrassah students have a greater taste for jihad than the students in other educational streams. It further suggests that Madrassah students are consistently more likely than students in private or public schools to support war with India and militants in Kashmir and are less likely to support equal rights for minorities and women.[20] And, with an increase in militancy, "the militant labour demand may evolve toward greater reliance on *madaris* for recruits."[21]

iv. Inter-Services Intelligence (ISI): US officials have been accusing the Pakistan army and the spy agency ISI of their complicity in militancy.[22] Immediately after the fall of the Taliban in Kabul they accused ISI officers of having ties with Taliban and for sheltering Mullah Omar in Quetta, which Pakistan has been denying persistently.[23] In February 2009 they reiterated their serious concern in this respect when the ISI chief was on a US visit.[24] Later on, Af-Pak Special Representative Richard Holbrooke and US Joint Chiefs of Staff Mike Mullen also blamed Pakistan of employing the policy of using terrorist groups, a tactic which had begun to consume Pakistan itself, besides endangering the world.[25] The Prime Minister of Pakistan reacted to these allegations and said, "The army and ISI are working in the ambit of constitution and under the command of the Prime Minister. It is the same ISI that had been working with the United States in the past."[26] The ISI also reacted by cancelling Holbrook's visit to ISI headquarters, Islamabad, at the last minute on March 27, 2009. He was to be briefed on the security situation in Swat and FATA.[27] Later on the ISI chief told the visiting Chairman of the Senate Committee on Foreign Relations, John Kerry, that the US allegations were "totally absurd" and US intelligence agencies were doing it to cover up their mistakes in Afghanistan and this was being done largely on the behest of Indian spy agency RAW, which was engaged in efforts to destabilize Pakistan through its own networks in Afghanistan.[28] Besides this clarification, Pakistan insinuated that due to India's growing influence in Afghanistan it was imperative to have influence in these organizations.[29] Pakistan's concerns and clarifications aside, the US impression of ISI is not favourable. This mistrust is an irritant that keeps cropping up to mar the smooth sailings of the allies.

The Core Concern

These factors revolve around the core concern — al-Qaeda, Taliban and TTP.

Al-Qaeda

Does al-Qaeda really exist? This disbelief was more widespread among the Pakistani community eight years earlier as they shared the perceptions of a myriad around the world who considered the 9/11 catastrophe the handiwork of the US instead of an organization called al-Qaeda. Most among them did not believe that Osama bin Laden ever existed and if he was a reality, he was killed in Tora Bora by the US Daisy Cutters.[30]

Despite this widespread ambiguity, most Pakistanis from the lower and middle classes saw bin Laden as an "imagined hero," whereas the educated upper-middle class heaped the onus on the CIA for creating him.[31] These myths, confusions and ambiguities were mainly due to lack of trust in the US, mistrust against the military rule of General Musharraf, al-Qaeda's elusive form and structure, and weak coverage of events by Pakistani media.

The apprehension and deportation of nearly 700 al-Qaeda terrorists by Pakistan did little to improve the level of this disbelief.[32] In fact the bombing of Afghanistan and the consistent news of collateral damage kept the people fixated on viewing the US as the aggressor. Thus bin Laden's popularity soared, which can be gauged from one particular incident. At the end of December 2002, the funeral prayer for Aimal Kansi, who was put to death by the courts for killing CIA officers outside the agency headquarters in Langley, in January 1993, was held at the Quetta stadium. According to various estimates, the number of mourners, which included army officers, police officers, civil bureaucrats, politicians and people from all walks of life, was so large that even the political parties and General Musharraf could not attract the same numbers in their election campaigns in the same venue.[33]

In 2002, as a result of the US operation "Anaconda," al-Qaeda was dispersed and pressed to move towards the treacherous mountains of Hindu Kush along the Pak-Afghan border. Many of them sneaked into FATA. Since then, they have been changing shelters from FATA to urban areas of Punjab and Sindh, and back to FATA to avoid annihilation at the hands of the US and Pakistani security forces. Al-Qaeda has defied obliteration due to its mercurial form and structure. Once pressed hard it vanishes from one area and appears at another.

In the first phase it grouped in FATA, where its old connections established during Afghan Jihad helped its leadership get the shelter. However, very soon the Pakistan security forces started operation against them and the Taliban. Resultantly the leadership started leaving FATA and moved towards bigger cities of Pakistan, especially in the Punjab, where they operated clandestinely, far away from the area under scrutiny.

In phase two, al-Qaeda leadership found safe houses, logistic support and transport in these cities with the help of the activists of religious parties and Jihadi organizations.[34] Hamza Rabia, the operational chief of al-Qaeda, and his family lived in Lahore for six months in 2003–04.[35] A number of al-Qaeda commanders were arrested from the cities from 2002–05, which included

Abu Zubaydah (Faisalabad), Khalid Sheikh Mohammed (Rawalpindi), Ahmed Khilfan Ghailani (Gujrat), Amjad Farooqi (killed in Nawabshah), and Abu Faraj Al-Liby (Mardan, near Peshawar). After the arrests of al-Qaeda key leaders in Punjab, it returned to its original safe haven, the FATA, and started regrouping there.[36] This was the beginning of the third phase, which is continuing now. However, they are again under intense pressure from the Pakistani military operation and US drone attacks. They might once again start trickling out into the cities of Pakistan or to other countries; the beginning of a fourth phase.

Documents recovered from the hideout of Hamza Rabia, in Gujrat, 2004, revealed that the al-Qaeda leadership hiding on the Pak-Afghan border was not in favour of fighting with the Pakistani army. They wanted to keep their focus on the "snake head" (the US) and avoid loosing their strength and focus by fighting with others. Most of the army encounters therefore took place with Uzbek desperadoes. The rationale of the birth of the TTP can be seen in this logic and policy of al-Qaeda to avoid direct skirmishes with the Pakistan army and let the locals perform this job.

It is estimated that after 2001 the membership of al-Qaeda depleted from 3,000–4,000 to a few hundred.[37] In Pakistan, top al-Qaeda leadership, excluding bin Laden and Ayman al-Zawahiri, has been neutralized and there should not be more than hundred core group members of al-Qaeda left in FATA.[38] It is hard for al-Qaeda to replenish its strength from within Pakistan, as it does not have a system and structure to recruit Pakistanis. It relies on groups based in Pakistan to recruit helpers and facilitators to continue their activities within Pakistan.[39] But its asymmetrical system to run loose federation works well for it, as other like-minded groups operating under its umbrella become its strength. In addition to the Uzbeks, Chechens, Turks and Afghanis, TTP is the largest and fiercest group raised by it in FATA and Swat.

Taliban

After the Taliban's fall in November 2001, the US expressed concern that many Taliban had moved across the porous Afghan border to regroup in Pakistan. There were instances where the Taliban fighters crossed over from the mostly unmanned Durand Line for rest and respite and returned to Afghanistan to fight again with the US-led forces. But the fact is that unlike al-Qaeda, the Taliban did not make their base in FATA to launch attacks in Afghanistan. They mostly remained in Afghanistan because more than 45 percent of the Afghan population is Pushtun, which makes it more convenient for them to assimilate in their own tribes. Thus they regrouped in Afghanistan and initiated their guerrilla struggle within two months of their fall.

Nevertheless, Pakistan established hundreds of pickets on the border to check Taliban infiltration. Afghanistan, on the other hand, has less than half of these pickets and has not agreed to Pakistan's suggestion to barricade the entire border. It is unthinkable that the Afghan Taliban have survived for eight years entirely on hit and run operations from FATA and by Pakistan's alleged secret help. It also belies British Foreign Minister David Miliband's misplaced optimism that Taliban are "deeply unpopular" and that only 8 percent of Afghans want the Taliban back.[40] Conversely, the facts show that Taliban are surviving on local strength and with support from within, which means the conflict could continue for a long time. And its intensity has already soared.[41] Consequently now Pakistan expresses apprehension of possible Taliban spill-over into Pakistan, especially after the initiation of Operation "Panther's Claw" by the British forces and later on, the US operation against the Taliban in Helmand in July 2009.[42] The US has "assured to take all steps to stop infiltration of fleeing militants into Pakistan."[43] Holbrooke also saw little evidence that Taliban fighters had fled from Helmand into Pakistan. However, he had to discover how the Taliban had melted away within Afghanistan.[44]

Interestingly, the Taliban chief Mullah Omar has never approved TTP's activities in Pakistan, though he did them to come to Afghanistan for jihad.[45] Baitullah Mehsud, however, did not pay heed to his instructions and concentrated on insurgency in FATA and terrorism in cities of Pakistan. This dichotomy rebuffs the assertions that the TTP has provided an "essential rear base for the Taliban insurgency in Afghanistan."[46]

Tehreek-e-Taliban Pakistan

Since 2002 some groups of tribesmen in FATA had been supporting the Afghan Taliban and al-Qaeda elements that had escaped the US onslaught in Afghanistan. These tribesmen, mostly Sunni Muslims of the Deobandi sect, joined forces and formed Tehreek-e-Taliban Pakistan (TTP) (the Students' Movement of Pakistan) on December 14, 2007. It was led by Baitullah Mehsud, who came to prominence after the death of famous militant tribal leaders, Nek Muhammad Wazir and Abdullah Mehsud.[47]

The TTP activists are not students of madaris like Afghan Taliban. But they adopted this name to take advantage of it to get quick recognition and the support of the Pashtuns of the tribal areas in particular and the people of Pakistan in general.

The stated objectives of TTP are resistance against the Pakistani security forces, enforcement of Sharia and support of Afghan Taliban against NATO forces in Afghanistan.[48] In an interview Baitullah Mehsud declared, "Our main aim is to finish Britain and the United States and to crush the pride of the non-Muslims. We pray to God to give us the ability to destroy the White House, New York and London."[49]

Ideological rhetoric aside, monetary benefits are a big incentive for the TTP. As per intelligence reports TTP receives money from al-Qaeda for keeping the security forces of Pakistan engaged so that they can operate around the Pak-Afghan border unchallenged.[50] Similar sources have information that it is receiving money from India also.

Due to funds and fundamentalism, TTP soon became the largest organization of Pakistani militants. It is active in most of the 24 districts, seven tribal agencies and six frontier regions in the North-West Frontier Province. Its strongholds are in South Waziristan, North Waziristan, Orakzai, Kurram, Khyber, Mohmand, Bajaur and Darra Adam Khel, and in the settled districts of Swat, Upper Dir, Lower Dir, Bannu, Lakki Marwat, Tank, Peshawar, Dera Ismail Khan, Mardan, Charsadda and Kohat.[51] South Waziristan, home of Hakimullah Mehsud, the new chief of TTP and its HQ has a very rugged mountainous terrain, an extension of Tora Bora in Afghanistan, making it quite inaccessible, ideal for prolonged guerrilla warfare.[52] TTP's strength in FATA is estimated to be 10,000[53] to 35,000.[54]

Most of the TTP fighters are not intransigent ideological extremists. They belong to different segments, and have different reasons for joining TTP:

a. they are unemployed youth, of which there are a lot in FATA, are recruited on payment of Rs. 15–20,000 per month (£100–120);

b. they are criminals, lured by the incentive of money and guns;

c. they are hardcore extremists of proscribed sectarian and Jihadi organizations like SSP, LJ, and JeM;

d. they are the angry and aggrieved relatives of those killed in the military operation and drone attacks.[55]

In addition to the TTP, a number of militant groups have mushroomed, mostly to receive foreign funds. These include non-Taliban Islamist militant groups in the Khyber Agency, mostly in the Bara areas like Mangal Bagh's Lashkar-i-Islam, the late Haji Namdar's Amr Bil Maruf wa Nahi Anil Munkar (Promotion of Virtue and Prevention of Vice) party, and Ustad Mahbubul Haq's Ansar-ul-Islam.[56]

The religious extremist Muttahida Majlis-e-Amal (MMA) government of NWFP, that had won the elections with the connivance of General Pervez Musharraf and ruled the province from 2002 till 2008, had a soft spot for the TTP. Moreover, the federal government of Pakistan remained ambivalent in tackling it. The security forces of Pakistan had launched an operation against the local militants in 2002 to prevent them from providing a safe haven to the Afghan Taliban and al-Qaeda in North and South Waziristan. But it started relying on negotiations a bit too early. Hence the TTP gained strength and became a menace for Pakistan.

On August 25, 2008, the Government of Pakistan imposed a ban on theTTP, froze its bank accounts and assets, and barred it from media appearances. The government also announced bounties on its prominent leaders.[57]

TTP in Swat

The militants operating in the Swat area of NWFP are as destructive and brutal, if not more so, as the Waziristani Taliban. They are headed by Maulvi Fazlullah, who is known as Maulvi FM for running unauthorized FM radio to propagate his militant views of "imagined Islam."[58] Their numerical strength is estimated to be 3,000[59] to 5,000.[60] They have resorted to bombing, destroying schools or seizing them as their bases, beheading opponents and capturing security personnel.[61]

Swat, a formerly princely state, is a picturesque valley in the north-west of Pakistan. It falls in the Malakand Division of the North-West Frontier

Province but is a settled area and is not part of FATA. Unlike Waziristan it shares no border with Afghanistan. Its population is about 3 million. It is only 160 kms (80 miles) away from Islamabad, a geographical proximity to the capital of Pakistan that is often referred to as a matter of concern.

The roots of this militant group of Swat can be traced back to the late 1980s, when Maulvi Fazlullah's father-in-law, Sufi Muhammad, formed the organization Tehreek-e-Nifaz-e-Shariat-e-Muhammadi (TNSM) or the Movement for the Establishment of the Law of Prophet Muhammad, a Wahhabi group, in Swat to strive to enforce his brand of Sharia in the area. In a bid to achieve this objective, TNSM created lot of trouble in the 1990s, including taking over the local airport and blocking the highway connecting Pakistan to China.[62] Its motto is *Shariat ya shahadat* (Islamic laws or martyrdom), and Sufi says, "Those opposing the imposition of *Sharia* in Pakistan are *wajibu-lqatl* worth being killed)." TNSM denounces democracy as un-Islamic.[63]

In 2001 Sufi raised a lashkar (militia) of ill-equipped and untrained Mujahideen to fight on the side of the Afghan Taliban against the US invasion. The lashkar was annihilated by the US air attacks and the brutal Northern Alliance forces. Sufi managed to survive but was arrested by the Government of Pakistan and imprisoned.[64] He was released only in 2008 at the initiative of the Awami National Party government, to broker a peace deal between the government and Maulvi Fazlullah's militant group. The loosely organized TNSM and its offshoots are still strong in the Matta Tehsil of Swat and in villages on the banks of river Swat. Sufi Mohammad led the campaign for enforcement of Sharia in 1994 and now his 32-year-old son-in-law Maulana Fazlullah is in command. He has been operating in a more brutal and aggressive manner. His group of militants has been trying to implement its uncouth brand of Sharia. The Swati Taliban have strong links with Waziristani TTP. At a higher level, they are a component of the Hakimullah Mehsud-led TTP.[65]

TTP's tactics involve both elements of "insurgency" and "terrorism." In FATA the TTP has undermined the administration and is trying to run a parallel government. The political agent, the powerful representative of the federal government, is confined to his office only. The age-old system of handling the tribes through Maliks has been shattered as more than 200 Maliks have been killed in FATA. TTP extremists frequently resort to beheadings, killing for petty reasons, inhuman treatment of opponents, occupying girls" schools and destruction of government and private property with a view to establishing their writ in the area and creating fear.[66]

In Swat, Maulana Fazlullah has been trying to enforce its writ by similar tactics, including closing down barber shops, CD and music shops, and girls' schools. His militants have been destroying or occupying government buildings and blowing up bridges. The basic health units and hotels, electricity and gas installations have been bombed and road blockades and checkpoints were set up. Beheadings of security force and police personnel and political rivals were common. Bodies of people slain overnight were dumped in the morning by the roadside everywhere in Swat.[67]

The TTP started expanding its area of influence and activities out of the region of Pushtun ethnicity and the precincts of FATA and NWFP by employing mega terrorist attacks, such as FIA Building Lahore, Naval War College, Lahore, Marriot Hotel, Islamabad, Wah Ordnance Factory, Sri Lankan cricket team, Lahore, police training school, Manawan, Lahore, GHQ, Rawalpindi, Elite Police School, and bomb blasts in Peshawar.

A better picture of the terror sans frontiers was revealed during the investigation of the September 2008 bombing of the Marriot hotel, Islamabad. Of the more than 250 suspects arrested from southern Punjab, a large number of them belonged to the LJ, JeM, LeT, SSP, TJP and SMP. It was clear now that the Taliban were no longer a purely Pashtun movement. The members of terrorist and sectarian organizations from Punjab had started joining forces with them to carry out activities within Pakistan.[68] It struck repeatedly in Islamabad, Lahore and Peshawar.

Al-Qaeda — TTP Nexus, Activities and Concerns

The basic cause of al-Qaeda's birth was disenchantment of its leaders with the systems of their Arab homelands, mostly in Saudi Arabia and Egypt. America became its number one target due to its influence on the leaders and systems of these homelands. Pakistan was not a target of al-Qaeda. In 2002 the army operations against them in FATA made them turn against General Musharraf. Pakistan, as a country, was still not the target. And it is still not the target.

But al-Qaeda wanted access to the FATA safe haven in order to carry on its agenda unhindered and of course without clashing with the Pakistan army and security agencies. For this purpose another "force" was needed that could engage the Pakistan government and army so that al-Qaeda could focus on the US and the rest on its list. The scattered tribesmen, mostly with jihadi backgrounds, who were already hosting them, were the most suitable to fit in with this. Thus, the TTP took birth as the frontrunner of al-Qaeda, which the Pakistani Taliban has proven with their activities in FATA, Swat and the rest of Pakistan.

The US concern was about the al-Qaeda in FATA. Initially it viewed TTP as insurgents focused on Pakistan. Pakistan failed to fathom the gravity of al-Qaeda's presence in FATA as it was not targeting Pakistan. But soon both Pakistan and the US realized the nexus between the two and the lethality of the combination that had expanded its nature and scope of operation. US President Barack Obama stated loud and clearly, "Multiple intelligence estimates have warned that al-Qaeda is actively planning attacks on the US homeland from its safe heavens in Pakistan."[69] He added, "The single greatest threat to their (US & Pakistan) interests comes from al-Qaeda and its extremist allies. That is why we must stand together."[70]

He then warned that Pakistan would be held accountable for its potential failure to act against terrorism on its soil.[71] He further asserted, "The situation is increasingly perilous. The world cannot afford the price that will come due if Afghanistan slides back into chaos or al-Qaeda operates unchecked."[72]

These statements mirror four US concerns that have become one big concern for Pakistan: first, al-Qaeda is planning a big attack on the US from Pakistani soil; second, its local allies are a threat to the US and Pakistan and the latter could become a failed state; third, Pakistan would be responsible if these two (TTP and al-Qaeda) carry out such attacks on the US; and fourth, these elements in FATA are adversely effecting US efforts in Afghanistan. Al-Qaeda, true to its elusive nature, is not visible and so far no spectacular attack, as feared by the US, has taken place. The fact is al-Qaeda has no specific base or particular country where it belongs. It has cells in almost forty countries. Its rules of engagement are also exceptional, as it never engages in direct armed conflict or guerrilla war. It strikes surreptitiously and snakes away, leaving behind trails, enough to reveal its imprints but not enough to discern its operational plans and preparations. This strategy prevents disruption of its manpower and command and control structure. Its structure is fragmented

Table 5.1 List of suicide attacks in Pakistan since 2002 (until 2009)

Year	Suicide Attacks
2002	2
2003	2
2004	7
2005	4
2006	7
2007	56
2008	61
2009	36 till July
Total	175

and layered in sub-groups, often formed on the basis of nationalities, headed by the respective nationals. Thus drones and military actions might be able to disperse al-Qaeda in Pakistan but destroying it may not be possible. Dozens of its fighters have reportedly fled from FATA and relocated to cities of Pakistan and as far as Somalia and Indonesia.[73]

The TTP, on the other hand, accelerated its actions in FATA, Swat, NWFP and the rest of Pakistan, especially after General Musharraf's "Operation Silence" in July 2007. Out of 56 suicide attacks in 2007, 27 occurred in NWFP, 13 in FATA and five in Islamabad. In 2008, out of 59 total suicide attacks in the country, 32 occurred in NWFP, 13 in FATA, 12 in Punjab and one each in Balochistan and Sindh provinces, as the graph below demonstrates. Thus, it has shown its ability to kill at will throughout Pakistan.

The Counter Strategies

Pakistan's Strategy

An army operation was launched against the clerics and students of Lal Masjid, Islamabad on July 16, 2007, resulting in a large number of casualties on both sides. Most analysts think that the situation could have been tackled by the local administration at the initial stages, without the army assistance, but it was allowed to simmer for six months till it reached a level where an army operation would seem the only viable option. Though even at that time many thought that the elite police force could have been used. When the situation worsened the politicians tried to find out a negotiated settlement. But the ruling party leaders, Chaudry Shujaat Hussain and Ijaz-ul-Haq, had to cut a sorry figure when the military operation was launched while they were engaged in talks with the holed-up cleric leader Maulana Abdul Rasheed Ghazi.[74]

General Musharraf's strategy was to create a situation that could be resolved through the army. He wanted to make the international community believe that only the army could tackle these militants. The army was his constituency on which he could survive and thrive. The objective was to get foreign aid for counter-terrorism through army action. He wrote in his biography that millions of dollars were "earned" by arresting 657 al-Qaeda activists.[75] Nevertheless after his departure the army has gradually changed the strategy. It is following the decisions of the democratic government to annihilate the insurgents with full zeal.

Counter-insurgency (COIN)

In July 2002, Pakistani troops entered the Khyber Agency for the first time since Pakistani independence in 1947. It intensified operations against the militants after two attacks on General Pervez Musharraf in December 2003. In 2004 the Pakistan army sustained heavy casualties.[76] In early 2005 it resorted to negotiations and peace deals with militants to avoid Pushtun backlash from the local populace and within the army cadres. All-out assault was avoided for three reasons; one, to avoid the dangers of battling multiple groups in multiple theaters in most rugged terrain; two, a lack of consensus within the state; and three, a dearth of support from the Pakistani public.[77]

The turning point came when despite the peace deal with TTP in Swat and acceptance of their demands for the imposition of Nizam-e-Adl (the justice system) the subversive and terrorist activities of Baitullah and Fazlullah continued unabated. In addition to immense US pressure, the public and the state also realized the gravity of situation. Thus the Pakistan army started Operation Rah-e-Rast (the virtuous path) against the Swat TTP on April 26, 2009.[78]

Within ten days of the operation the militants were on the run. The army rapidly cleared town after town and made quick progress. The ferocious Swat TTP melted away in the fire and fury of the army. Air power was also used to destroy their hideouts and underground tunnels in the mountains. More than 1,700 militants were killed, as claimed by the Inter Services Public Relations (ISPR).[79] At least 260 soldiers were killed. About 3 million people were internally displaced.

The US Chairman of the Joint Chiefs of Staff, Admiral Mike Muller, acknowledged that Pakistan made an "awful lot of progress in its fight against the Taliban insurgency in Swat."[80] The operation was therefore declared to have entered the wrapping-up stage on July 8, 2009.

But three aspects are perplexing. First, there was no element of surprise, second, most of the top leaders of Swat TTP fled, and finally, the melting away of TTP forces created a scare. The Afghan Taliban had also melted away within 35 days of the US attack on Afghanistan. Within two months they started the guerrilla war and eight years down the track they are still fighting with the international forces. All the militants, 3,000 or 5,000, need to be accounted for: how many are killed? How many are arrested? How many have slipped away — and more importantly where?

While this operation was being wrapped up, the operation "Rah-e-Najat" (the salvation path) was been launched against the TTP in Waziristan. Pakistani Air Force fighter jets pounded the hideouts and compounds of TTP militants. ISPR reported that hundreds were killed, injured and arrested. The rest are on the run, looking for shelter.[81] But this operation might be tougher than the one against the Swat TTP because the terrain is harsh and closer to the Afghan border and their numerical strength is more than the Swat TTP. But one big consolation is that Pakistan's most wanted man, Baitullah Mehsud, was been killed in a US drone attack.[82]

The strategic difference in this operation is that while 20,000 troops were used in the Swat operation, more reliance would be on air power to destroy the TTP hide outs in the mountainous region of Waziristan.[83] Analysts do not consider it an appropriate approach to annihilate the hardened militants who are fighting guerrilla war in harsh terrains.[84]

Is Military Method the Right Solution?

Military operations should be the last resort to tackle an insurgency. In the Battle of Algiers, the commanders of the French army, General Massu and

Colonel Bigeard, were reluctant to carry out a counter-terrorism operation as they considered it "un travail de flic" or "cops" work.[85] Even the soldiers of the French army considered it a job they were not trained for. But once the operation started, the French army went in with the typical mindset of an army in war — to kill and destroy.[86] Nevertheless the defeat of the FLN was regarded a tactical victory, at the cost of the ultimate defeat of the French army.

In present times, the Indian army operation against the Kashmiri militants seeking self-determination, continuing for the last 20 years, speaks volumes of its failure, as despite horrendous repressions[87] the insurgency is thriving. Similarly, the military solution against the Liberation Tigers of Tamil Eelam LTTE in Sri Lanka was extremely violent and only came to an end after 25 years of bloody fighting and 70,000 deaths.

Therefore, now when Pakistan has achieved initial success against the militants, the emphasis should be on intelligence-based dedicated operations to pursue the higher echelon, dispersed command structure and most importantly their sources of funding. Even the use of lashkars against the Taliban in FATA and Swat, encouraged by the army, requires extra caution as it might trigger inter-tribe strife and thus, more violence.[88]

Peace Deal Politics

The government of Pakistan has signed at least four prominent peace deals, three in South Waziristan (2004 and 2005) and one in North Waziristan (Sept 2006), but all have ended in smoke very quickly as both the parties involved blamed each other for the violations.[89]

The latest peace deal between the NWFP government, led by the secular Awami National Party (ANP) and TNSM in Swat was signed on February 16, 2009. It met the same fate because of two main reasons: one, the government had failed to learn from the previous peace deal experiences that the nature of dispute and the form of the militants was quite different from the traditional tribal disputes between clans, tribes or individuals or even an invading force, which could be resolved through traditional Sulah (truce) accords; two, ironically, Sufi Muhammad, a party to the issue, posed as mediator between the NWFP Government and TTP leader Maulvi Fazlullah and signed the deal.[90]

Many, within Pakistan but especially in the West, considered it a surrender of Swat valley to the militants after a bloody two-year battle.[91] In pursuance of the peace deal, the Nizam-e-Adl Regulation 2009 was passed by the National Assembly of Pakistan by unanimous resolution, after a debate of less than 30 minutes, on April 14, 2009. Only the MQM abstained. The next day the governor of the NWFP promulgated the regulation. It sparked criticism at home and abroad.[92]

Even after the signing of the peace deal and the imposition of Nizam-e-Adl, devastating suicide attacks were carried out in Dera Ismail Khan, Lahore, Peshawar, Rawalpindi, Jamrud, Charsadda, etc.[93] The heavily armed militants of TTP moved from Swat towards Buner. The Western media raised an alarm that Islamabad was now just 80 miles away. It created a scare that the militants might ultimately capture the capital and with it the nuclear weapons.[94] Once again the situation had worsened enough to be resolved through military might. It generated mass public support for the military operation. Thus the army moved ahead to launch Operation Rah-e-Rast, which paid dividends.

Some still argue that despite the repeated failures of peace deals, negotiations should remain an integral part of the COIN strategy to encourage breathing space, which can ultimately help in achieving lasting peace.

Counter-terrorism

While COIN was underway in Swat and FATA, suicide bombings escalated in the big cities. Successful strikes by the suicide bombers have exposed the lack of a comprehensive counter-terrorism strategy to cope with this situation. The police and their intelligence set-ups are deficient in temperament, training, experience, paraphernalia and at times, will to tackle this sort of terrorism. Immediately after the attack on the Sri Lankan cricket team in Lahore the Inspector General of Police, Punjab, stated that countering terrorism was not a police job.

As the suicide attacks generally emanate from FATA and Swat, outside the respective provinces, it becomes difficult for the provincial set-ups to pre-empt and prevent them. It requires relentless coordination of the provincial police/intelligence set-ups with the federal intelligence agencies like the Intelligence Bureau (IB) and ISI to have advance information originating from FATA and elsewhere. This coordination is patchy and inconsistent.

Usually the forewarnings, indicators and insinuations provided by the federal agencies are taken lightly by the police. They resent the paucity of information provided to them and therefore are reluctant to take action on it. Unfortunately these information reports turn out to be corret quite often. Mostly the police investigations into suicide attacks have been found too insipid and half-hearted to stand up in the courts. As a result, a number of perpetrators have been exonerated by the courts and they have re-joined their militant groups to continue with future actions.

The dispersal and destruction of the militants in Swat resulted in a lull in suicide terrorism. Nipping the bud of perpetrators in their areas is a good counter-terrorism strategy. But it has not been done properly. The death of Baitullah and the operation against the TTP in Waziristan triggered a renewed spate of terrorism. Baitullah had claimed that he had more than 200 suicide bombers who would strike the cities of Pakistan. Thus, even after his death they have retaliated with more force and ferocity.

Irritants and Impediments

These strategies and policies are, however, not having a smooth sailing. The flared-up Pushtun sentiments, the "drone effects," myths and conspiracy theories — genuine, manufactured or invented — are taking their toll in a silent and surreptitious manner.

Pushtun Nature

History is full of lessons to be learnt about the Pashtuns' religious and tribal sensibilities, which get triggered quite quickly. Badal (revenge) is the first and greatest commandment of "Pashtunwali," "the way of the Pathan" or the "Pathan (Pushtun) code."[95] Pashtuns are devout Muslims who revere, practice and preserve Islam.

The Drone Effects

Baitullah claimed that each drone attack brought him three or four suicide bombers, who were usually from the families of the drone's victims.[96] This is the badal nature of Pashtuns, which is now being capitalized on by the TTP in terms of gaining more support and more volunteers.

The CIA-operated unmanned intelligence aircrafts, the Predator and the Reaper, have been launching drone attacks on al-Qaeda members in FATA since 2006. The CIA claims to have killed 20 high profile al-Qaeda commanders and destroyed many of its bases and safe houses.[97] Pakistani media stated that from 2006 till June 2009, the drones have killed 14 al-Qaeda leaders and 687 civilians.[98]

There is resentment among the Pashtuns in particular and the Pakistanis in general over this invisible invasion and the innocent civilian casualties. This sentiment had flared up when the first drone on a seminary in Damadola, Bajaur in 2006 resulted in the deaths of locals, including young students. This one incident played a vital role in the unpopularity of General Musharraf and subsequent rout of the PML (Q) in the 2008 general election.[99] But Baitullah's death-through-drone might diminish the diatribe at least for the time being.

Role of security agencies

After the end of General Pervez Musharraf's rule and the initiation of democratic order in 2008, the army has ostensibly been withdrawn from exercising direct government power in order to to let the elected civilians do their job, but the security turf, internal and external, is still being held by it. This job had let it grab the lion's share of the more than $10 billion in US assistance and reimbursements given to Pakistan since 9/11.[100]

Principally, minimal use of armed forces is recommended to curb an insurgency within a country but the situation in FATA and Swat has been allowed to reach a point where the army's involvement has become inevitable. The timely use of intelligence, police and paramilitary forces could have prevented the situation to becoming so volatile it had to be handled by the army and air force.

The army's prolonged involvement in FATA and Swat gave rise to fears that Pushtun ethnic sentiment and religious sensibilities might affect the armed forces, which has 20 percent Pushtun soldiers and officers. So far, however, there is little credible evidence to suggest that anything like this has happened.[101] There are no reported cases of insubordination or disobedience on these bases during the military operations in FATA and Swat. The Pakistan army is considered to be a disciplined and professional organization.

Emphasis on intelligence solution has been inadequate and monopolized by the ISI, which has been involved in these affairs and areas ever since the Afghan Jihad. The ISI is often accused of having created the Taliban and local militants or for having close links with them. General Mahmood, the close aide of General Musharraf, who helped him come into power, was made the scapegoat and removed as the Director General of the ISI, in order to give positive signals to the US. But till very recently the US has been expressing mistrust towards ISI's role.

"Unlike the UK's MI5 and MI6 or the U.S.'s FBI and CIA, the ISI faces no equivalent turf-war with a powerful internal rival."[102] The Intelligence Bureau (IB), the national civil intelligence agency, has been a casualty of this monopoly. It has been held back to play a secondary role, much below its capacity and capability. In the past it delivered whenever the government tasked it to tackle insurgency or terrorism. It handled the urban terrorism of MQM in Karachi in 1993–1995. Similarly, in 2004–2005, IB played an effective role against al-Qaeda in urban areas of Punjab.

Police, especially in the NWFP and in insurgency-hit areas "are not trained, equipped or geared to fight insurgency."[103] Talat Masood, a military analyst, said that the government had been slow to train and equip the police for a wave of attacks.[104] Even the Punjab police performed poorly during the terrorist attack on the Sri Lankan cricket team in Lahore.[105] Elite police are a highly trained force that can face any sort of terrorist situation. Provincial police intelligence agencies like the special branch are neither trained nor willing to counter this sort of terrorism. CID Punjab played a substantial role in quelling the sectarian terrorism in 1990s. But now its performance is hardly better than the special branch. Professor Anatol Lieven observed, "The Pakistani State, with its overstretched, demoralised and desperately under funded police, just does not have the resources to defend against a threat on this scale."[106]

Myths, Conspiracy Theories and Facts

In the whirlpool of accusations, myths and conspiracy theories taking rounds in Pakistan, two countries figure prominently, the US and India.

Three things seem to have spurred anti-US sentiments and given birth to conspiracy theories. One, most Pakistanis see the US through its role in Iraq and Afghanistan, which they consider an attack on Muslims resulting in mass-scale killings of innocent people. The reports that the US and UK concocted evidence of WMDs in Iraq further fed these views. The second reason is more localized — the drone attacks resulting in the killing of innocent people in FATA. The third reason is the recent US tilt towards India, evidenced by its nuclear program deal and the billions of dollars worth of weapons contracts made during Hillary Clinton's visit to India.[107]

Historically speaking, many Pakistanis consider the US as unfriendly and unreliable because of three complaints: first, Washington's refusal to help Pakistan during the 1965 war with India; second, the US's discarding of Pakistan "like a Kleenex" when it was no longer needed after the Afghan war; and, third, the indiscriminate nature of US nuclear sanctions, which, until the May 1998 nuclear tests, affected Pakistan and not India.[108]

There is also a belief that the US wants to take Pakistan's nuclear bombs. This indication is enough to stir the adverse sensibilities of most Pakistanis, who consider the nuclear program as their pride, and the way to be secure from arch rival India. They see a Indo-Israel nexus behind this conspiracy. Mike Muller said, "We actually sanctioned Pakistan from about 1990 to 2002. And so they're wary of what is going to be our sustained position."[109] Adding to this wariness was the myth that the US was funding Baitullah Mehsud to destabilize Pakistan.[110]

These public perceptions, arising out of half-truths, are problematic for the governments of Pakistan and the US in the formation and implementation of their policies against terrorism.

The US wants Pakistan to concentrate on al-Qaeda and religious militants in Pakistan and stop worrying about India.[111] But nobody in Pakistan will believe anybody from the West that India is not a threat to Pakistan. The creation of Pakistan was detested by the Congress leaders of India, who dreamt of ruling a united India. Kashmir, the eternal bone of contention between the two, three wars, dismemberment of East Pakistan, and the Siachen issue are just a few examples of the hostility and enmity between the two. Even now, about 80 percent of the Pakistan army is dedicated to countering the threat from India. Similarly, seven out of thirteen corps of the Indian army are "pointing their guns at Pakistan."[112]

The cases of secret back-stabbing are many. Three days after 9/11, the Indian intelligence agency RAW informed the CIA that Pakistani jihadi organizations were planning an "imminent attack" on the White House. President Bush refused to believe it until shown the exact information. Obviously no such information could be presented, as "it was an effort on the part of India to push the US Administration to include Pakistan on the hit list."[113]

Christine Fair's observations regarding India's covert operations against Pakistan are worth noting:

i. Having visited the Indian mission in Zahedan, Iran, I can assure you they are not issuing visas as the main activity.

ii. India has run operations from its mission in Mazar (through which it supported the Northern Alliance) and is likely doing so from the other consulates it has reopened in Jalalabad and Qandahar along the border.

iii. Indian officials have told me privately that they are pumping money into Balochistan.

iv. Kabul has encouraged India to engage in provocative activities such as using the Border Roads Organization to build sensitive parts of the Ring Road and use the Indo-Tibetan police force for security.

v. It is also building schools on a sensitive part of the border in Kunar — across from Bajaur.[114]

It is a common myth that Indians and Gorkhas were found among the dead fighting on the Taliban side in Swat against the Pakistani security forces. It was revealed that they were found uncircumcised.[115] But it is a fact that in August 2008, three arrested terrorists belonging to TTP's Qari Hussain, known as "Ustad-e-Fidayeen" (mentor of suicide bombers),[116] revealed that he received Rs. 68 million from "an enemy country" (India).[117]

The Prime Minister of Pakistan, Yousuf Reza Gilani, handed over a dossier containing proof of India's involvement in subversive activities in Pakistan to Indian Prime Minister Dr. Manmohan Singh during their meeting at Sharm el-Sheikh in Egypt in July 2009.[118] These reasons are enough for the people and the government of Pakistan to keep India at the top of its security priorities.

The Implications

Economic Downturn

The economy has been the worst victim, as the losses of foreign direct investment and tourism are indeed substantial. According to Pakistani Foreign Minister Shah Mahmood Qureshi, Pakistan has suffered a monetary loss amounting to US $34.5 billion since 2001. The loss of $5 billion has been estimated in foreign direct investment, more than $5 billion in exports and $5.5 billion in privatization. Visa and job opportunities for Pakistanis to the Middle East are being increasingly curtailed.[119]

In 2009, following military operations in Swat, over 3 million people were internally displaced (IDPs). The expenditure on their support and rehabilitation is a substantial strain on the fragile economy.

Social, Cultural and Psychological Fallouts

According to a doctor from NWFP, every second person in Waziristan suffers from depression. Stress has emerged as a new sociological phenomenon in insurgency hit areas.[120] Similarly, the residents of cities are suffering from the effects of terrorism and psychological war. The terrorist threats to educational institutions especially co-ed private schools in Islamabad, Karachi, and Lahore, and suicide attacks on the International Islamic University in Islamabad resulting in the deaths of five female students, has added to the deep sense of insecurity among teachers, students and parents.[121] Simultaneously, religious bigots have harassed women on the streets by telling them to observe the so-called Islamic dress code. This trend petered out as soon the government showed a resolve to handle the terrorists with an iron fist. The beard, a symbol of religiousness and piety in this society, is becoming a symbol of extremism and is seen with fear and suspicion. Conversely, moderate Muslim men with beards consider themselves odd men out in their own society. Anxiety and mistrust have seeped into the society.

Expansion Across the Country

A new scare was caused when the interior minister of Pakistan declared that South Punjab could be the next Swat.[122] He gave two reasons for it; first, Jihadi militia groups like the Lashkar-e-Jhangvi (LeJ) and Jaish-e-Mohammed (JeM) hail from South Punjab; second, all of the terrorists who fled from Waziristan or Swat might have taken refuge in South Punjab. Three aspects are, however, often ignored when predicting the emergence of a Swat-like situation in South Punjab; one, the presence of Punjabis in the ranks of TTP should not come as a surprise because Punjabis have always been a major part of Mujahideen, from the Afghan Jihad period; two, organizations like the SSP, LeJ and JeM have lost their militant command and structure, so they are not part of TTP as organizations but some of its extremist members have joined forces with the TTP; three, unlike FATA and Swat, the Punjab's terrain is not suitable for guerrilla warfare.[123] These aspects do not, however, diminish the danger. The scattered members of these organizations are the "sleeper agents" and facilitators who can provide shelter to fleeing TTP fighters, offer hideouts for training and planning and join the active cadres of fighters and suicide bombers. The blast caused by stored suicide jackets and rocket launchers in the house of a militant in Mian Channu, which killed 22 people, including seven children, confirmed this fear.[124]

The security situation in insurgency-hit Balochistan could go from bad to worse if the fleeing TTP fighters regroup there to carry out their terrorist activities. They may join forces with the Baluchi insurgents. The fallout of the undesirable army action by General Musharraf against Nawab Bugti and other Baluchi dissidents, the alleged Indian support of Baluchi insurgents and Western claims of the presence of Mullah Omer and Afghan Taliban leadership in Quetta have already made Balochistan a hotbed of unrest and uncertainty. Even terrorists challenging the Iranian government have set up bases in Balochistan.[125]

The metropolis Karachi, the home of terrorist ethnic party MQM, is a troubled spot, with various armed groups resorting to violence there. During the first six months of 2009, about 100 people, belonging to different groups, were killed in various incidents.[126] The TTP has been fishing in these troubled waters, and has committed robberies and kidnappings to raise funds for the resistance. The CID held financiers of TTP from Mauripur and youngsters from Karachi, in order to raise funds.[127] But the TTP has refrained from resorting to violence in Karachi because they want to use it for fundraising, recruitment and as a resting place.[128] The TTP is therefore making its presence felt in different forms in many cities across Pakistan.

Conclusion

After the catastrophic incident of 9/11 the US is not ready to take any chances with al-Qaeda, which has regrouped in FATA and is planning further attacks on it. Its indigenous helper, the TTP, has caused immense damage to the serenity, stability, economy and social fibre of Pakistan to a level that its existence is threatened. These grave threats to Pakistan and the US have brought them together to beat the combined forces of terrorism. They have been able to disperse and dislodge the terrorists through US drone attacks and the Pakistan army actions. But the ultimate goal of destroying them needs much more coordination, understanding, time and action.

The Af-Pak policy is the product of this realization and that the COIN campaign needs much more than military action. But what has not been realized is that Af-Pak without the consideration of India may not meet quick and sustainable success. The US needs to take a more even-handed approach to India and Pakistan, to calm the latter's apprehensions. Recently, Pakistan has been concentrating on internal terrorism but just one act of hostility from the eastern border, which comes quite easily, will make it refocus on India.

A substantial focus from the Pakistan Government and the army on curbing the militants has paid dividends, as there is a visible decrease in the insurgency in Swat after the successful military operation there. The IDPs have started going back home. But most of the TTP leadership, like of al-Qaeda and Afghan Taliban, is alive. They have not given up the resolve to strike back. The follow-up stage is therefore crucial. The insurgents have the capacity and history to regroup and resume their activities afresh.

To achieve sustainable success, the Government of Pakistan will have to devise a comprehensive and transparent counter-terrorism policy to take decision-making in its own hands and not allow any other organization to monopolize the issue. The civilian agencies like IB must figure prominently in the counter-terrorism strategy. Moreover, police and provincial intelligence agencies should be revamped and reactivated to face terrorism in the urban centres. Fortunately public mood is in favour of action against the terrorists and extremists. Further, drastic measures for improvements to socio-economic conditions in FATA and control over madaris ought to be ensured. There needs to be an emphasis on education, health and employment.

These measures may help the situation, but they won't resolve it unless the Taliban-US conflict in Afghanistan comes to an end. Though a new surge in Helmand and South Afghanistan has given birth to the fear of escalated violence, the hope is alive that the Obama Administration might use a saner approach and initiate some sort of negotiations with the Taliban. Only with this optimism can one hope to end militancy in Pakistan, which has for the most part emanated from Afghanistan.

Notes

1   *The Nation*, March 28, 2009.
2   *Dawn*, March 19, 2009.
3   Shaun Gregory, "The ISI and the War on Terrorism," *Studies in Conflict & Terrorism*, 30:12, (2001) pp. 1,013–1,031.
4   *The Nation*, July 24, 2009.
5   Ibid p. 154.
6   *The News*, March 22, 2009.
7   Pakistan Intelligence source.
8   *Asia Times Online*, August 20, 2002.
9   *The News*, March 22, 2009.
10 *The Pakistan Development Review* (winter 1996), p. 628.
11 www.khyber.org, July 22, 2009
12 Christine Fair, *The Madrassah Challenge: Militancy and Religious education in Pakistan*. Lahore: Vanguard Books, 2009.
13 Ibid.
14 Ibid., p. 4.

15   Ibid., p. 35.
16   Ibid., p. 94.
17   Ibid., p. 95.
18   Ibid.
19   Ibid., p. 94–95.
20   Ibid., p. 74.
21   Ibid., p. 80.
22   *Dawn*, April 9, 2009.
23   *New York Times*, March 26, 2009.
24   *The Nation*, April 10, 2009.
25   *The Nation*, April 10, 2009.
26   *Daily Times*, April 2009.
27   ISI source.
28   *The Nation*, April 14, 2009.
29   *Daily Times*, April 2009.
30   Interviews with Pakistanis, March 2009.
31   Ibid. July 2, 2009.
32   *The Post*, October 18, 2005.
33   Interview Durrani, June 25, 2009.
34   Fair, p. 495.
35   Pakistan Intelligence source.
36   Musharraf (2006), p. 263.
37   Gregory, p. 778.
38   Pakistan Intelligence source.
39   Fair, p. 490.
40   *Daily Times*, July 28, 2009.
41   Ibid.
42   *Daily Times*, July 28, 2009.
43   *Daily Times*, July 27, 2009.
44   *The Nation*, July 24, 2009.
45   *New York Times*, March 26, 2009.
46   Ibid.
47   *Defence Against Terrorism Review* (Fall 2008), p. 71.
48   Council on Foreign Relations, Feb 6, 2008.
49   *The News*, March 22, 2009.
50   Ibid.
51   *Terrorism Monitor*, March 3, 2009.
52   Gregory.
53   Intelligence sources.
54   Council on Foreign Relations, 6 Feb 2009.

55 *Time*, June 1, 2009.
56 *Terrorism Monitor*, March 3, 2009.
57 *The News*, August 26, 2008.
58 *Dawn*, April 17, 2009.
59 *Democracy News Analysis*, February 23, 2009.
60 *The News*, March 22, 2009.
61 Ibid.
62 *The Nation*, April 8, 2009.
63 *The News*, March 22, 2009.
64 *The Nation*, April 8, 2009.
65 *The News International*, January 3, 2008.
66 *The News International*, February 7, 2009.
67 *The News International*, January 17, 2009.
68 Ibid.
69 *The Nation*, March 28, 2009.
70 Ibid.
71 *The Nation*, April 7, 2009.
72 *The Nation*, April 9, 2009.
73 *Dawn*, July 6, 2009.
74 *Daily Times*, July 28, 2009.
75 Musharraf (2008), back flap.
76 *New York Times*, September 10, 2006.
77 *The Nation*, August 15, 2009.
78 Ibid.
79 *The Nation*, July 10, 2009.
80 Ibid.
81 *The Nation*, July 10, 2009.
82 Ibid., August 9, 2009.
83 Ibid., July 10, 2009.
84 Ibid.
85 Cradock and Smith (2007), p. 84.
86 Ibid.
87 Iffat Malik, *Kashmir: Ethnic Conflict International Dispute*. Oxford: Oxford University Press, 2005.
88 *Asia Times*, July 16, 2009.
89 *Terrorism Monitor*, October 5, 2006.
90 *The Nation*, March 26, 2009.
91 *The Nation*, March 28, 2009.
92 *The Nation*, April 16, 2009.
93 *Dawn*, April 16, 2009.

94 *The Nation*, April 9, 2009.
95 Spain (1962), p. 46.
96 *Time*, June 1, 2009.
97 Ibid.
98 Ibid.
99 Interview with Saeed Elahi, MPA.
100 *RAND Review* (Fall 2008).
101 *Foreign Affairs*, March 31, 2009.
102 Gregory, p. 1,014.
103 *Daily Times*, July 10, 2009.
104 Ibid.
105 *Dawn*, March 26, 2009
106 *The Times*, September 22, 2008
107 *The Nation*, August 2, 2009.
108 Kux (2001), p. 365.
109 *The Nation*, July 10, 2009.
110 *Asian Tribune*, July 10, 2009.
111 *Press Trust of India*, July 7, 2009.
112 *The News*, April 26, 2009.
113 Hassan Abbas, *Pakistan's Drift into Extremism: Allah, the Army, and America's War on Terror*. New Delhi: Pentagon Press, 2005.
114 *Foreign Affairs*, March 31, 2009.
115 *Times Online*, June 7, 2009.
116 *Dawn*, June 14, 2009.
117 Pakistan Intelligence source.
118 Dawn, July 22, 2009.
119 Cheema, http://www.sassu.org.uk/pdfs/
120 IPS, December 24, 2007.
121 *Dawn*, May 7, 2009.
122 *Daily Times*, June 27, 2009.
123 *Daily Times*, July 18, 2009.
124 *The Nation*, July 7, 2009.
125 *Dawn*, July 6, 2008.
126 *The Nation*, July 17, 2009.
127 *The News*, August 25, 2008.
128 *Dawn*, June 28, 2009.

CHAPTER SIX

Al-Qaeda: The Threat from Tribal Pakistan

Rohan Gunaratna[1]

Abstract

Since the beginning of the movement, al-Qaeda has been a strong influential force behind other Islamist movements, including Taliban and Tehrek-e-Taliban Pakistan. Its influence is both ideological and operational. Based on his many visits to the FATA region and exclusive access to security agencies and law enforcement institutions in Pakistan, the author analyzes and explores al-Qaeda's ideological and operational influence on other militant groups, with special reference to Pakistan and elaborates on its current role in FATA. The main argument of the chapter is that al-Qaeda not only severely threatens Pakistani and regional stability and security but its impacts are profound on global security, particularly to the West, as many of the previous and current terrorists plots trace back to this volatile region.

Introduction

When US-led coalition forces intervened in Afghanistan, of al-Qaeda numbered about 3,000. Today, the centre of gravity of al-Qaeda and other foreign fighters has shifted from Afghanistan to tribal Pakistan. Nonetheless, the number of foreign fighters in tribal Pakistan has dramatically decreased both due to Pakistani military operations and US drone attacks.

Today, a group of about 90 hardcore members led by Osama bin Laden and his deputy and designated successor, Ayman al-Zawahiri, are spearheading the fight against the US, its allies and its friends.[2] In addition to working with both tribal and mainland Pakistani groups, they cooperate with about 900 foreign fighters in the Federally Administered Tribal Area (FATA). Among the Tajiks, Uighar's, Turks and foreign fighters of other nationalities, approximately 350 are Uzbek.

The foreign fighters work with about 15,000 Afghan and Pakistani insurgents on both sides of the border. Approximately 60 percent of these fighters are from tribal Pakistan.[3] The tribal belt separating Afghanistan from mainland Pakistan has become the strategic epicenter sustaining the fight in the region and beyond.

Terrorism, guerrilla warfare and insurgency have emerged as the pre-eminent national security threat to most countries in the early twentieth century. The threat is spreading from conflict zones to neighboring regions and countries far away. Iraq, Afghanistan and Pakistan are among the best known case studies. The spectrum of threat groups includes both Muslim and non-Muslim groups, but al-Qaeda presents the most formidable threat.

Afghanistan, a victim of international neglect after Soviet withdrawal, emerged as the epicenter of terrorism until the US-led coalition intervention. Since then, the ground zero of international terrorism has shifted from Afghanistan to Pakistan's tribal region. Many of the major terrorist attacks attempted or conducted in the West after 9/11 have been organized, directed or inspired by al-Qaeda's senior leadership located in this rugged and inaccessible mountainous region. Three profound developments characterize the post-9/11 global threat.

First, after the US-led intervention in Afghanistan, the ground zero of terrorism has moved from Afghanistan to the FATA. Today, FATA is the single most important base of operations, a place where leaders, trainers and planners are all located.

Second, after the US invasion and occupation of Iraq, al-Qaeda has gained a foothold in the Middle East, establishing a forward operational base 2,290 km (1,420 miles) closer to the West. From FATA, al-Qaeda has directed its battle globally, including in Iraq.

Third, by investing in sustained communication and propaganda from FATA, al-Qaeda co-opted several like-minded groups in Asia and the Middle East. In place of one single al-Qaeda, there are several al-Qaedas — Tawhid wal-jihad became al-Qaeda in Iraq, the Salafist Group for Call and Combat became Al-Qaeda Organization of the Islamic Maghreb, and Al-Jemaah Al-Islamiyah's Noordin Mohammed Top Faction became Al-Qaeda Organization for the Malay Archipelago.[4]

The long-term strategic significance of al-Qaeda successfully carving out a semi-safe haven in FATA is yet to be realized. In addition to the inaccessible Pak-Afghan border emerging as the new headquarters of the global jihad movement, al-Qaeda and its like-minded groups are seeking to change the geopolitics of the region. Using FATA, al-Qaeda, its associated groups and self-radicalized homegrown cells have recruited globally and struck al-Qaeda's enemies both through its operational network and inspired and instigated cells. Operating from FATA, groups trained in that region are mounting attacks in Western China (Xingjian), North India (Kashmir), Iraq, Algeria, Somalia and other conflict zones. As the assassinations and assassination attempts on leaders both in Pakistan and Afghanistan show, the philosophy of al-Qaeda and its associated groups is to put in place leaders that are not hostile to the terrorists and the extremists. The subject of al-Qaeda dominates the international media, but until the London bombings in July 2005, its active presence in FATA was not a subject of intense international debate.

Tribal Pakistan

Located along the 2,446 km long rugged border separating Afghanistan and Pakistan, is the isolated region known as the FATA. A 27,220 km^2 area, FATA is comprised of seven agencies — Bajaur, Mohmand, Khyber, Orakzai, Kurrum, and North and South Waziristan (see map in front matter). While the population of FATA is 3.1 million, its adjacent NWFP has a population of 17.5 million.

FATA has always been ruled through political agents. The Pashtunwali, or the Pukhtun code, governed the way of life. The code included hujra, the center of Pukhtun society, jirga, a council formed to settle conflicts, melmastia, which regulates host/guest relations, and "da khazoo dranaway," respect for females. Furthermore, they adhered to jaba, promise, nanawatee, to seek mercy, panah, to give shelter, nang, to honour, badal, revenge, and swara, a female given to affect compromise.

These traditions and customs were affected by the steadfast Islamization of FATA in the 1980s and 1990s. The emergence of the Afghan Taliban gave rise to like-minded forces in FATA. There was the resurgence of politico-religious parties and their militant wings. The number of madaris, including those preaching hatred, grew. Nonetheless, an admirable security situation prevailed in FATA despite decades of conflict in neighbouring Afghanistan and limited economic development.

To maintain control, Pakistan traditionally deployed five military and paramilitary organizations in FATA: Frontier Corps on the Afghan border; Frontier Constabulary between FATA and settled areas; police in settled areas; levies in parts of FATA; and Khassadars, deployed in FATA, irregular and based on inheritance.

Threat Displacement

After al-Qaeda was dislodged from Tora Bora in Afghanistan in early 2002, the group retreated to FATA. After relocating to Waziristan, both al-Qaeda and the Afghan Taliban linked up with the Pakistan Taliban and other Pakistani mainland groups. These two entities survived by reaching out to FATA's politico-religious parties, their host. Thereafter, al-Qaeda used its historical affiliations and nurtured and built a clerical support base.

Al-Qaeda's deputy leader, Ayman al-Zawahiri, moved to Waziristan and stayed there during part of 2002 and eventually moved to Bajaur Agency.[5] As his wife and two children were killed during US attacks in Afghanistan, al-Zawahiri married a woman from the Mohmand tribe in Bajaur Agency.[6] Similar to the manner in which bin Laden had married a women from Yemen to strengthen his ties to the Yemeni tribes, al-Zawahiri's marriage enabled the deputy leader of al-Qaeda to develop strong tribal ties to the leadership of Tehreek-e-Nifaz-e-Shariat Mohammadi (TNSM) in Bajaur Agency.[7] Maulana Faqir Muhammad, also from the Mohmand tribe, represented TNSM in Bajaur Agency.[8] Similarly, al-Zawahiri built a relationship with Liaquat Hussain, who ran the Ziaul Uloom Taleemul Qur'an seminary in Chingai in Bajaur until his death in October 2006.[9] Through these contacts al-Zawahiri was able to avoid arrest and reconstitute a scattered al-Qaeda. As the de-facto head of the Majlis-e-Shura (consultative council) of al-Qaeda, al-Zawahiri re-established contact with al-Qaeda cells in Pakistan and overseas. He also built alliances with groups in the Arabian Peninsula, the Horn of Africa, Southeast Asia and Iran.

After the arrival of both groups in 2002, the situation in FATA began to change. Immediately after al-Qaeda and its associates retreated from Afghanistan to FATA, they began to plan attacks against coalition forces in Afghanistan. They were initially supported by multiple Pakistani groups, which later formed TTP. In addition to the Afghan Taliban, Hizb-e-Islami, led by Gulbadin Hikmatyar, and the Haqqani network also joined them. As the local Pakistani groups grew in strength, the Pakistani military responded, spawning an insurgency. As the Pakistani military had difficulties of mounting land operations to neutralize al-Qaeda and its associates in FATA, the US conducted about 60 drone attacks from June 2004 until January 2009.[10] The first drone attack by the US killed Nek Muhammad, who was a staunch supporter of al-Qaeda and other foreign fighters and who facilitated operations against US led coalition forces, and two of his associates in Wana, North Waziristan on June 18, 2004.[11] The Pakistan government stated that the attack was mounted by the Pakistani security forces.[12]

Nek Muhammad was replaced by Abdullah Mehsud, a former detainee at Guantanamo Bay, as the most significant leader in FATA. After his death on July 24, 2007, Baitullah Mehsud emerged as the most prominent leader in FATA. Under the leadership of Baitullah Mehsud both Afghanistan and Pakistan experienced unprecedented levels of violence. Furthermore, al-Qaeda has become more assertive, often using the Pakistani Taliban as its strike arm.

With the emergence of local militias in their support, Pakistan deployed its regular military in FATA. Since then, Pakistan has been facing an insurgency in FATA. In many ways, FATA drifted away from the state of Pakistan. Pukhtun wali, a system that governed the day-to-day lives of the people in FATA, was shattered. Furthermore, faith in religion dwindled. In the name of Islam, un-Islamic acts were carried out by foreign fighters.

Pakistani Al-Qaeda

Among the terrorist leaders and operatives of Pakistani origin that have emerged since 9/11, the best known is Khalid Sheikh Mohammed, alias KSM, alias Mukhtar. The mastermind of the 9/11 attacks, KSM was a Western-educated Pakistani terrorist.[13] If it wasn't for KSM, al-Qaeda would not be well known globally. Both he and his nephew, Ramzi Ahmed Yousuf, grew up in Kuwait. Together they planned the February 1993 attack on the World Trade Center and the foiled plan to bomb a dozen aircraft over the Pacific (Operation Bojinka) in 1995. Having grown up in the Middle East, Ramzi Ahmed Yousuf and KSM were comfortable operating with both Asian and Arab terrorists. KSM planned several other attacks, such as a second wave against the US in 2002, including plans to strike the Bank of America building in Los Angeles using Southeast Asian terrorists. KSM partially funded the Bali bombing in 2002, and claims to have personally beheaded Daniel Pearl, the first American to be killed in an act of terrorism after 9/11.

KSM's partner in the Pearl murder was Ahmed Saeed Omar Sheikh, a British-born Pakistani educated at the London School of Economics. After joining Harakat-ul-Mujahideen, Omar Sheikh kidnapped Westerners in India in 1994. Released in return for hostages held in the hijacking of Indian Airlines Flight 814, Omar Sheikh lured Pearl, the respected *Wall Street Journal* reporter, to Karachi, kidnapped him and gave him to al-Qaeda in 2002.

Another Asian terrorist was Muhammad Naeem Noor Khan, alias Abu Talal, a computer specialist serving as the communications coordinator of al-Qaeda. Arrested in Pakistan on July 13, 2004, his laptop contained surveillance profiles of Heathrow Airport in London, the New York Stock Exchange and Citigroup headquarters in New York, the Prudential Building in New Jersey, and the International Monetary Fund and World Bank buildings in Washington DC. A protégé of KSM, Dhiren Barot, the al-Qaeda leader in the UK, had surveillance on these targets. Barot envisioned placing 12 or 13 explosive cylinders inside limousines, and detonating them in underground carparks to collapse the buildings; he called this the "Gas Limos Project." He travelled to the US in August 2000 and in March 2001 to study the targets in minute detail and briefed the al-Qaeda leadership on the Pak-Afghan border. Barot's cell members were mostly young British nationals of Pakistani heritage, none older than 31. Although known to the British intelligence community and New Scotland Yard since December 2001, Barot was identified and arrested only in August 2004. The dominance of Asians in European and North American operations was inevitable. After the 9/11 attacks, it was recognized, even within al-Qaeda, that it was difficult for Arabs to operate in the West. As Arabs were suspect, al-Qaeda relied on its Asian members, including those living in the West, to take charge of its operations. While Europe-based South Asian members who were either trained or inspired by al-Qaeda dominated the threat landscape, there were also Southeast Asians determined to strike the US, its allies and friends. For instance, Encep Nurjaman, alias Riduan Isamuddin, alias Hambali, from Indonesia, working together with KSM, spearheaded the bombing of churches in Indonesia in December 2000, the first Bali bombing, and arranged to house the 9/11 hijackers in Malaysia.

Threat

Almost all the terrorist and extremist groups that existed in Afghanistan under Taliban rule have reconstituted themselves and maintain a robust presence in FATA. Al-Qaeda is providing the crucial knowledge and methodology to mobilize not only the foreign but the domestic terrorist groups. Traditionally, the tribes in FATA supported the anti-Soviet multinational Afghan Mujahideen campaign (December 1979 to February 1989).

The tribes in FATA perceived Western intervention in Afghanistan in 2001 as an extension of the past, where non-Muslims occupied Muslim land. Henceforth, the hard-line Pashtun nationalists and the Islamists are supporting the fight against the US, their allies and friends. Like Sudan from 1991–96 and Afghanistan from 1996–2001, FATA has emerged as the most important terrorist sanctuary in recent history.

Today, FATA is of unprecedented significance to the international security and intelligence community for three reasons. First, the leadership of al-Qaeda, the Afghan Taliban, the Pakistan Taliban, the Eastern Turkistan Islamic Movement, the Islamic Movement of Uzbekistan, the Islamic Jihad Group, the Libyan Islamic Fighting Group, and a dozen other groups are located in FATA.[14] Both their operational and ideological leaders are protected by the Pakistani Taliban, a group that emerged after al-Qaeda and the Afghan Taliban moved to FATA in early 2002.

Second, FATA has become a sanctuary for research and development in explosives, training and directing operations globally. This included the attacks against not only Afghanistan and mainland Pakistan but the Middle East and the West. As long as FATA remains a sanctuary, the incessant attacks against coalition forces in Afghanistan will not stop. Furthermore, the spate of attacks on mainland Pakistan will continue. This included the multiple assassination attempts on Pervez Musharraf and the successful assassination of Benazir Bhutto. Attacks in the UK and several other operations disrupted in the West, such as the liquid explosives plot, were planned in FATA. Rashid Rauf, the mastermind of the foiled liquid explosives plot in August 2006 to blow up airplanes traveling over the Atlantic Ocean, escaped during his appearance in a Pakistani court. He was later killed, along with an al-Qaeda leader, Abu Zubair al-Masri, in a predator drone strike in the Mir Ali area of the North Waziristan Agency on November 22, 2008.[15]

Third, al-Qaeda is working together with like-minded groups and has invested in sustained propaganda to radicalize the Muslim masses. Even in migrant communities, al-Qaeda has unleashed a homegrown threat. In 2007 and 2008, al-Qaeda produced a video every three to four days.[16] The aim of al-Qaeda is to politicize, radicalize and mobilize Muslims worldwide into supporting and participating in the fight against the West. In the absence of a robust government response to counter al-Qaeda's message, Muslims are susceptible to extremist propaganda. Heightened extremism leads to support and participation in terrorism.

Despite intermittent pressure, al-Qaeda and many other foreign and Pakistani militant groups have re-established a smaller and more rudimentary version of their Afghan training infrastructure in the Shakai Valley of South Waziristan.[17] Operating out of FATA and the neighbouring settled area, the NWFP, al-Qaeda trained over 100 Westerners of Pakistani heritage to mount attacks in Europe and North America. For example, the leader of the 7/7 bombers, Mohammed Siddique Khan, and the leader of the failed 7/21 attacks were both trained in NWFP.[18] Furthermore, the al-Qaeda leader in the UK Dhiren Barot, alias Abu Issa al-Brittani, visited Waziristan to consult the al-Qaeda leadership when planning to attack multiple targets in the UK and the US, including the Prudential Building, New York Stock Exchange and Citigroup's headquarters in New York, as well as the International Monetary Fund's headquarters in Washington DC.[19]

Al-Qaeda's Pakistan-Iraq Links

The aforementioned threat can be best explained by examining al-Qaeda's role in Iraq and Afghanistan, operated through FATA. After the US invasion of Iraq in March 2003, Abdul Hadi al Iraqi acted as a conduit between bin Laden and al-Zarqawi, the leader of Tawhid wal-jihad.[20] As an Iraqi Kurdish member of al-Qaeda's Majlis Shura, Abdul Hadi brokered bringing bin Laden and al-Zarqawi into an alliance. The al-Qaeda leadership accepted the proposal by Abu Musab to name his group al-Qaeda in Iraq. As Abu Musab swore a "baya," an oath of allegiance to bin Laden, Tawhid wal-jihad was integrated into al-Qaeda.[21] The al-Qaeda leadership guided al-Zarqawi not only to wage the local jihad but also the global jihad from his base in Iraq. Another al-Qaeda leader, Mustafa al-Uzayti, alias Abu Faraj Al-Liby, head of al-Qaeda Internal Operations from 2002 until he was captured in May 2005, asked al-Zarqawi to target US interests outside of Iraq.[22] In September 2004, several members of al-Qaeda involved in terrorist operations, including Faraj Al-Liby, met in Syria to discuss a variety of terrorist operations, including planned operations in the US, Europe and Australia.[23] In the al-Qaeda strategy to use Iraq to strike the West, Abdul Hadi was a key figure.

Abdul Hadi and Ammar al-Ruqa'I, alias Abu Layth al-Liby, worked mainly from bases in the Shakai Valley in the South Waziristan Agency and from Sedgi and the Shawal Valley in the North Waziristan Agency of FATA.[24] Al-Qaeda operations in Afghanistan were conducted under the overall leadership of Taliban leader Mullah Mohammad Omar. Abdul Hadi conducted attacks in south-eastern Afghanistan, while Abu Layth al-Libi commanded al-Qaeda attacks in south-western Afghanistan. They personally trained the fighters and led operations from the front. As Abdul Hadi spoke not only Kurdish, Arabic and Persian but also Urdu and the Waziri tribal dialect of Pashto,[25] like Abu Layth, he built a strong relationship with the Pakistani tribes. They both had long-standing ties to the Taliban that went back to the 1990s and he acted as a liaison between al-Qaeda and the Afghan Taliban. As a brilliant military commander, Abdul Hadi was respected by both the Pakistani and Afghan Taliban. However, his tough personality brought him into conflict with other senior commanders, and the Egyptians in al-Qaeda. In August 2004, Abdul Hadi requested to be removed from his position as leader of al-Qaeda operations in Afghanistan and was intent on returning to his native country and serving with Abu Musab. However, knowing of the great disenfranchisement among al-Qaeda's leadership in Pakistan, with his leadership in Iraq, Abu Musab feared that Abdul Hadi was sent to replace him and refused to assist his entry into Iraq. In Abdul Hadi's absence, bin Laden appointed the Egyptian, Khalid Habib, as his Abdul Hadi replacement. Khalid Habib is a very able commander and a close friend of both Hamza Rabia and al-Zawahiri, also Egyptians. However, Khalid Habib, an introvert, is a less inspiring military commander than Abdul Hadi. When Abdul Hadi failed to enter Iraq and returned to North Waziristan, al-Qaeda decided his military skills were too important to leave unused, and they reappointed him as the commander of al-Qaeda operations in south-western Afghanistan. Khalid Habib remained in overall command of operations in Afghanistan and regionally in command of operations in south-eastern Afghanistan. Although cross-border attacks on coalition and Afghan forces in Afghanistan were Abdul Hadi's priority, he worked with Abu Faraj al Libbiin the multiple targeted operations to assassinate Pakistan's President Pervez Musharraf.

After Pakistan arrested Abu Faraj al-Libbi in May 2005, the Egyptians Hamza Rabia and Abu Abd-al Rahman al-Muhajir assumed the respective roles as number three and four in the organization. However, after the death of Hamza Rabia in December 2005, his post as head of External Operations was assumed by Abdul Hadi. Even before Abdul Hadi was appointed the Chief of External Operations, he worked with various al-Qaeda commanders in FATA and with al-Qaeda cells in the West to mount operations. As Abdul Hadi's interaction with Iraq grew, he almost relocated to Iraq with a view of creating a second safe haven for al-Qaeda.

Capable in multitasking, Abdul Hadi conducted both battlefield and off-the-battlefield operations. Abdul Hadi understood and knew the value of using Muslim migrants and the diaspora residing in the West to target the West. Instead of infiltrating operatives from Asia and the Middle East to the West, Abdul Hadi arranged several hundred British Muslims to travel both to Pakistan and to Iraq to receive training and then dispatched them to their host countries. In 2006 alone, the number of British Muslims that travelled to Iraq was assessed at 150.[26] Abdul Hadi's important role first came to the attention of the international intelligence community after the UK authorities intercepted a phone call between Abdul Hadi and Mohammed Quayyum Khan, alias Q, a British citizen of Pakistani heritage.[27] A part-time taxi driver from Luton in Bedfordshire, Q provided funds and equipment to al-Qaeda and facilitated the travel to Pakistan of Omar Khyam, another British citizen of Pakistani heritage. Before Omar Khyam joined Al-Muhajirun, a pro-al-Qaeda group in the UK, he had visited Pakistan in January 2000 and trained with Lashkar-e-Tayyiba. Afterwards, he built a cell of well-to-do British Muslims, almost all British-educated university graduates. When Omar Khyam returned to Pakistan in March 2003 with his cell members to fight in Afghanistan, Abdul Hadi sent word to them that because al-Qaeda had enough people, if they really wanted to do something they could go back [to the UK] and do something there.[28] Abdul Hadi's deputy then met Khyam in Kohat, Pakistan and instructed him to carry out "multiple bombings" either "simultaneously" or "one after the other on the same day."[29]

Under Abdul Hadi's orders, Khyam's cell exploited their contacts with Kashmiri groups to set up a training camp in Malakand, adjacent to Bajaur in FATA. Together with Mohammed Siddique Khan and Shehzad Tanwir, the leader and deputy leader of the cell that carried out the London bombing on July 7, 2005, they were instructed in bomb-making techniques.[30] After returning to the UK in the fall of 2003, they purchased 1,300 pounds of fertiliser to bomb Bluewater Shopping Centre in Kent, the Ministry of Sound nightclub in London, high-pressure gas pipelines around the south-east and trains and synagogues. On preparation of the device, Khyam remained in contact with Abdul Hadi's deputy. Khyam testified at his trial that the 2001 war in Afghanistan against the Taliban turned his group of friends against their home country for the first time and that the war in Iraq was "just sort of the final [straw]."[31] Similar to the way in which Abdul Hadi re-tasked the Khyam cell, he also met with and re-tasked Mohammad Siddique Khan and Shehzad Tanwir during a visit to Pakistan from November 2004 to February 2005.[32] Al-Qaeda claimed responsibility for the coordinated simultaneous suicide attacks by the cell led by Mohammad Siddique Khan in the UK, which killed 52 bus and underground train commuters. A similar bombing on July 21, 2005, led by Ibrahim Said Mokhtar, also trained in the Malakand camp, was unsuccessful. Abdul Hadi's interests included striking both Europe and the US. Together with Abu Zubaydah, Abdul Hadimet with Jose Padilla from the US and other operatives in 2002 to organize training on building remote-controlled detonation devices for explosives. In 2003, Abdul Hadi also controlled the American Pakistani Mohomed Junaid Babar of Queens in New York who provided money, night-vision goggles and sleeping bags to al-Qaeda attacking coalition forces in Afghanistan. Babar met with Abdul Hadi four times. Before returning to New York in early 2004, Babar conceptualized an attack on Times Square during New Year's Eve celebrations. Abdul Hadi worked on a range of operations to hit the US from 2005 onwards. He also tasked a key operative between al-Qaeda and Kashmiri groups and Rashid Rauf, from Birmingham, to coordinate the operation to blow up transatlantic airliners in mid-flight and on US soil. UK authorities, working with several foreign security agencies, mounted Operation Overt to disrupt al-Qaeda plans and preparations in August 2006.[33]

After Abu Musab was killed in June 2006, Abu Ayyub al-Masri from the Egyptian Islamic Jihad replaced him,[34] but bin Laden also dispatched Abdul Hadi to replace him. Al-Qaeda was determined to use Iraq as a forward operational base to hit the West, particularly the US, and Abdul Hadi was already in contact with multiple cells in the West. On his way, Abdul Hadi met with an al-Qaeda cell in Iran, but before he could enter Iraq, he was covertly captured in Turkey in late 2006. In April 2007, US authorities announced that they had detained Abdul Hadi and that he had been relocated to the US detention facility at Guantanamo Bay in Cuba.[35] As head of external operations, Abdul Hadi was replaced by an Egyptian, Abu Ubayda al-Masri. Abdul Hadi also worked with Abu Ubayda al Masri, the al-Qaeda leader in Kunar Province, to plan several operations in the West. He was preferred to two other contenders for the post, Khalid Habib al Masri and the Gulf Arab Hamza al-Jawfi.

Impact on FATA and the Neighbourhood

The population of FATA has suffered more than any other region of Pakistan. After al-Qaeda and its erstwhile host Afghan Taliban linked up with like-minded Pakistani groups and leaders, FATA emerged as a zone of sustained violence. The tribal belt has witnessed an unprecedented scale of violence and new tactics, including suicide bombings, attacking jirgas, killing women, beheadings, attacking mosques, funeral prayers, mutilating dead bodies and target killing of rallying points/icons.

Seeking to exercise their control, Pakistani groups influenced by the ideology of al-Qaeda have killed over 600 tribal elders, or maliks, as seen in the chart below.[36]

No.	Elder assassinated	Agency
1	Senator Faridullah Khan	SWA
2	Relatives Senator Abdul Malik	Khyber
3	Malik Afzal Khan	Mohmand
4	Malik Tuti Gul	NWA
5	Malik Mirzalam Khan	SWA
6	Malik Ahmed Khan	Khyber
7	Malik Khandan	SWA
8	Malik Shah Jehan	Bajaur

Despite an increase in military and law enforcement personnel, the wave of crime continued to increase. It has spilled over from FATA to the settled areas, provincially administered tribal areas, and frontier regions and to de-facto tribal areas. The rise of violence from 2007 to 2008 indicates a trend into 2009, as the Table 6.1 demonstrates.

While the number of military personnel killed exceeded 2,000 since the beginning of the insurgency, the number of law enforcement personnel being killed continued to rise. After the Lal Masjid tragedy in July 2007, both violence and the support for violence in FATA and the adjacent areas grew significantly, as noted in Table 6.2.[37]

Table 6.1 Growth of violence in the aftermath of the "Lal Masjid" (Red Mosque) incident (July 2007)

Offences	2007	2008	Difference
Total reported crime	109475	114089	+4614
Against person	8309	8830	+521
Kidnapping	669	810	+141
Assault on police	315	341	+26
Against property	1829	1959	+130
Vehicle theft	445	484	+39

Table 6.2 Comparison of the security personnel killed before and after July 2007

Year	Police officers killed	Police officers injured
2006	25	31
2007	108	234
2008	166	300

Today, FATA is suffering from a double flight, both in terms of capital and in "brain drain" to other parts of the country and overseas. The insecurity has caused economic activity to come to a near standstill. With utilities and other infrastructure destroyed, development funds are being diverted to law enforcement activities. The education system has suffered gravely, affecting the future of the region. In Swat alone, over 200 schools have been destroyed and female education has been banned by the Taliban.[38]

Conclusion

Al-Qaeda, the most hunted terrorist group in the world, has created another robust and resilient sanctuary in Pakistan. Since the October 2001 US-led coalition intervention in Afghanistan, bin Laden and the core leadership of al-Qaeda has made tribal Pakistan their new base. Both al-Qaeda and its associated groups, notably the Pakistani Taliban, target Afghanistan and Pakistan.

Today, the violence in Afghanistan has surpassed the violence in Iraq. Afghanistan witnessed a 33 percent rise in attacks in 2008.[39] In addition to its existing contingent 36,000 troops, Washington plans to send in another 30,000 troops to Afghanistan in 2009.[40] Despite the increase of coalition forces in Afghanistan, the terrorist threat will persist. The answer to stability in Afghanistan rests in clearing the terrorist enclave on the Pak-Afghan border. FATA remains the epicenter of global terrorism, where multiple al-Qaeda-led and al-Qaeda-driven groups plan, prepare and execute attacks globally.

Unless and until the international community recognizes and assists Islamabad in dismantling al-Qaeda and the Pakistani Taliban infrastructure in tribal Pakistan, the threat to the world will continue. With the influx of Pakistani fighters from mainland Pakistan to tribal Pakistan, the proportion of attacks in Afghanistan by the Pakistani Taliban will increase.

Since al-Qaeda relocated to tribal Pakistan, it has transformed from an operational group to both a training organization and an ideological movement. Al-Qaeda's ability to influence local Muslim groups in Pakistan and globally, particularly in Iraq, has been profound. Today, more Muslim groups are adopting al-Qaeda's methodology of suicide attacks and ideology of global jihad. Using vehicle- and human-borne suicide bombers, terrorist groups in Asia, Africa and the Middle East are mounting spectacular attacks against high-profile, symbolic and iconic targets in urban cities.

Al-Qaeda's displacement from Afghanistan to tribal Pakistan enabled both the ideology and organization of al-Qaeda to survive and revive. From FATA, al-Qaeda achieved four major successes.

First, al-Qaeda using Pakistan as a base built partnerships with groups in Asia, Africa and the Middle East. As they are influenced by ideology and operational practices such as suicide, these local and regional clones of al-Qaeda pose a threat greater than al-Qaeda itself. Although al-Qaeda as an organization is likely to fade away in the coming years, these regional associates are likely to endure and threaten the world. These structured groups enjoy close operational cooperation with core al-Qaeda leadership in tribal Pakistan.

Second, al-Qaeda's vicious ideology has infected a new generation of Muslims globally. While those politicized and radicalized people join groups in the East, others in the West either travel to the East and join structured groups or form homegrown cells to carry out attacks at home or elsewhere in the West. While the threat from well-structured hierarchical groups will persist, the new generation of homegrown cells will pose a greater threat to the West, especially to the US. Governments worldwide are today challenged by homegrown cells that are difficult to detect. Governments worldwide are still in a very early stage of building the platforms to counter the ideology of al-Qaeda that is leading to the formation of these cells.

Third, al-Qaeda created a front closer to the West by co-opting Tawhid wal-jihad in Iraq. Renamed al-Qaeda in Iraq, al-Qaeda leaders in Pakistan fully control this group after the death of al-Zarqawi. By using al-Qaeda in Iraq beyond its purpose in Iraq, al-Qaeda has created bases of support for violence in the Middle East as well as in Europe itself. Al-Qaeda in Iraq was joined by a few thousand European, African and Middle Eastern youth and several tens of thousands of supporters. The intentions of al-Qaeda in Iraq after freeing Iraq of Western influence is to use the networks developed beyond Iraq to target the Levant, the greater Middle East, and to strike the West. The threat in Iraq after Western retreat is extends to North America, and both Canada and the US. Even if al-Qaeda in Pakistan is crushed, al-Qaeda in Iraq, shaped and influenced by it, is likely to adopt bin Laden's vision and continue the fight.

Fourth, al-Qaeda in Pakistan has not only built ideological and operational ties to Pakistani groups in the tribal and mainland Pakistan but also to the Pakistani Diaspora in Europe. The groups infected by al-Qaeda pose a sustained threat to Afghanistan, both to the government and to coalition forces. Furthermore, they pose a real threat to Pakistan. After Afghanistan, Pakistanis have suffered more from terrorism than any other country in Asia and Pakistani youth both in Pakistan and overseas are undergoing extensive politicization and radicalization. Like a segment of the Middle Eastern youth were swayed by the violent ideology of the Palestinian and Lebanese groups in the 1980s, mobilized segments of the Pakistani diaspora will pose a long-term threat to the security of the West and the rest of the world. As Operation Overt, the investigation onto the British cell that planned to strike the US, demonstrated, the threat from radicalized Pakistanis in Europe and its spill-over effects are profound. Unless the ideologies of the threat groups are countered, they will pose a profound threat.

Notes

1 The author is indebted to the editor, Usama Butt, for the editing and updating of this chapter.

2 As of January 2009, the intelligence community of Pakistan estimated the total number of Arabs serving in al-Qaeda in FATA at 90. Visit to Pakistan, January 17–23, 2009.

3 US assessments based on intelligence and debriefing of captives, January 2009.

4 "Indonesia 'terror chief' questioned," Al Jazeera English http://english.aljazeera.net/news/asia-pacific/2007/06/2008525143040777971.html (accessed February 14, 2009).

5 "Bajaur mission fulfilled: army: chance to net Zawahiri 'missed,' says govt," *Dawn*, Pakistan, September 2, 2008.

6 http://www.zmong-afghanistan.com/profiles/zwahiri.asp (accessed February 14,

2009), and Akram Gizabi, "Bajaur: Tribe and Custom Continue to Protect al-Qaeda," *Terrorism Focus*, vol. 3, issue 2, January 18, 2006.

7   Mushtaq Yusufzai, Maulana Faqir, "Govt may ink peace deal after Eid," *The News*, Pakistan, October 22, 2006.

8   Jayshree Bajoria, "Pakistan's New Generation of Terrorists," Council on Foreign Relations, *Backgrounder*, February 6, 2008. Available at: www.cfr.org/publication/ 15422/pakistans_new_generation_of_terrorists.html?breadcrumb=%2Fbios%2F136 11%2Fjayshree_bajoria (accessed February 24, 2010).

9   Justin Huggler, "Eighty die as Pakistan bombs Madrassah linked to militants," *The Independent*, UK, October 31, 2006.

10   Global Pathfinder II, The Database of the International Centre for Political Violence and Terrorism Research, S. Rajaratnam School of International Studies, Nanyang Technological University, Singapore (accessed February 14, 2009).

11   Zulf Khan Afridi and Azka Jameel, "Operation in Wana: wanted al-Qaeda ally killed," *Pakistan Times*, June 19, 2004.

12   Ibid.

13   According to the 9/11 Commission, KSM studied at the North Carolina Agricultural and Technical State University, in Greensboro, North Carolina, where he graduated as a mechanical engineer.

14   Pervez Musharraf, *In the Line of Fire*. London: Simon and Schuster, 2006, pp. 265–270.

15   "Rashid Rauf among five killed in North Waziristan drone strike," *Daily Times*, Pakistan, November 23, 2008.

16   Interview with Sheikh Ayman al-Zawahiri, Intelligence Centre, al-Qaeda Videos, No. 74, May 5, 2007 and ICPVTR research on al Sahab Institute for Media Production.

17   Musharraf, p. 268.

18   The London Bombings, Briefing by the Secret Intelligence Service (SIS), UK, July 2006.

19   Ibid.

20   Sami Yusufzai and Ron Moreau, "Terror Broker: Bin Laden needed a role in the Iraqi insurgency, and Zarqawi needed outside support. How a deadly deal was made." *Newsweek*, April 11, 2006. When Al Qaeda negotiated with leaders of other groups, bin Laden chose al-Qaeda personalities similar to them. Like Abu Musab, Abdul Hadi was very direct and candid: this made Abdul Hadi the natural choice. Interview, Anders Nielsen, Research Fellow, International Centre for Political Violence and Terrorism Research, Singapore, December 2007.

21   Ibid.

22   Office of the Director of National Intelligence September 2006 "Profile on Abu Faraj al-Liby."

23   Verbatim Transcript of Open Session Combatant Status Review Tribunal Hearing ISN 10017.

24 "Accounts after 2005 London bombing point to Al Qaeda role from Pakistan," *New York Times*, August 13, 2006.

25 Yusufzai and Moreau.

26 Dipesh Gadher, "Al-Qaeda planning big British attack," *The Sunday Times*, UK, April 22, 2007.

27 Ian Cobain and Richard Norton-Taylor, "The phone call that asked: how do you make a bomb?," *The Guardian*, May 1, 2007.

28 Peter Bergen and Paul Cruickshank, "Al Qaeda-on-Thames," *The Washington Post*, April 30, 2007. Available at: http://newsweek.washingtonpost.com/postglobal/need toknow/2007/04/al_qaedaonthames_plotters_well.html accessed on February 24, 2010.

29 Ibid.

30 Mohammed Sidique Khan also knew Khyam and his associate Muhammad Junaid Babar from the US. Nonetheless, neither he nor his deputy Shehzad Tanwir were monitored by the UK authorities. There was a failure of security.

31 Bergen and Cruickshank.

32 "7/7 'mastermind' is seized in Iraq," *The Times*, UK, April 28, 2007.

33 "Accounts after 2005 London Bombing Point to Al Qaeda role From Pakistan," *New York Times*, August 13, 2006.

34 Abu Ayyub al-Masri, a heavy weapons instructor at al Farooq in Afghanistan, was in Iraq before the US invasion. Unlike Abu Musab, he maintained a low profile. Interview with high value detainees, Camp Cropper, December 2006.

35 "7/7 'mastermind' is seized in Iraq."

36 Terrorist Threat in FATA/NWFP, Briefing by Intelligence Bureau, Pakistan, January 2009.

37 Ibid.

38 Ibid.

39 Syed Salahuddin, "Afghanistan Says Foreign Fighters Coming from Iraq," *Reuters*, February 4, 2009.

40 Karen de Young, "Afghan Conflict Will Be Reviewed: Obama Sees Troops As Buying Time, Not Turning Tide," *Washington Post*, January 13, 2009.

CHAPTER SEVEN

Safety and Security of Pakistan's Nuclear Assets

Rabia Akhtar and Nazir Hussain

Abstract

Pakistan has been in the eye of the storm ever since it embarked on the nuclear weapon program in early 1970s. Beginning with the US pressures to roll back its nuclear program and economic/military sanctions to the cancellation of the French reprocessing plant, Pakistan's quest for restoring a balance of power in the region has met with stiff opposition from the Western states. More importantly, in the aftermath of 9/11, the regional and global security environment and the disclosure of AQ Khan episode, Pakistan has been under intense international scrutiny about the safety and security of its nuclear weapons. International media reports, academic analyses, intelligence commentaries and world leaders have been pointing towards the fragility of Pakistan's nuclear arsenal. There are three reasons cited for concern: (1) deteriorating law and order situation in the wake of growing militancy and terrorism, (2) collapse of the plural democratic political system and (3) nuclear weapons or materials falling in the hands of militants with insider-outsider scenarios.

However, despite the negative propaganda and concerns raised about its nuclear weapons, Pakistan has been following a strict and secure national command and control system. Although Pakistan is a non-signatory to the Nuclear Non-Proliferation Treaty (NPT) it complies with all international conventions and agreements concerning safety and security of nuclear materials. This chapter endeavours to analyze the safety and security of Pakistan's nuclear weapons in the light of international concerns and propaganda. To achieve this objective the chapter empirically evaluates Pakistan's command and control system, the multilayered safety mechanisms and contingency planning to meet any unforeseen eventuality. It also addresses international concerns on the safety and security of Pakistan's nuclear weapons and material raised in various international independent and official assessment reports in an effort to evaluate Pakistan's nuclear safety and security regime.

Introduction

Pakistan's nuclear journey has been long and arduous. Forced by the circumstances of its threat perception, Pakistan was a reluctant entrant into the nuclear weapons club. The separation of former East Pakistan, now Bangladesh, in 1971 and the Indian Pokhran-I nuclear test in 1974, created a whole set of events that eventually led to the shaping of Pakistan's determination to acquire nuclear weapons capability of its own. Prime Minister Zulfikar Ali Bhutto's promise to the nation in the gloomy post-1971 era pioneered the determination to build the bomb at any cost. The rest, as is typically said, is history. The nuclear weapons capability of the two South Asian nations remained largely covert until India decided to carry out a set of nuclear explosions in May 1998, which were swiftly followed by Pakistan's own tests within a span of two weeks, to restore the regional balance. Ten years of overt nuclearization from 1998–2008 in Pakistan has been an experience of numerous challenges and significant achievements. The position that Pakistan was a reluctant entrant in the nuclear weapons club stands to reason, since it was spread over 24 years from 1974–98.[1]

Since May 1998, perceptions about Pakistan's nuclear program have changed in myriad ways. In view of the opacity about its nuclear program, a perception of a "risk-acceptant" Pakistan developed, ostensibly due to Indian perceptions. Despite the negative overtone of this perception, it can be argued that it was helpful in stabilizing deterrence, such as during the 2001–02 escalation as, despite the presence of war-ready forces on both sides of the border, deterrence did not fail. After 10 years of overt nuclearization, this definition merits revision. Pakistan has taken significant measures to strengthen the Command and Control (C2) of its nuclear forces post-1998. This past decade stands witness to painstakingly created and carefully maintained nuclear management and capabilities.

Pakistan has come a long way in its first decade of nuclearization. The setting-up of the National Command Authority (NCA), with its highly professional secretariat, the Strategic Plans Division (SPD); the establishment of the Pakistan Nuclear Regulatory Authority (PNRA) to address nuclear safety issues and the creation of a highly versatile Bureau, the Security Division, to regulate and administer security in four tiers — physical, human, technical and counter intelligence — are some of the extraordinary steps that define the professionalism in which the nuclear establishment operates. Pakistan has adopted the doctrine of credible minimum deterrence and the operational readiness of its nuclear weapons program safely entails a "force in being"[2] bordering on the "always-never" nexus.[3] In its nuclear policy, Pakistan always maintains that its weapons are not for war. Even after a decade of nuclearization, this realization is still the main pillar of Pakistan's "rationality and restraint" logic that a survivable, small nuclear force can and will thwart any future nuclear blackmail or coercion. The progress achieved in this ten-year period provides the confidence that the vulnerabilities of the formative years no longer exist. While unfounded fears might still persist about possibilities of a rollback through coercion, Pakistan's nuclear establishment is confident that no one can thwart its nuclear capability.

A declassified US State Department document summarized the progress of Pakistan's nuclear weapons program by identifying that there was "unambiguous evidence" that Pakistan was actively pursuing a nuclear weapons development program. It went on to suggest that Pakistan's long-term goal was to establish a nuclear deterrent to aggression by India, which was Pakistan's greatest security concern.[4] This assessment, which was declassified in 1983, correctly predicted that Pakistan wanted to achieve nuclear weapons capability in response to the threat it perceived from India. The Indian-led dismemberment of Pakistan in 1971 was followed by the famous Multan meeting on January 20, 1972, in which Bhutto urged the Pakistani scientist community to embark upon the journey of acquiring nuclear weapons capability, providing Pakistan with a nuclear deterrent to curb military asymmetry vis-à-vis India. Bhutto appointed Munir Ahmed Khan as Chairman of the Pakistan Atomic Energy Commission (PAEC) and entrusted him with the responsibility to undertake this arduous challenge. Munir Ahmed Khan was thus the pioneer of the nuclear weapons program in Pakistan, with many significant milestones to his credit. Much to the dismay of the international community, Pakistan's nuclear development continued with great intensity during the 1990s, eventually leading to overt nuclearization in 1998. In 1993, the *New York Times* quoted Prime Minister Benazir Bhutto as saying, "We will protect Pakistan's nuclear program and will not allow our national interest to be sacrificed."[5] This statement, however, was denied by Pakistan's press attaché in Washington. In tacit acknowledgement, he identified that during the process of developing its peaceful nuclear program, "Pakistan has acquired a certain technical capability in the nuclear field."[6] Thus it was through the use of effective ambiguity that Pakistan managed nuclear testing in 1998 to counter the Indian explosion. As a non-NPT state, like India and Israel, Pakistan had no legal obligation to refrain from acquiring nuclear capability. Nevertheless, the achievement of this capability, despite decades of severe international criticism and sanctions, was no mean feat.

The broader contours of Pakistan's nuclear doctrine are determined by its adherence to a policy of credible minimum deterrence, which is often thought to be India-centric. Pakistan does not subscribe to the NFU (No First Use) doctrine that India does, suggesting that just like the NATO, Pakistan has chosen to keep its options open.[7] Consequently, the nuclear doctrine does not preclude the option of choosing any counter-value targeting, with a "force-in-being" arsenal (implying "ready to use" posture) and the institutionalized nuclear "command and control" structure, which is *assertive* rather than being *delegative* in nature. The command and control system has been designed to circumvent all possible eventualities related to human and material management.

Command and Control

Soon after the nuclear explosions in May 1998, Pakistan's command and control structure was informally put in place (in 1999). On February 2, 2000, the National Security Council approved the establishment of the National Command Authority (NCA).[8] Pakistan's nuclear command organization is a multi-layered system, which is structurally grouped in three tiers — the NCA, the SPD and the Strategic Forces Commands.

Pakistan's National Command Authority

The first constituent, the NCA, is the pinnacle decision-making organ for strategic matters in Pakistan. It is comprised of the top highest decision-makers of the country and is a mix of political and military leadership. The NCA is responsible for nuclear policy formulation and is the central authority for the development, deployment and employment of strategic assets.[9] In a re-promulgated ordinance of NCA 2009 issued on November 27, 2009, the President is no longer the Chairman of NCA.[10] It is believed that the rest of the arrangement remains the same, which is described below. One can, however, assume that the post of the Vice Chairman now stands abolished. According to the new arrangement, with the Prime Minister of Pakistan as the Chairman of the NCA, it operates with two main committees, the Employment Control Committee (ECC) and the Development Control Committee (DCC). The two committees function separately for operational and developmental aspects. The Director General of SPD is a member and secretary of both Committees.

Committees of the NCA

The Employment Control Committee (ECC) of the NCA is a superior committee that functions to review strategic weapons program deployment and employment issues and also decides on various response options in the face of continuous developments. The composition of the ECC is politico-military. On the political side, apart from the Prime Minister, are four federal ministers that are elected civilian representatives from the parliament. These are Foreign, Defence, Interior and Finance Ministers. The military members are the Chairman of the Joint Chiefs of Staff Committee (CJCSC) and the three services chiefs. The ECC is entrusted with the responsibility for providing policy direction during peacetime, whereas in wartime, it would exercise complete authority to order, control and direct the use or employment of the three services strategic forces. Therefore, ECC ensures fail-safe command and control during both peace- and wartime as well as during periods of crisis. The Development Control Committee (DCC) of the NCA is a subordinate committee, which oversees implementation of the policies and decisions taken by the ECC. This is a military-scientific committee, with the scientific

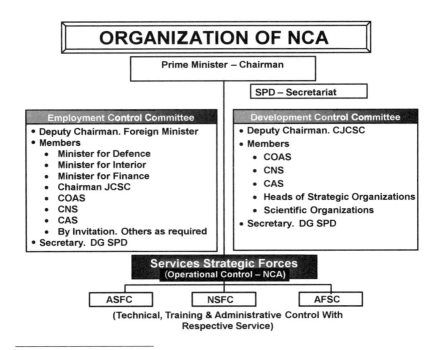

The structure of NCA with its constituent committees represented in Figure 7.1 is a widely circulated source. However, the change in the structure after re-promulgation is authors own construction whereby we assume that the post of Vice Chairman may now no longer exist in the structure.

Figure 7.1 Pakistan's National Command Authority

component represented by the heads of strategic commissions. The major strategic organizations include PAEC, KRL, NESCOM and SUPARCO. The committee exercises complete control over day-to-day technical, financial and administrative matters of strategic organizations. It also ensures that the systematic development of the strategic weapons program is executed according to the approved developmental strategy.[11]

Strategic Plans Division (SPD)

The SPD is the second constituent of the command and control organization. As the secretariat of the NCA, the SPD manages Pakistan's nuclear capability in an all-encompassing manner, including all dimensions-policy formulation, operations, plans, weapons development, arms control and disarmament, command and control, storage, budgets, safety and security. "On behalf of the NCA, SPD exercises firm control over all strategic organizations and coordinates their financial, technical, developmental, and administrative aspects. SPD is also responsible, in collaboration with the foreign ministry, for providing military inputs in the formulation of Pakistan's position on disarmament, non-proliferation and arms control issues."[12]

The SPD undertakes measures to ensure the safety and security of strategic assets in both the short and long term. While coordinating financial, technical, developmental and administrative matters, the SPD helps the NCA to exercise effective control over strategic organizations, facilities and assets. On the inter-agency side, it coordinates its work with the Foreign Office and key Pakistani ambassadors at the Conference on Disarmament (CD) Geneva, IAEA Vienna, the UN Headquarters at New York, and at the major capitals around the world, to provide strategic inputs. Similarly, coordination to establish a C4I2SR system for command and control of strategic assets for the NCA, with real-time linkages to the Services C4I2SR networks and Strategic Forces, is another responsibility of this division. The security bureau function that is accomplished by the SPD's Security Division, is another significant, and in some ways, stand-alone achievement.[13]

In brief, the SPD's functions include formulation of nuclear policy, nuclear strategy and nuclear doctrine. It envisions safety and security of Pakistan's nuclear program including strategic assets in the short and long term. This involves technical solutions, human factor reliability and counter intelligence. It conceives and facilitates advanced development, expansion and coordination of nuclear power and other peaceful uses of nuclear energy. Finally, it assists in implementing national obligations relating to non-proliferation, safety, security, accidents and WMD terrorism.

As depicted in Figure 7.2, the Operations and Plans Branch of the SPD resembles the structure of a military headquarters with operations, plans, intelligence and C4I2SR as essential elements. The Strategic Weapons Development (SWD) function provides the linkage to the classified side of the program, whereas Conventional & Open Programmes (COPD) was created to separate the civilian and peaceful uses of nuclear technology as well as the conventional spin-offs from the engineering outfits. Arms Control

Figure 7.2 Organization of the Strategic Plans Division

& Disarmament Affairs (ACDA) provides the linkage with the federal government's policy elements, i.e. the Ministry of Foreign Affairs (MFA) and Pakistan's Ambassadors in major capitals and UN headquarters. It is also a nuclear establishment's research outfit and keeps a watch on Pakistan's international obligations as well as the evolving geo-strategic environment.[14]

The Strategic Forces Commands at three service levels represent the third constituent of the NCA. Independent and operationalized Strategic Forces Commands have been raised in the Pakistan Army, Air Force and Navy to handle and operate nuclear weapons, when required. The three services retain responsibility for training, technical and administrative control of respective strategic forces. This notwithstanding, the NCA is solely responsible for operational planning and executive control over these forces, under the overall command of the CJCSC. For all operations-related aspects, the SPD is the main coordinating agency for the three services.[15]

Security Division

The security mechanism in Pakistan's nuclear establishment has been significantly augmented in the last few years. Physical security is multi-layered and has an elaborate system of access control. The current system comprises more than 10,000 specialized workers,[16] with multi-faceted training in counter-intelligence, human factor oversight, technical solutions, state of the art equipment and training facilities and special security directorates for each scientific commission.

An elaborate mechanism called a personnel reliability program (PRP) has been instituted to ensure a good "induction to grave" arrangement of oversight.[17] This system also serves as an effective enforcement measure for internal compliance. Since Pakistan's strategic organizations are all state-controlled or public organizations, it becomes relatively easier to implement enforcement measures.

With regard to physical security of Pakistan's nuclear assets, well-developed multi-tiered physical security mechanisms are in place, with firewalls in weapons and in the chain of command, to ensure that no unauthorized or inadvertent use can take place. Just like other aspects of the program, access control to the sensitive places is on "need basis." This makes the physical security system easier to manage. Similarly, when the radiation sources are on the move, elaborate transportation security arrangements designed in full consideration of the international standards ensure foolproof security.

The NCA ordinance, which was promulgated on December 14, 2007 and re-promulgated in November 2009, is an overarching legislation.[18] The safety and security system that Pakistan has created for the management of its nuclear capability continues to be improved, with various additional measures incorporated in it. One such measure is an view on the scientific manpower; Pakistan realized the need to regulate the movements of scientific manpower from its nuclear establishment. Through a system of reporting, approvals and monitoring of key personnel possessing sensitive information, the entire scientific community is under the strict control of the SPD. Furthermore, for any international travel to IAEA or any other international agencies, for either educational or private purposes, a clearance from SPD is a requirement that is provided after extensive scrutiny. Regular intelligence updates ensures an overview of all aspects.

Pakistan follows a strict regime of material control and accounting on modern scientific lines, which makes pilferage unlikely. Surprise checks are reportedly carried out on a regular basis to check sensitive material production and account for wastes to the last gram. For ensuring transportation security, Pakistan has instituted special measures to ensure transportation of

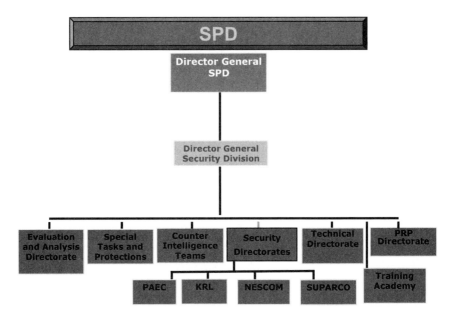

Figure 7.3 Security Division of SPD

sensitive materials through the acquisition of specialist vehicles with theft and tamper proofing under professionally organized escorts. A "two man rule" is operational and Pakistan has installed indigenously designed Permissive Action Links (PALs) on its nuclear weapons.[19] With specific reference to "the two man rule," it is a concept whereby control mechanism is established and thus no single individual is authorized with access codes where materials and operations of nuclear weapons are concerned. While no details about the nature of Pakistani PALs are available, generically speaking PALs are 6- or 12-digit-long alphanumerical codes, which according to various sources protect the weapon from detonating even if it has been accidentally dropped. The weapon automatically becomes disabled if the codes are fed incorrectly too many times.[20]

Although mechanisms to thwart any inadvertent use of nuclear weapons are in place, the weapons will be ready when and if they are required at a short notice. This mechanism in itself ensures strategic stability because unlike the Cold War model, Pakistan's nuclear weapons are not on hair trigger alert but rather in a "force-in-being mode." Also, on the classified side, the weapon system security remains stand-alone and independent. However, being a member of the PNRA, the Director General of the SPD remains a high tier, formal link that enables staying apace with international best practices.[21]

Technology Controls

While Pakistan's state structures and the existing legislations remained effective from its formative years, it undertook a review of its export control instruments soon after the May 1998 nuclear tests. It is noteworthy that while the international concerns arose out of the traumatic experience of the 9/11 attacks, Pakistan had already embarked upon structuring a new legislation in view of its overt nuclear capability. While the spade work commenced on legal review process, the SPD issued elaborate export policy guidelines to its strategic organizations in September 2000. Considering that the NCA was formalized in February 2000, issuance of export policy guidelines was speedy work. The Ministry of Foreign Affairs (MFA), however, interacted closely with the SPD to incorporate availability of technical inputs into the initial drafting of the legislation.

Pakistan's "Export Control on Goods, Technologies, Material and Equipment related to Nuclear and Biological Weapons and their Delivery System Act 2004," or simply, the Export Control Act 2004, includes all important elements of an effective national export control system.[22] It enhances control over exports, re-exports, trans-shipment and transit of goods, technologies, material and equipment. It also prohibits the diversion of controlled goods and technologies and provides for penalties up to 14 years" imprisonment, a Rs. 5 million fine and confiscation of property in Pakistan or elsewhere.[23]

Pursuant to the enactment of the Export Control Act 2004, a National Export Control List (NCL) was notified on October 19, 2005 (S.R.O. 1078(I)/2005).[24] It contains items that are to be subjected to strict regulatory requirements. It is consistent with the scope of export controls maintained by the Nuclear Suppliers' Group (NSG) as it incorporates items listed in NSG Part I and II; the Australia Group (as related to biological agents, toxins and associated dual use technologies); and the delivery systems and components according to the Missile Technology Control Regime (MTCR) lists.

As a measure of enforcement of the export control act, the Strategic Export

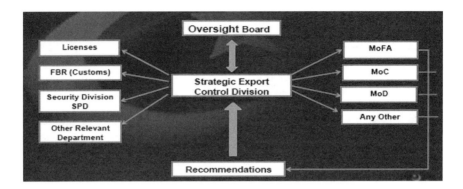

Figure 7.4 Interagency linkages — SECDIV

Source: www.partnershipforglobalsecurity.org/documents/zafar_export.pdf

Control Division (SECDIV)[25] was created at MFA. The SECDIV is run through a multi-disciplinary approach where experts from Pakistan Customs, Ministries of Foreign Affairs, Commerce, Defence, on one hand, and Federal Board of Revenue (FBR), PAEC, PNRA and SPD on the other, work closely to ensure successful implementation of export control mechanism.

An Oversight Board, comprising senior officials of the Government of Pakistan, was established in July 2007. This Board is mandated to independently review the implementation of export controls, in particular the Export Control Act 2004 and to supervise the functioning of the SECDIV. The Board is chaired by the Foreign Secretary and includes members from the Ministries of Foreign Affairs, Defence, Interior, Cabinet Division, Federal Board of Revenue, PNRA and the SPD.[26] Finally, within the strategic organizations, an internal compliance mechanism has been introduced. All together, the stringent export control mechanism not only provides a comprehensive structure within Pakistan, it also matches with the international requirements in general and acts as a swift response to UN obligations in particular.

Pakistan Nuclear Regulatory Authority (PNRA)

The PNRA was established under the PNRA Ordinance No. III of 2001. Its core goals are safety and security of radioactive materials, radiation protection, ensuring physical protection of radioactive materials as per IAEA INFCIRC/225, transport safety, waste safety. PNRA was created in 2001 ". . .

for regulation of nuclear safety and radiation protection in Pakistan and the extent of civil liability for nuclear damage resulting from any nuclear incident."[27]

The PNRA was created partly in compliance of Pakistan's obligations under the Convention on Nuclear Safety (CNS). It is the main agency in Pakistan that coordinates emergency preparedness at a national level and also collaborates with international agencies for nuclear and radiological emergencies. In order to strengthen and enhance the existing regulatory capabilities towards safety and security of nuclear/radioactive materials and facilities Pakistan has launched a five-year National Nuclear Security Action Plan (NSAP). Approved by the Government in May 2006, the NSAP implementation commenced in July 2006, for which the PNRA remains the sponsor agency. Pakistan has taken various steps towards ensuring the safety and security of its nuclear installations.[28] The NSAP has five main objectives, which include the management of radioactive sources and evaluation of vulnerable facilities; the establishment of Nuclear Safety and Security Training Centre; the establishment of National Nuclear Security Emergency Co-ordination Centre; detection equipment at entry/exit points to obviate chances of illicit trafficking; and locating and securing orphan sources.

The establishment of the Nuclear Safety and Security Training Centre is one such step. The training centre imparts training in nuclear safety and security. Its laboratories are equipped with state-of-the-art equipment. Besides imparting training to the first responders, the centre also trains customs and border officials for nuclear and radioactive material detection at borders. A memorandum of understanding (MoU) has been signed between the PNRA and the Federal Board Revenue (FBR) "to promote cooperation and organize mutual assistance against illicit trafficking of radioactive and nuclear materials."[29] Another step in securing Pakistan's nuclear complex is the creation of National Nuclear Security Emergency Co-ordination Centre (NuSECC).[30] The main objective of establishing this center, which functions round the clock, is to assess, coordinate and respond in case of a nuclear security emergency in Pakistan. The level of preparedness for any radiological or nuclear emergency exhibits Pakistan's consciousness about disaster management in case of a nuclear accident.

In order to ensure nuclear safety, the Nuclear Security Directorate (NSD)[31]

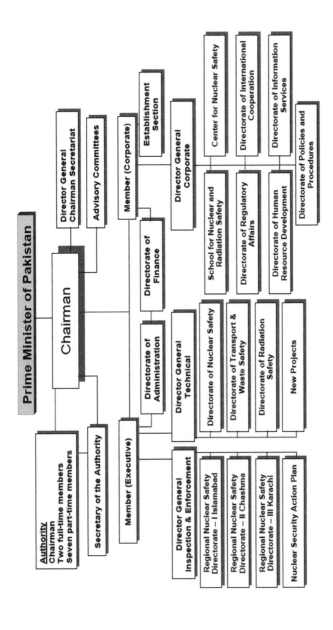

Figure 7.5 Organizational Chart of PNRA

Source: www.pnra.org

was established to undertake licensing of nuclear power plants, including modifications; periodic safety reviews and re-licensing; licensing and inspections of nuclear grade equipment manufacturing facilities; establishing and maintaining regulatory framework for nuclear safety; reviews and assessments; self assessment; coordinating with regional directorates in activities related to nuclear safety; maintaining and disseminating information on nuclear safety within PNRA; preparation of regulations, working procedures and guidelines.

Pakistan and the Nuclear Security Instruments

Following are the international instruments that contribute to the framework of the nuclear security regime, of which Pakistan is a responsible state party, the Convention on the Physical Protection of Nuclear Material (CPPNM);[32] Convention on Nuclear Safety;[33] UN Security Council Resolution 1540;[34] and the IAEA Code of Conduct on Safety and Security of Radioactive Sources.[35] Pakistan is amongst many countries that have made a political commitment with regard to the Code of Conduct and the supplementary guidance on the import and export of radioactive sources.

The CPPNM was opened for signature on March 3, 1980 and entered into force on February 8, 1987. "Pursuant to Article 2, the Convention applies to nuclear material used for peaceful purposes while in international nuclear transport."[36] Pakistan acceded to CPPNM on September 12, 2000.[37] Following are the legal instruments that constitute Pakistan's export control framework, the Import and Exports (Control) Act, 1950 (Act No. XXXIX of 1950).[38] Through this act the Federal Government is authorized to prohibit, restrict or control the import/export of goods and regulate practices and procedures connected therewith. Provisions for control of import/export of nuclear substances and radioactive materials are laid down under this ordinance the Pakistan Nuclear Safety and Radiation Protection (PNSRP) Ordinance of 1984 and Regulation of 1990;[39] Statutory Notification No. SRO-782 (1), 1998 to prohibit the export of fissionable materials; the Chemical Weapons Convention Implementation Ordinance 2000 to regulate and control import and export of chemicals in accordance with the provisions of CWC and penalties in case of violations; the Export Control Act on Goods, Technologies,

Material and Equipment related to Nuclear and Biological Weapons and their Delivery Means, 2004.[40] Export control guidelines were issued to strategic organizations in September 2000 and the National Control List (NCL) was notified in October 2005.

Challenges to Pakistan's Nuclear Security Framework

According to the IAEA, nuclear security framework is referred to as "the combination of international binding and non-binding legal instruments together with IAEA nuclear security guidance." Pakistan adheres to this legal framework and is an active participant on all IAEA forums of training, information exchange, legislative assistance and capacity-building that constitutes its nuclear security regime. The insinuations raised in the international media about the safety and security of Pakistani nuclear weapons, assets, materials and personnel have crossed all limits of projecting worst-case doomsday scenarios but none of the reports that have been published about Pakistan's nuclear weapons program can highlight tangible issues with the system.

The insider threat, the outsider threat, the insider-outsider collusion, the wrong hands, the rogue hands and the theorizing about militant extremists eyeing Pakistani nuclear weapons — all these have become a standard to bash Pakistan and pressurize it into accepting programs akin to those of Cooperative Threat Reduction (CTR) between the US and the former Soviet Union. But Pakistan is not the Soviet Union. The kind of transparency that the West or the international community demands of Pakistan's nuclear establishment is unprecedented. Despite having fulfilled all obligations as ascertained by IAEA nuclear security framework, confidence in Pakistan's ability to secure its personnel and assets remains questionable. Pakistan is a signatory of both the Biological and Toxin Weapons Convention and Chemical Weapons Convention and does not produce or possess biological or chemical weapons. Yet as unfortunate as it remains, reports like "World at Risk"[41] by the Commission on the Prevention of WMD Proliferation and Terrorism continue to speculate that Pakistan poses a grave danger of WMD attack, given the alleged vulnerability of its nuclear stockpile. Such reports[42] derail confidence-building mechanisms and thus render the entire process counterproductive.

A considerable amount of speculation regarding Pakistan's nuclear security culture arose after the AQ Khan revelations of an illicit nuclear proliferation network. However, according to some scholars "The nuclear security culture was originally designed to protect the autonomy of the scientists so that their work could continue unhindered. Because of the significance of the cause, managers of the program had no authority to question the motives and practices of the scientists. This enabled Khan to take advantage of the lack of proper accountability."[43]

Conclusion

Pakistan maintains a reasonable amount of strategic ambiguity where its nuclear policies, doctrines and strategy are concerned "No one knows the location of our weapons. The system is close-looped and the rules very stringent due to a strict 'need to know' policy. Such strict compartmentalization of knowledge facilitates strategic ambiguity."[44] However, Pakistan has been transparent about its command and control structure, its nuclear safety arrangements, and the processes involved in physical safeguarding of the assets and the materials. The security of its facilities and the safeguarding of its nuclear materials are according to the internationally established norms followed by all nuclear and non-nuclear states. The most commonly known information is about the civil-military structure of the NCA itself, which brings in a balanced mix of civil and military personnel where the decision-making of the NCA is concerned.

Pakistan has survived several political and technical challenges and made significant achievements. In the political dimension, Pakistan has achieved a demonstrable nuclear weapons capability, managed its nuclear assets by creating a robust command and control infrastructure, instituted nuclear safety and security regime, fulfilled its international non-proliferation obligations, established credible minimum deterrence and taken considerable steps in support of strengthening strategic stability in South Asia. The creation of the NCA consequent to the May 1998 tests signifies a well-conceived and well-deliberated management structure. It projects Pakistan as a responsible nuclear weapons state in complete control of its security arrangements. On the technical side, the successful and safe achievement of the nuclear tests, soon after the Indian tests, moving swiftly to establish technologically feasible C2 structures, ensuring that a "force-in-being" remains credible and relevant and launching an elaborate nuclear safety and security regime have been ensured with consistency. Pakistan's nuclear program continues to be India-specific given its past and present threat perception but reliance on minimum deterrence, which is credible, will remain the central pillar of Pakistan's nuclear policy thereby reasserting Pakistan's seriousness towards maintaining strategic stability in South Asia.

Since Pakistan has been engaged in fighting the US-led war on terrorism since 2001, speculation of an extreme nature have been conducted in the international media. Although the US has the most extensive nuclear security infrastructure in the world, cases of lack of oversight[45] and errors[46] have managed to over-blow the concerns for new nuclear states like Pakistan. Despite Pakistan's emphasis on its nuclear safety and security arrangements and its command and control structure before the world, a significant amount of unease still exists in the international community — simply because Pakistan stands grossly misunderstood. For Pakistan's nuclear establishment, the doomsday scenarios are dismissed with an air of confidence, "We have the advantage of hindsight. We have worked hard, we have trained hard, and we are very sure of what we have. We have learned from the best international practices."[47] Since no security system in the world is foolproof, there can never be absolute measures in place to counter the unforeseen. However, contingency planning is constantly being reviewed and tested with all possible threat scenarios catered for. To put it simply, Pakistan's nuclear weapons are as vulnerable or as safe as any other country with such capabilities, including the P5 states. The approach has been all-encompassing, with special emphasis on nuclear safety and physical and other aspects of security. Much of this has been acknowledged by international observers.[48]

There is a dire need for the creation of an atmosphere of trust and confidence with Pakistan's nuclear establishment and the people of Pakistan, who take pride in being a responsible nuclear state. Pakistan is outside the fold of the NPT yet follows all international non-proliferation norms, follows IAEA safeguards on all its civilian nuclear facilities in letter and spirit, has no record of smuggling or trafficking of uranium or other fissile materials that can be confirmed from IAEA's Illicit Trafficking Database (ITDB), has no record of nuclear accidents, maintains an impeccable record of nuclear safety and is part of various binding and non-binding international instruments on nuclear safety and security. The most immediate and significant political challenge that Pakistan will continue to face for some time, given the constant pressure by the international community, is battling international misperceptions, and convincing the world that the problem of internal stability that Pakistan faces today does not and will not lead to vulnerability of its nuclear assets.

Notes

1 Despite the fact that Pakistan's nuclear program is highly secretive in nature with very little information available about its various arrangements; the authors would like to thank DG Strategic Plans Divisions Lt. Gen. (Retd) Khalid Ahmed Kidwai and his outreach team in the SPD for providing transparency on issues of physical safety and security of Pakistan's nuclear assets.

For a quick reference matrix on Pakistan's efforts, see Khalid Banuri, "Pakistan's Role in Global Non-Proliferation," Partnership for Global Security (PGS), Washington DC, April 30, 2007. Available at: http://www.partnershipforglobalsecurity.org/documents/banuri_acda.pdf

2 The expression of "force in being" is borrowed from Ashley Tellis's views regarding India, which in the author's opinion is equally applicable to Pakistan. According to Tellis "force in being" is defined as a nuclear posture which "exhibits a deterrent capability based on available but dispersed components capable of being constituted into usable nuclear weapon systems during a supreme emergency, and even after enduring an enemy nuclear strike." For a detailed discussion on "force in being" please see Ashley Tellis," "Toward a 'force-in-being': the logic, structure, and utility of India's emerging nuclear posture," *Journal of Strategic Studies*, vol. 25, December 4, 2002, pp. 61–108.

3 The "always-never" relates to the level of readiness and usability alongside safety from accidents and unintended consequences. For further details, see Peter Feavor, "Command and Control in Emerging Nuclear Nations," *International Security*, vol. 17, no. 3 (Winter 1992–1993), pp. 160–187.

4 "The Pakistani Nuclear Program," State Department Briefing Paper, June 23, 1983. Available at: www.gwu.edu/~nsarchiv/NSAEBB/NSAEBB6/ipn22_1.htm

5 Edward A. Gargan, "Bhutto stands by the nuclear program," *The New York Times*, October 21, 1993. Available at: www.nytimes.com/1993/10/21/world/bhutto-stands-by-nuclear-program.html

6 "Pakistan isn't building any nuclear weapons," *The New York Times*, December 2, 1993.

Available at: www.nytimes.com/1993/12/02/opinion/l-pakistan-isn-t-building-any-nuclear-weapons-011193.html

7 These views were expressed by Air Commodore Khalid Banuri, Director Arms Control and Disarmament Affairs (ACDA) SPD at a Seminar in National Defense University, Islamabad on May 30, 2008.

8 "National Command Authority established," *Global Security*, February 3, 2000. Available at: www.globalsecurity.org/wmd/library/news/pakistan/2000/000203-pak-app1.htm (accessed November 06, 2009). For a detailed reference on Pakistan's management structure of nuclear capability see Mahmud Ali Durrani, "Pakistan's Strategic Thinking and the Role of Nuclear Weapons," Cooperative Monitoring Center Occasional Paper 37, Sandia National Laboratories, July 2004. Available at: http://www.cmc.sandia.gov/cmc-papers/sand2004-3375p.pdf (accessed November 6, 2009).

9 Khalid Banuri and Adil Sultan, "Managing and Securing the Bomb," *Daily Times*, Pakistan, May 30, 2008.

10 "President sheds powers of NCA Chairman," *The Nation*, Pakistan, November 28, 2009. Available at: www.nation.com.pk/pakistan-news-newspaper-daily-english-online/Politics/28-Nov-2009/President-sheds-powers-of-NCA-Chairman

11 Air Commodore Khalid Banuri's lecture on Pakistan's Command and Control structures at Fatima Jinnah Women University Rawalpindi on April 2009.

12 Banuri and Sultan, op. cit.

13 The authors were present at the background brief given to the local and foreign journalists by the Director General of the SPD on February 4, 2008.

14 Ibid.

15 Ibid.

16 "10,000 men protecting the nuclear assets," *Dawn*, May 28, 2009. Air Commodore Khalid Banuri quoted on security of nuclear assets. Available at: www.dawn.com/wps/wcm/connect/dawn-content-library/dawn/news/pakistan/13+10000+men+protecting+n-assets+official-za-09

17 For a Western perspective on nuclear security pattern, see Peter Wonacott, "Inside Pakistan's Drive to Guard it's a-Bombs," *The Wall Street Journal*, November 29, 2007.

18 Text of NCA Ordinance December 14, 2007. Available at: www.brecorder.com/index.php?id=663841&currPageNo=1&query=&search=&term=&supDate

19 Peter Wonacott, op. cit.

20 S. M. Bellovin, "PALs, Nuclear Weapons and History of Cryptography," 2005 lecture notes from Department of Computer Science, Columbia University. Available at: www.stanford.edu/class/ee380/Abstracts/060315-slides-bellovin.pdf

21 For comments on Pakistan's nuclear security and the role of DG SPD, see Ashley J. Tellis, Testimony to US House Committee on Foreign Affairs, Sub-Committee on Middle East and South Asia, January 16, 2008.

22   IAEA INFCIRC/712 Pakistan's Export Control Act, September 6, 2007. Available at: www.iaea.org/Publications/Documents/Infcircs/2007/infcirc712.pdf

23   Ibid.

24   For the complete text of the NCL, see IAEA INFCIRC/669.

25   IAEA INFCIRC 712 Pakistan's Export Control Act, op. cit.

26   SRO 693(I)/2007 Establishment of the oversight board. Available at: www.mofa.gov. pk/SECDIV/Oversight%20Board.PDF

27   Text of PNRA Ordinance 2001. Available at: www.pnra.org/regulations.asp

28   For a discussion on NSAP, see Jamshed Azim Hashmi and Muhammad Khaliq, "Pakistan's Nuclear Safety and Security Action Plan" Partnership for Global Security (PGS), April 30, 2007. Available at: www.ransac.org/PDFFrameset.asp?PDF=hashmi_pnra.pdf

29   "FBR, PNRA to jointly combat illicit trafficking of radioactive, nuclear materials," *Associated Press of Pakistan*, June 21, 2008.

30   Kenneth Luongo and Naeem Salik, "Building Confidence in Pakistan's Nuclear Security," *Arms Control Today*, December 2007. Available at: www.armscontrol. org/act/2007_12/Luongo. Also see Jamshed Azim Hashmi and Muhammad Khaliq, op. cit.

31   Nuclear Safety Directorate. Available at: www.pnra.org/ns.asp

32   Text of the Convention on the Physical Protection of Nuclear Material (CPPNM). Available at: http://www.iaea.org/Publications/Documents/Infcircs/Others/inf274r1. shtml (accessed November 19, 2009).

33   Text of the Convention on Nuclear Safety (CNS) that Pakistan ratified on September 30, 1997. Available at: www.iaea.org/Publications/Documents/Infcircs/Others/inf449. shtml

34   Text of UNSCR 1540. Available at: www.un.org/News/Press/docs/2004/sc8076.doc. htm

35   For a complete text of the IAEA Code on Safety and Security of Radioactive Sources please see: www-pub.iaea.org/MTCD/publications/PDF/Code-2004_web.pdf

36   Op. cit. text of the CPPNM. Available at http://www.iaea.org/Publications/Documents/ Infcircs/Others/inf274r1.shtml (accessed November 19, 2009).

37   Status of CPPNM available at http://www.iaea.org/Publications/Documents/ Conventions/cppnm_status.pdf (accessed November 19, 2009).

38   For a comprehensive appraisal of Pakistan's strategic export control mechanism please see http://www.sassi.uk.com/pdfs/Report-28.pdf (accessed December 03, 2009).

39   PNSRP Ordinance text. Available at: www.pnra.org/legal_basis/1984.pdf

40   INFCIRC/636 Text of Pakistan's Export Control Legislation. Available at: www.iaea. org/Publications/Documents/Infcircs/2004/infcirc636.pdf

41   "World at Risk: Report of the Commission on the Prevention of WMD Proliferation and Terrorism." Available at: www.cfr.org/publication/17910/world_at_risk.html

42   A plethora of material is available on the worldwide web on Pakistan's nuclear security, mostly targeting Pakistan's nuclear safety and security arrangements and dismissing its capability to deal with any eventuality. Latest reports include Seymour P. Hersh's "US nuclear security plan" *New Yorker*, November 8, 2009, speculating on Pakistan compromising nuclear secrecy, which was rebutted very strongly both by the Foreign Office and Chairman of the Joint Chiefs of Staff Committee (CJCSC) General Tariq Majid, who stated, "I reiterate in very unambiguous terms that there is absolutely no question of sharing or allowing any foreign individual, entity or state any access to sensitive information about our nuclear assets," quoted in *DAWN Report "N-assets report mischievous, absurd: Gen Majid" DAWN*, November 10, 2009. Available at: http://www.dawn.com/wps/wcm/connect/dawn-content-library/dawn/news/pakistan/13+gen+tariq+majid+calls+hersh+article+mischievous-za-01+ (accessed December 03, 2009).

43   Feroz Hassan Khan, "Nuclear Security in Pakistan: Separating Myth from Reality," *Arms Control Today*, July-August 2009. Available at: http://www.armscontrol.org/act/2009_07-08/khan (accessed December 11, 2009).

44   Authors' interview with Air Commodore Khalid Banuri, Director Arms Control and Disarmament, Strategic Plans Division (SPD), JSHQ on December 18, 2009.

45   The Minot Air Force base incident where six AGM-129 ACM cruise missiles with nuclear warheads remained missing for 36 hours without any security precautions or protections. See: http://news.bbc.co.uk/2/hi/6980204.stm (accessed December 11, 2009).

46   "Nuclear parts sent to Taiwan in error." See: www.washingtonpost.com/wp-dyn/content/article/2008/03/25/AR2008032501309.html (accessed December 12, 2009).

47   Air Commodore Khalid Banuri Director Arms Control and Disarmament Strategic Plans Division (SPD) in a televised interview 2007–2008. Transcript can be accessed at: www.globalpolitician.com/24013-pakistan

48   See "Pakistan's Nuclear Oversight Reforms," (chapter 5) in International Institute for Strategic Studies, *Nuclear Black Markets: Pakistan, A. Q. Khan and the Rise of Proliferation Networks — A Net Assessment*. London: IISS Strategic Dossier, May 2007. Also see Kenneth N. Luongo and Naeem Salik, "Building Confidence in Pakistan's Nuclear Security," op. cit.

CHAPTER EIGHT

The Politics of IDPs: A Fallout of Politics of Domestic and Foreign Actors

Sajjad Naseer

Abstract

A severe conflict has been raging in Afghanistan since the 1980s. First, it involved the Soviet Union, which fought a losing war as an occupation force until its withdrawal in 1988. Since 9/11 it is now the American occupation force, aided by coalition partners, struggling to prevail without success. The global agenda of the surviving superpower is clashing with the interests of the actors in the region. The non-state actors, the state actors, the ethno-religious and tribal variants, the role of the invisible hands and competing perception of national interest are interacting in an uneasy relationship. So many discordant notes have been struck in the ongoing conflict rendering the overarching policy and its implementation problematic. Even the coalition partner, Pakistan, is not fully adhering to the policy as it is understood in Washington. Because of the policy conundrum, a coherent policy and its implementation is facing persistent hiccups. The politics of the internally displaced persons (IDPs) is a manifestation of the ongoing conflict. This chapter explores the various dimensions of this conflict, and it is argued that without a political system enjoying support and legitimacy of its own people, the conflict is likely to persist in varying degrees and forms.

Introduction

The phenomenon of IDPs is visiting different parts of the world in varying forms, degrees, intensity and consequences. Untold misery and suffering are fated for these human beings, who have lost their material and psychological wellbeing and remain unsure of their future prospects. Being uprooted from one's home is not only tragic, but as victims of the ongoing conflict, it adds various intended and unintended dimensions to the predicament. Coerced into the situation, the prospects of sustainability, homecoming and stability remain distant, fleeting and elusive, though claims are made by the national governments and international community of big plans for the rehabilitation of the displaced persons. The saga of the Palestinian refugees and displaced persons with their agonizing plight continues to test and challenge the competence of international managers to come up with reasonable solutions. What happened in the aftermath of Yugoslavia's break-up is another case in point. The chaotic and messy end to the overlapping civil wars across much of former Yugoslavia and within Bosnia-Herzegovina (ethnic cleansing) is a grim reminder to scholars to evaluate the competence of international managers in the areas of rehabilitation, state-building and democracy. The current situation of IDPs in Pakistan presents yet another test case.

It is worth noting that the origins of the Dayton agreement in 1995 are surrounded by controversy and disputes, though it is referred to as a consensus document and was virtually a mantra of international officials. This agreement was a treaty designed to end a war, not to build a state.[1] The post-Dayton process from 2000 to 2005 marginalized the elected bodies, paving the way for direct and indirect European Union interference. The routine argument of the commentators is that Dayton was negotiated by the nationalist parties, whose leaders caused the war in the first place, and it, therefore, secured the power of these ethnically-based political parties.[2] One sees clearly that the political process since Dayton as the "continuation of war by other means" is an inversion of Clausewitz's often repeated and used doctrine.[3] The way the situation is unfolding in Pakistan, there may be the potential of a repeat exercise of Dayton agreement with different features but surely the role of international officials seems ominous.

Historically, humans have a track record of moving from place to place under specific circumstances, compulsions (domestic and foreign) or as an act of choice. Around the middle of the twentieth century, South Asia witnessed huge migrations across borders of the newly-born states of India and Pakistan and subsequently in the wake of the civil war in East Pakistan leading to the birth of Bangladesh in 1971. In 1964 and 1973, the military action of the Pakistan army in Balochistan forced Baluchi people to move across the border into Afghanistan. The 1980s saw Pakistan's engagement in the proxy war against the Red Army in Afghanistan, the consequence of which was the movement of over 3 million Afghans into the Pakistani provinces of Balochistan and Frontier (NWFP). Still, after the withdrawal of the Soviet army, 2 million persons reside in the two provinces with serious social, economic, political, law and order and military implications.

The 9/11 episode engaged Pakistan as an American-led coalition partner and a non-NATO ally in the war on terrorism and was initially inducted into this global project called the "war on terrorism" to provide logistic support and facilitate military action in Afghanistan, but the war theatre has now shifted to the northern areas of Pakistan. In the last two years, violence characterized by "suicide bombing" has engulfed the whole of Pakistan, including its major urban centers. Even sensitive security installations (police and military) were hit with precision along with the bombing of five-star hotels in Islamabad and Peshawar. The visiting Sri Lankan cricket team was not spared from this violent action, despite stringent security arrangements guiding their movement in the city of Lahore in February 2008. This presented such a horrific spectre to the outside world that Pakistan was labeled as an "epicenter of terrorism" and a "failing state" in the international media. Without getting into a discussion to evaluate the substance of these labels, it is pertinent to point out that no attempt was made to project Pakistan in a positive way or build its image as a partner by the Western allies. Then there were intriguing questions regarding the frequency of violence and certain explanations pointing towards foreign invisible hands seeking to undermine Pakistan. Indian involvement was repeatedly mentioned by government spokespersons, while speculating about other actors.

The situation within Pakistan became so bleak that the life of the common man was seriously affected. The elite was the prime target but the attacks on them also killed innocent citizens in large numbers. Panicked by the deteriorating law and order conditions, the educational institutions in Lahore were closed down in July 2009 as a result of threats issued by the Taliban. A sense of insecurity permeated throughout the country.

Besides the pervasive insecurity, the national security paradigm defined and held tightly by the Pakistan army appeared to have been punctured. The nuclear-armed state apparently faced real or exaggerated existential threats, attracting comments and debates regarding its survival.[4] Facing a virtual insurgency in the Malakand districts ("settled areas"), the Taliban asserted and took over most of these areas through force and violence. The writ of the government of Pakistan faded away and the Tehreek-e-Taliban Pakistan leader Maulvi Sufi Muhammad demanded the introduction of Islamic laws under the nomenclature of Nizam-e-Adl (Sharia-based justice system). The NWFP government negotiated the Nizam-e-Adl agreement on February 16, 2009, and it was approved by the national assembly of Pakistan and signed by President Asif Ali Zardari in order to have the stamp of legitimacy.[5] As the implementation process was underway, Sufi Muhammad issued statements disapproving the existing parliamentary system in Pakistan and demanded the introduction of an Islamic system in the entire country. The peace deal could not hold amidst heated controversy and contested claims of violation of the agreement by each side. Under mounting pressure from the US, coupled with the compulsion of domestic dynamics, the Pakistan army launched it's operation "Rah-e-Rast" (The Virtuous Path) on April 26, to re-establish the writ of the government of Pakistan. The military operation caused the displacement of over 2 million people. While this operation entered a conclusive stage on July 8, another operation — "Rah-e-Najat" — was "partially" launched in Waziristan, but full-scale attack is still on hold. If the military goes ahead with this plan, another wave of displaced persons seems imminent.

The conditions in Pakistan are threatening and critical. Pushed into military operation, the "war on terror" has become Pakistan's war of survival, as proclaimed by official spokespersons, including the Prime Minister Yousuf Raza Gillani. In addition to these operations, insurgency is prevalent in the Balochistan Province. The political parties belonging to the opposition are critical of government policies relating to the "war on terror." Food and energy shortages are other serious constraints on the capacity of the present government. The economic meltdown has forced the government to seek financial assistance from the International Monetary Fund just to sustain itself, but as a consequence it loses autonomy to make independent decisions. Whether the conditions of the IMF coincide with national interest or serve the interest of the donors is indeed a debatable issue. The Indian pressure in the wake of the Mumbai blasts of November 2008 is another issue to be addressed and surely strains Pakistan to stabilize itself internally and continue to fight the "war on terror." The interaction with the US is another stressful exercise — often requiring Pakistan to do things that are only correct from the American perspective.

Pakistan had fought in the past and is still fighting a proxy war stretching over 16 long years, besides pursuing an active role in Afghanistan and Kashmir during the 90s. Can a small to medium-size state like Pakistan, belonging to the developing world, square well with the regional and global agenda? Even the superpowers have manifested a fatigue syndrome after eight years (America in Vietnam and Soviets in Afghanistan), how justified would it be to expect Pakistan to continue in its role? This issue has never attracted the attention of policy-makers and think tanks in Washington.

As Pakistan stands on the crossroads of history, the issue of IDPs is testing its fatigued nerve and stamina. The tragedy is a fallout of politics pursued by domestic and foreign actors. This chapter seeks to make some sense out of the unfolding politics by examining the term IDP, the changed international scenario, the role of national and international actors and the capacity of the government to manage this unwieldy heavy agenda. It will be refreshing to remember the realist school formulation that politics is indeed "a struggle for power" and it is a continuing contest domestically and internationally. This struggle is directed to achieve "what, when and how" as Harold Lasswell, a noted American Political Scientist asserts.[6]

The Term "Internally Displaced Persons"

The term "IDPs," when relating to Pakistan, is understood as a reference to the people driven out of their homes as fallout of the military operation in Swat, Pakistan. Is the term just jargon used by UN bureaucrats along with national bureaucrats for their mutual convenience to operate a project or has it a basis in some international treaty or law? It is worth noting that there is no international treaty that applies specifically to IDPs. Recognizing this gap, the then UN Secretary General, Boutros Boutros-Ghali, appointed Francis Deng in 1992 as his representative for IDPs. In 1994, at the request of the UN General Assembly, Deng set out to examine and bring together existing international laws relating to the protection of the IDPs.[7] This resulting document spells out the responsibilities of status before, during and after displacement. They have been endorsed by the UN General Assembly, the African Commission on Human and Peoples" Rights (ACHPR) and by Sudan, the Democratic Republic of Congo and Uganda. Unfortunately for the IDPs, the "guiding principles" are non-binding. Bahame Tom Nyanduga, Special Rapporteur on Refugees, Asylum Seekers and Internally Displaced Persons in Africa for the ACHPR has stated, "the absence of a binding international legal regime on internal displacement is a grave lacuna in international law."[8] In September 2004, the then Secretary General of the UN demonstrated the continuing concern of his office by appointing Walter Lain as his representative on the human rights of internally displaced persons. Part of his mandate included the promotion of the "guiding principles."[9]

As the term "war on terror" has been crying out for a proper UN definition since 9/11, the phenomenon of "IDPs" lacks a legal regime also. The "guiding principles," which are not binding, leave a lot of open space for manipulations and interventions of many kinds, locally and internationally. This renders the task of IDP management problematic and in the process different actors play the game of politics, serving their particular interests. In some cases, the IDP phenomenon injects another irritant in the body politics on a continuous basis, to emerge as an issue in national, provincial and local politics.

It is pertinent to point out that states generally ignore or fail to observe these criteria. There is no evidence to suggest that the government of Pakistan or the Pakistan army made an assessment of the consequences of military action to be launched in the Malakand district or the Swat district. The armed clash with the militants uprooted more than 2 million people, who moved mostly in the vicinity of North-West Frontier Province, where no facilities existed to receive them. The US, which had been urging the government of Pakistan to take military action, either ignored or failed to advise the government to take necessary steps to deal with the consequences of the aforementioned military action. It was only in the aftermath of the tragedy that the government machinery moved to arrange tent accommodation, food and other basic facilities to sustain the affected persons.

There was no ready response from the UN or the international community to the human catastrophe that was unfolding. President Asif Ali Zardari appealed for global aid and said, "The civilians are losing their crops, they are losing their earnings, their livelihood and their homes, so we want the world to help us."[10]

It is unfortunate that the thinking process and subsequent actions to address the problems started after the tragedy. The situation in neighbouring Afghanistan is no better, where the numbers of IDPs are at least 235,000, which is 0.8 percent of the population. The newly displaced persons in 2008 are estimated to be over 42,000.[11]

The IDP crisis hit Pakistan while it was pursuing the American agenda of "war on terror," as a coalition partner. The Pakistani government, with its limited resources and management capabilities, is struggling to address the critical situation. The international community and the UN response came in slowly and remained inadequate, while the military action is still ongoing; the return of the IDPs has begun. What are the reconstruction plans for those returning without a home? Without serious socio-economic and political engineering, the situation has the potential of erupting in violence.

Should we use the term IDPs for people who were coerced to leave their homes to move to other places within their own country? Can we confer this status on them when there is no international legal regime governing their rights? How are these people to be treated in the absence of any national legislation in Pakistan? Are they not the citizens of Pakistan, enjoying the same rights enshrined in the constitution? These questions demand an urgent response from the national government and the international communities as the movement of these multitudes assumes different forms and manifestations in the wake of military operations. Surely, this raises questions about the prudence of government policy. Why is the government pursuing military action, while it fails to provide food, electricity and law enforcement in the midst of a fragile and precarious economy trapped in the conditions of the International Monetary Fund? The IDPs, even after their return, will certainly throw up problems to be addressed by the local, provincial and national governments, injecting many issues into the politics of Pakistan.

Paradigm Shift in Global Politics

The collapse of the Soviet Union in 1990 is interpreted as the end of the

Cold War era (1946–90). A nuclear superpower imploded in the most unprecedented and unceremonial way. Even the brilliant Sovietologists in Washington were taken by surprise. The unexpected event had no parallel in human history. This was proclaimed as the triumph of capitalism and democracy over communism, which also signified the end of the political divide of the globe on the basis of ideology.

When the Cold War paradigm ended abruptly, the emerging realities in its wake challenged the academics and political leaders alike, to formulate a new construct to explain global politics. In this transition phase, there was competition between different expressions and terms attempting to make sense of the post-1990 world. Francis Fukuyama coined the term "End of History," but this theory failed to capture attention and became irrelevant within a year.[12] George Bush Senior used the expression "New World Order" during "Operation Desert Storm" to describe the global politics without desalinating its features.[13] Very soon, the White House stopped referring to it, thereby causing the problem of its acceptance and legitimacy. However, academics started writing articles and books to explain the New World Order. Samuel P. Huntington theorized in an article that appeared in 1993 entitled "The Clash of the Civilizations," projecting the future global conflicts/fault lines through clashes between civilizations.[14]

These attempts fell short of describing the emerging realities. The new concepts and expressions traded and competed for acceptance by the policy-makers. The transition phase led to tentative but seemingly indefinitive policy responses generating uncertainties of sorts.

This conceptualization transition ended when the "globalization" paradigm was inaugurated, with some clear features. It had three components — political, economic and military. The "political" implied that the future form and shape of the world will be one of democracy and human rights. In economic terms, the policies will be characterized by free-market economy, privatization and deregulation. Militarily, the emphasis will be on denuclearization and disarmament.

Without making any significant achievement in the military and political context, the much-trumpeted economic achievements of the past 15 years have melted into global recession. The US, as the leader of this paradigm, is the worst hit and the economies of other countries are experiencing its impact in a variety of ways. Needless to say, the developing countries are the worst hit, with food insecurity and violence.

As the policy initiatives of the globalization paradigm failed to register any significant success, another aspect of global politics is facing challenges and serious resistance. With the demise of the Soviet Union, the "bipolar" world order gave way to "unipolarity."

The current power configuration of the world system is one of unipolarity without hegemony. Non-hegemonic unipolarity is little understood but deserves indepth study. The hypothesis that the US is the leader of the unipolar system, acting as a hegemon or non-hegemon, deserves careful study and analysis. What evidence do we have in favour of the hypothesis of US hegemony? The removal and installation of governments in Panama and Haiti; the restoration of order in Bosnia; good offices and mediation in Northern Ireland; subsidies to reward actions in the Middle East and consensual command in the Persian Gulf and the Kosovo operation. It is also true that the collective military action by major powers seems impossible in most places without American leadership and participation. The internal policies of many states bear prints of American influence and through institutions like the International Monetary Fund and the World Bank, which have a strong American presence.

Let us now examine the evidence against the hypothesis that the US is now the system-wide hegemon. US failure to restore order in Somalia and Colombia, to prevent nuclear proliferation in India, Pakistan and North Korea and threats/sanctions failed to produce the desired change in Iran regarding its nuclear programme, removed Saddam Hussain in Iraq at what cost and the manner it is withdrawing from the scene. America cannot push Japan, France and the European Union to change economic policies nor can it discipline China on human rights policies. Also it did not succeed in ensuring actual compliance with, rather than expressed respect for actual compliance regarding drug, trade and sanction policies.

In contemporary times, the globalization paradigm is failing and the American attempts to operationalize don't inspire confidence. Unipolarity with a hegemon also appears to be problematic. In fact, most of the evidence that might he offered to prove the existence of US hegemony is to be found in American relationships with small- and medium-size powers. Even in this context, the record is mixed. The defiance demonstrated by Iran in recent times is a glaring example.

It will be pertinent here to examine and evaluate Pakistan-US relations in the context of America as a hegemon. In 1990, President Bush refused to issue a certificate stating that Pakistan was not pursuing its nuclear program, thereby invoking the Symington Amendment to suspend the military and economic assistance to Pakistan. During the summer of 1993, the US media became active in labeling Pakistan as a "failed state." This pressure was mounted to discourage Pakistan from advancing its nuclear programme. This made hardly any impression on the Benazir and Nawaz governments during the 1990s. The US policy was discriminatory, as it ignored Indian efforts to acquire nuclear capability. When India tested a nuclear device in 1998, Pakistan followed and again the Clinton administration failed to deter the Nawaz government. Pakistan conducted the tests and sanctions were slapped on Pakistan and India. Thus on the nuclear issue, the US failed to act as a hegemon.

After the military takeover by General Musharraf on October 12, 1999, and since 9/11, the nature of relationship between the two countries changed. Musharraf, who was struggling for legitimacy at home and acceptance abroad, found the US offer too tempting. In a 20-minute telephone conversation with foreign secretary Collin Powell, Musharraf agreed to "all the demands" to become a coalition partner in the "war on terror."

The post-9/11 phase suggests that the US is conducting itself as a hegemon in directing and controlling the decisions and events in Pakistan. The military assistance of US$11 billion and non-NATO ally status were the incentives offered by the US to assume a dominant role in the military strategy as it increased its enhanced power and leverage to influence the decision-making in the domestic politics of Pakistan.

Over the last 29 years, Pakistan has been grappling with the problem of Afghan refugees and now it is up against IDPs. How long it will take to rehabilitate these multitudes is an open question, keeping in view the past track record. A restive and frustrated people such as these are vulnerable for the opponents to exploit. The refusal of the governments of Sindh and Punjab to receive these uprooted people injects yet another lethal dimension to the already strained inter-provincial relations and the hostile sentiments of the minority provinces towards the federal government. The issue of IDPs has many more serious implications, rendering the task of governance very difficult.

Sharing a "common" long unguarded border with Afghanistan, the military operations there had the inevitable consequences for Pakistan. Why this dimension was not considered by the decision-makers remains an open and controversial issue. The safe havens for al–Qaeda, the Taliban and the emergence of the Pakistani Taliban in the northern areas of Pakistan changed the dynamics of this war. The spate of suicide bombing and challenges to the writ of the Pakistan government finally drove the army of Pakistan to launch decisive military action in Swat and other settled districts of the northern areas. This is what caused the tragedy of IDPs.

The continued military operation made the government of Pakistan own this war. It was declared to be Pakistan's war and it is intriguing to see this transition from proxy war to the stated position today. Prior to reaching this stage, the US administration was pushing Pakistan "to do more." The pressure under this mantra had the desired results in pushing the army to a full-scale operation under the "legitimate" democratically elected government after February 18, 2008. It is intriguing to note that Musharraf was sustained during two years of lawyer's movements against him. Even the entry of Benazir and others in the political process was brokered through the Anglo-American initiatives including the "National Reconciliation Ordinance," whitewashing the acts of omission and commission by the politicians. The newly elected government imposed "Governor Raj" in the Province of Punjab to frustrate the attempts to restore judiciary to its pre-November 2008 position. The present political setup, actualized through the elections, continues with the same policies of Musharraf. The drone attacks flying out from the Pakistani bases to target al-Qaeda and Taliban hideouts in northern areas kill some elements but cause collateral damage, killing men, women and children in large numbers. This inevitably fuels anti-American sentiment. The drone issue is a major irritant and has embarrassed the government on a routine basis for the last two or so years. Starting from Musharraf's later years, the drone attacks have become more frequent in the last two months. Even the National Assembly has passed a resolution against drone attacks but this failed to make any impression on US administration. However, there is a perception that Musharraf and the present government allowed these attacks under an arrangement. Engaged in this war since 9/11, Pakistan's economy is badly hurt, the implications of global recession notwithstanding. This forces Pakistan to accept the IMF loan, along with its conditions. These funds are barely sufficient to keep Pakistan afloat. The Friends of Democratic Pakistan pledged over US$5 billion in a Tokyo meeting, but the money has yet to come. The Kerry-Lugar Bill assuring US$1.5 billion annually for the non-military sectors, with its conditions in fact make Pakistan lose its autonomy in decision-making. The interaction between Pakistan and the US surely suggests the latter's role as a hegemon.

The consequences of this hegemonic relationship have been difficult to fathom. Pakistan certainly was not a fit candidate to assume the role of a "frontline state." This engagement over the last eight years has disrupted its institutional, economic and political growth. It has manifested in a precarious law and order situation, poor economic conditions and an uncertain political environment. A nuclear-armed state seems most vulnerable and faces existential threat. With such poor indicators, it is intriguing that Pakistan has been pushed to "own" this war without the necessary support systems in place or the provision of adequate economic and military assistance, if it is compared with the American and NATO forces expenditure in Afghanistan. While the hegemon is getting ready to penetrate the domestic scene of Pakistan more deeply (Kerry-Lugar Bill), the policy issues governing this region present another perplexing puzzle.

Policy Conundrum — the American Perspective

The US invaded Afghanistan after 9/11 to punish al-Qaeda and remove the Taliban regime, which protected Osama bin Laden and his organization. Riding on the forces of the Northern Alliance (opposing the Taliban regime) the US installed anti-Taliban forces in Kabul. This was a non-Pushtun minority outfit to rule over the majority of Pushtun population; not the best beginning for an invading occupying force.

The other unorthodox feature of this military venture was that it was not a conventional war. A superpower targeted a non-state actor. Accordingly, the war design, planning and execution should have reflected such an approach to war. Robert Bunker, a counter-terrorist expert, describes criminal challengers to nation state (al Qaeda and Taliban) and argues that "the process involves the territorial shell of a dead nation-state, one with no central authority and devoid of state institutions, being overrun by non-state groups — such as landlords, armed gangs and drug cartels — that fill the power vacuum that develops."[15] In social sciences, it is asserted that without a theory the facts are silent. Where is theory though as facts are in hand? Where are the lessons of the Vietnam War and the jihad against the Red Army? Where is the policy response taking into consideration the reality on ground?

Another perceptive observation by Clausewitz's claims, "we see, therefore, that war is not merely an act of policy but a true political instrument, a continuation of political intercourse, carried on with other means."[16] Where is the political instrument? In a country ravaged by war for decades, an attempt was made to plant the semblance of democracy in a tribal society. Any student of comparative politics would refer to the political culture. The political system must be congruent/compatible with the political culture. There is a disconnection in the system, inhibiting it to perform its functions. Consequently, the Hamid Karzai government does not function beyond Kabul and conditions within the capital are far from satisfactory. The elections held recently lack legitimacy, as the Taliban and its nationalist allies reject the vote as fraud designed to validate foreign occupation and open the way for Western oil and gas pipelines.[17] Even the Obama administration is not happy with President Karzai for presiding over a corrupt administration but there is apparently no alternative. Amid charges of fraud and rigging, this election will add more problems to the already intractable situation. While President Obama contemplates another major military operation, the political instrument is not effective to address the issues.

The policy confusion further deepened when a South Asia expert and academic, Stephen Phillip Cohen stated, "the war on terror is not global [belies American official policy]. It is not all about terror. It is (sic) merely advertising slogans of the US administration [in order] to make its way in the world"[18] In fact, Cohen is testifying to the imperial agenda of the US under the cover of a slogan. Do we take Cohen's statement seriously or pay heed to President Obama's General Assembly speech that the US alone cannot fix the problems of the world. This is a hint for greater cooperation and suggests a withdrawal from the single leadership position.

It is an interesting exercise to look at the actors in the conflict. The US is the major actor with its imperial or "terror"-centered agenda. Pakistan as a coalition partner agreed to American demands yet has national interest-driven preferences that may not coincide with US decisions. Afghanistan, which is in occupation, has internal divisions along tribal, ethnic, religious and geographical lines. The Indian presence and its increasing influence in Kabul complicate the equation with Pakistan. Iran discreetly fishes in the troubled waters. Russia is smiling and hopes for a repeat in Afghanistan. Amid these fault lines there can be no coherent policy to be implemented. Hence US failure to control Afghanistan is understandable.

America has relied on its superior military power to address the problem. US Army General Stanley McChrystal states in his report to President Obama that "the eight year old war would end in a failure without additional troops."[19] This suggests a continuation of the current policies. This would hardly be successful, as military power has its limits and has to be supplemented by genuine political initiatives to have a legitimate government. In the absence of the latter, military action would be counter-productive and inevitably expand the conflict zones to the disadvantage of all actors, particularly Pakistan.

Pakistani Perspective

Pakistan was coerced into a "coalition partner" position on the "war on terror" and was labeled a "frontline state," and subsequently non-NATO member status was conferred on it. These labels are misnomers, as it was never treated as a partner or as a meaningful non-NATO member. Sucked into this situation, its actions became subservient to the US acting as a hegemon.

Political Order in Changing Societies, a pioneering work of Samuel P. Huntington' in the 1960s, was the set text for students of political development studies in the last three decades of the twentieth century. His concern was not the creation of states, which had the stamp of international approval because the ruling clique supported the policies of those in power in Washington. The key to state stability, according to him, was of the building of a domestic consensus, a sense of political community and establishing a government with popular legitimacy. The level of political community a society achieves reflects the relationship between its political institutions and the social forces that comprise it.[20]

The fallout of the 1980s and the current engagement have compounded the problems in Pakistan. The internal problems of governance have their own dynamics and they have been aggravated to critical proportions because of external variables. The issues of food and energy crises, the law and order situation, a poor economy, democracy in transition, subservience to the hegemon, institutional malfunctioning and political instability are deepening the crisis. The army is engaged in the war in Swat without enjoying popular support.

This presents, to say the least, a depressing and disappointing situation. The critical point is reached as there is no legitimate locus of authority in the political system. The emergence of powerful media and the restoration of a powerful judiciary have increased the power centers struggling to acquire legitimacy in the system. The other power centers like Parliament and Cabinet are in this race. The President wishes to continue with the same powers that Musharraf enjoyed. Through military action, the army is seeking to reclaim its image and reputation, which was badly tarnished by Musharraf. In this dangerous competition among power centers, there seems no one strong enough to blow the whistle if the situation gets out of hand. Without apportioning blame for the present explosive and precarious conditions, Pakistan's engagement in the proxy wars contributed substantially to the ongoing mess.

Conclusion

The IDPs present merely one minor dimension of the ongoing conflict, with serious implications for Pakistan within and without. The nature and dynamics of the conflict include much more than what meets the eye. The historical forces have turned topsy-turvy in the present explosive situation. The dialectical movement of this conflict is both intriguing and puzzling. Because of the protracted nature of the conflict, many more elements have entered to frustrate the initiatives towards its resolution.

Jihadi culture was enacted in 1980 and the Taliban were nurtured, energized, financed, equipped and trained by a (Western-led) US in concert with

Saudis and the Gulf States to fight the Red Army in Afghanistan, which was an "occupation force." Emboldened by the victory, the Taliban moved to assume power in Kabul in 1995 and exercise control over 90 percent of the Afghan territory. Post-9/11 saw an invading US force overthrow the Taliban government and since then the US has been viewed as an "occupation force." Once an ally of the West in the struggle against an "evil empire" (Reagan's expression for the former Soviet Union) now the Taliban are designated as evil. This is seen as "betrayal" by the Taliban, which acquires deeper meaning in tribal culture. The US commitment to construct a modern state in Afghanistan, where one has never existed, appears to be highly misplaced. It is a project that would most likely last many years, cost hundreds of billions of dollars and entail the deaths of many more Western troops, and massive destruction and deaths on the other side. And yet there is no success guaranteed in this venture.

The policy conundrum seems to be deepening, causing more fault lines to hamper a coherent, consensus-based agenda being operationalized in the region. As a unipolar world order hegemon, the US is facing many uneasy situations around the world, and the differences have come to the fore in Afghanistan and Pakistan. The political situation in Afghanistan after the rigged elections of August 2009 poses a serious threat to the political order and its future prospects. This adds to the complexities and the apparatus for implementing decisions will be inadequate, and it also lacks legitimacy. The nation-building efforts in this war zone dried up any meaning that the word "aid" generally has.

The confusion of how to deal with Pakistan is compounded by the inability of US policy-makers to distinguish a post-colonial modern state from tribal Afghanistan. The Obama Administration's "Af-Pak" policy of equating the two as one socio-cultural entity is highly misleading and is not owned by Pakistan. Amid controversies over policy, the Kerry-Lugar Bill attracted widespread public outcry, putting the Zardari government on the defensive. Any support of the Bill further undermines the already low level of legitimacy of the regime. It is ironic that the US finds itself on the wrong side of public opinion when it supports either dictatorial dispensation of General Musharraf or the present democratically elected government in Pakistan. The dialectical movement between the anti-American public opinion and the government support for American policies is causing political instability of sorts. A national policy lacking public support can hardly be a successful enterprise.

The war on terror and the phenomenon of IDPs proceed without any international legal regime. The imperial reach of the US, the regional approach, the competing and conflicting perspectives of major and covert players of the conflict, the recent ambivalent stance of the Obama Administration regarding future policy and the declining legitimacy of governments in Kabul and Islamabad are sources of confusion that are getting more confounded.

The ongoing conflict has already demonstrated the limits of military power or its overkill capacity without achieving the stated objectives. The missing and significant link in this enterprise is the political instrument. The governments in Islamabad and Kabul are suffering from political instability, which is further aggravated by the American support, widening the gulf between the people and the political dispensation. Samuel P. Huntington's prescription offers the way out from this cruel and messy situation. There is a need to build domestic consensus imbibing a sense of political community and ensuring a government that enjoys popular legitimacy. In the absence of a political order that connects people with government, the policy suffers from confusion, accentuating the governance crisis.

Pakistan is facing the consequences and challenges of this persisting conflict. Being an epicenter of terrorism now, the relevance of Pakistan as "frontline state" has lost its meaning. Engaged in the proxy war and now its own war, Pakistan has been badly shaken. The weak and exhausted state is up against multi-faceted challenges. Is this the destruction of the state? There appears to be no sign of immediate victory or exit strategy. Pakistan has landed in a bottomless quagmire.

Notes

1   Lord Paddy Ashdown, "International Law, Justice and Reconciliation in a Changing World," The Eighth Hauser Lecture on International Humanitarian Law, New York, March 3, 2004. See also B. Denitch's view that Dayton was a "terrible peace to end a terrible war," Postscript, in *Ethnic Nationalism: The Tragic Death of Yugoslavia* (rev. ed.). Minneapolis: University of Minnesota Press, 1996.

2 See for example, M. Kaldor, "One year After Dayton," in "Dayton Continued in Bosnia Herzegovina" in *The Hague: Helsinki Citizen's Assembly Publication Series* 11, 1997, pp. 28–30.

3 Ashdown, op. cit.

4 Sajjad Naseer, "Perspective on Political Kingdom," *Business Recorder*, Pakistan, August 14, 2009.

5 *The Nation*, February 17, 2009.

6 Harold Lasswell, *Politics: Who gets What, When, How.* New York: Whittlessey House, McGraw Hill, 1936.

7 Roberta Cohen in Anthony J. Marsella, *Fear of Persecution: Global Human Rights, International Law and Human Well-being.* Lexington, MA: Lexington Books, 2007.

8 Bohame Tom Nyanduga, "The challenge of international displacement ion Africa" (PDF) *Forced Migration Review* 21, September 2004.

9 Mandate, UNHCHR. Available at: http:/www.ohchr.org/English/issues/idp/mandae. htm (accessed October 24, 2009).

10 "Pakistan seeks world aid for IDPs," May 13, 2009. Available at: www.pakpoint.com/, posted by 123456 in Headline, News and Views.

11 IDMC: Internal Displacement Monitoring Centre, Global Overview 2008, p. 58. Available at: http://www.internaldisplacement.org/8025708f004BDODA3E2B69E88 2EDO (accessed July 15, 2009).

12 Sajjad Naseer, *South Asian Perceptions of National and Regional Security: Demand and Validity in Security in Europe and South Asia: Challenges and Options for the Twenty-First Century*, edited by Naveed Ahmad Tahir, Area Study Centre for Europe, University of Karachi, Summer 2000, p. 210.

13 Joseph Nye, "New World Order," Spring 1992, Foreign Affairs.

14 Samuel P. Huntington, "Clash of Civilizations," Summer 1993, Foreign Affairs.

15 Robert J Bunker (ed.) *Criminal-States and Criminal-Soldiers.* London: Routledge, 2008.

16 Khalid Ahmed of Carl von Clausewitz and "asymmetric war," book review August 2, 2009. Available at: http://groups.yahoo.com/group/cmk-Pak/message/15954

17 Eric S. Margolis, "Afghanistan Needs Peace-Making, Not Phony Polls," *Daily Times*, August 25, 2009.

18 "War on terror advertising slogan of the US Govt", *Khaleej Times*, http://www.khaleej-times.com/display article new.asp?col=]&section=subcontinent&xfile= . . . March 19, 2009.

19 Steve Holland, "It's up to Obama to decide on Afghanistan," *Dawn*, Lahore, September, 10, 2009.

20 Samuel P. Huntington, *Political Order in Changing Societies.* New Haven and London: Yale University Press, 1968, p. 8.

CHAPTER NINE

The Prospect of a Populist Islamist Takeover of Pakistan

Julian Schofield

Abstract

There is widespread concern that Pakistan may fall prey, with its nuclear arsenal, to extremist Islamist elements. The author considers the likelihood of three paths to this outcome: Islamist civil war (the current situation in the NWFP), Islamist revolution (the Iranian model), and an Islamist electoral victory (the Algerian model). The overall assessment is that the strength of Pakistan's bureaucracy combined with the autonomy of the military and its intelligence services make all of the scenarios unlikely. The Islamist civil war scenario considers the impact of a primarily Pashtun assault on the state of Pakistan. Important factors in this case are the historical precedents for both Pashtun and Jihadist penetration into the Punjab. The Islamist revolution examines the prospects of a mass uprising along the Iranian model in the Punjab. In this case, the balance of Deobandi versus Barelwi allegiance and violence, and the level of influence of Islamist Punjabi centers are considered. In the Islamist electoral model, a survey is done of historical successes and failures of Islamist parties in Pakistan, under different regional and ethnic contexts.

Introduction

In 2009 US Central Command General David Petraeus warned that Pakistan could be overwhelmed if it did not resist the Taliban.[1] Counter-insurgency expert David Kilcullen predicted that Pakistan could fall within six months once the Taliban were within 100 km of Islamabad.[2] US Secretary of State

Hillary Clinton and Harvard nuclear expert Graham Allison warned that if Pakistan were to fall, its nuclear arms could fall into the hands of the Taliban.[3] Though the crisis has passed since the Pakistan army re-established control of Swat in mid-2009, the immediate concern was what the consequences of the ongoing insurgency in the Pashtun areas would be on the widely characterized "failing" state of Pakistan.[4] More broadly there is a worry that Pakistan, the leading nuclear proliferator, could succumb to an Islamist government.

In this chapter, I explore three paths to an Islamist Pakistan.[5] First, the Islamist civil war scenario considers the impact of a primarily Pashtun assault on the state of Pakistan. Second, the Islamist revolutionary scenario examines the prospects of a mass uprising, along the lines of an Iranian revolution, in the Punjab. Third, the Islamist electoral model investigates the likelihood of Islamists achieving democratic success, along the lines of Algeria and Turkey. These scenarios are all based on a similar chain of events that ends with the Pakistani state and by extension, its nuclear arsenal, in the control of Islamists. My overall assessment, however, is that the strength of Pakistan's bureaucracy combined with the autonomy of the military and its intelligence services render all three scenarios unlikely. Most of the exaggerated fears of a Pakistani collapse have been widely criticized by regional experts as based on paranoia and a cartoonish ignorance of the structure of Pakistani state and society.[6] Furthermore, I will suggest that the military remains firmly in control of these Islamist elements as instruments of Pakistan's domestic and foreign policy.

First Scenario: Pakistani Civil War

Pakistan's current hostilities with the Taliban in the Northwest Frontier Province (NWFP) are the latest expression of the underlying aspirations and assertions of Pashtun nationalism. Though this current manifestation is in the form of a religious insurgency, it is similar in many respects to a civil war within Pakistan because of the scale of the resistance and the extent of territory held and administered by the Taliban. A Taliban victory war could have serious implications for the domestic role of Sharia law, and for the foreign policy of Pakistan. Pakistan's quick defeat of the Taliban in Swat demonstrates the overwhelming firepower of even a brigade-sized deployment of the Pakistan army, but less aggressively prosecuted operations elsewhere show that Pakistan is worried about provoking widespread Pashtun hostility. The prospect of a Taliban victory in this civil war is remote for three reasons: the strength of the Pakistan military, the containment of the insurgency in Pashtun areas, and the diversity of political ideas among the Pashtun.

The Pakistan Army

The military is coercively the strongest single grouping in Pakistan society, possessing over 600,000 troops (with their dependents, and retirees, and economically-associated populations probably exceeding 10 million), 2,400 tanks, 4,200 pieces of artillery, 380 combat aircraft, warships, submarines, strategic rockets and nuclear weapons. It is an army designed for the singular purpose of repelling an invasion from India, six times its size in population. The army has extensive counter-insurgency experience in the tribal regions, Balochistan, and East Pakistan in 1971, where 40,000 soldiers dominated 75 million people. Pakistan has 112,000 soldiers and paramilitaries in the tribal areas,[7] of which about half are the Frontier Corps and Frontier Constabulary. As of late 2009, Pakistan has had slow but firm success in Bajaur, Mohmand and Swat.[8] The Taliban, a predominantly Pashtun movement numbering no more than a few thousand, probably a few tens of thousands if sympathetic tribal militias are included, and armed only with infantry weapons, can at best only hope for survival in the rugged mountains of the tribal areas.

The material costs to Pakistan are minor compared to the damage the conflict has done to the reputation of Pakistan among the Pashtun Tribals. Since operations began in 2004, Pakistan has lost a few hundred soldiers, comparable to what it lost in fighting in 1960s suppressing an earlier Pashtun uprising in Dir.[9] However, Pakistan has suffered a significant loss to its influence in the tribal regions because of its support to US and NATO operations in Afghanistan.[10] It lacks the local support it needs to collect the intelligence used to govern the FATA (Federally Administered Tribal Areas), particularly the impact the Taliban have had on the traditional mullah-malik relationship in the region.[11] While very effective against foreign militants, the tribal militias, Frontier Constabulary and Frontier Corps are composed primarily of local Pashtun, and are therefore reluctant to act against their ethnic kin.[12] The army is constrained by the over-representation of Pashtuns in the Inter-Services Intelligence Agency (at 30–40 percent),[13] by its 22–25 percent share of the officer corps, and 22 percent share of the soldiery.[14] The army does not want a replay of its 1970 split, when its Bengali soldiers deserted en masse, ultimately splitting the country in two. Despite this restraint, the over 2 million Pashtun refugees produced by Pakistan's limited actions have weakened its popular support.[15] As late as 2009, the Pakistan legislature has consequently sought to negotiate with local Taliban leaders, with mixed results.[16]

Since 2007, the main Taliban response has been the use of terrorism, including suicide bombings, targeting parts of Pakistan facilitated by substantial Pashtun minorities, such Rawalpindi, Lahore and the Pakistan Ordnance Factories headquarters at Wah, in the Punjab, and cities adjacent to the NWFP like Dera Ghazi Khan.[17] Suicide bombings jumped from six in 2006 to 56 in 2007, and higher still in 2008.[18] Some project that the Taliban could strike large industrial targets like the Tarbela Dam, or shut down the airport and highway around Peshawar.[19]

Pashtun Ethnic Nationalism

The Taliban are overwhelmingly a tribal Pashtun movement, and are consequently restricted to the tribal areas of the NWFP.[20] While they have the ethnic sympathies of other Pashtun, such as the settled and more economically developed populations of Yusufzai, the Usman Kel, or Kataka, their Salafist lifestyles make them unpopular, and thus limit their appeal.[21] The essentially ethnic nature of the Taliban alienates the ethnically, religiously and linguistically diverse populations in Afghanistan and Pakistan.[22] Taliban chauvinism has, for example, led to the failure to unite with the adjacent Baloch, who share an even greater hostility to the Pakistan state, with their nearly continuous history of insurgent resistance: 1948, 1958–59, 1962–63, 1973–77, and 2002–2009+.[23] The Taliban phenomenon is a combination of the displaced youth of the Afghan uprisings beginning in 1974, propelled by the religious funding of overseas South Asian Muslims and coercive or absent governance of the tribal areas by Pakistan government agencies.[24]

The Taliban has come to control most of the marginalized Pashtun areas of Afghanistan and Pakistan because it has understood local politics, appeals to Pashtun cultural sensibilities (Pashtunwali), especially with regards to self-governance and autonomy, and has promised to reinstate Pashtun dominance in both Kabul and the NWFP.[25] For example, at least some of the Taliban's appeal in Swat was that it sought to replace the corrupted system of "Anglo-Saxon" law imposed by the Pakistani state in 1969, with Nizam-e-Adl (Rule of Justice), which is Pashtun customary law integrated with Sharia.

The Pakistan Taliban, or Tehrek-e-Taliban, in conjunction with al Qaeda, seeks the ambitious goal of establishing an Islamic state in Pakistan and Afghanistan.[26] This bravado is, however, based on centuries-old memories of opportunities no longer obtainable. A Pashtun homeland was created by a rare coincidence of the simultaneous decline of the Uzbek, Safavid Persian and Mughal Indian empires in the early eighteenth century.[27] Under Ahmad Shah, the Pashtuns defeated the Marathis in 1761 and the Sikhs at Lahore the following year, expanding from Afghanistan into the Sindh and Punjab. However, the re-emergence of the Sikhs in the Punjab reduced the independent Pashtuns to modern-day Afghanistan by 1818.[28] Syed Ahmad's subsequent attempt to conquer the Punjab resulted in the complete defeat of his 100,000 Pashtun army by a much smaller force of Sikhs in 1831 at Balakot.[29] Another attempted jihad by Maulana Obaidullah Sindhi, with an army of 100,000 against the British in 1919, failed as dramatically and quickly.[30] Thereafter, aside from raids by lashkars seeking plunder, and the invitation of 7,000 tribal warriors to intervene in Kashmir in 1947, no significant Pashtun military force has ever crossed over to the east side of the Indus River.[31] This is because the Pashtun have simply become too weak compared to the industrialization of the settled Punjab and Sindh, and those in Afghanistan have become hemmed in between Pakistan, Iran and the Central Asian allies of Russia. Most of the Pashtun who do travel to the rest of Pakistan come as economic migrants and settle in the poorer urban areas of Karachi and the Punjab.

Pashtun Diversity

Although Pashtuns on both sides of the Durand Line share a mutual affinity, and consequently resist any recognition of the Pakistan-Afghan border, they express their search for autonomy through a diversity of political views that precludes the possibility of an overarching Taliban victory.[32] For example, Abdul Ghaffar Khan was the pre-eminent leader of the Pashtun immediately prior to Partition in 1947, and he rejected a separate Muslim homeland and sought instead to join India to avoid Punjabi domination. Though not a mullah, he was a devout Muslim, who also embraced the pacifist views of Hindu Mohandas Gandhi. His grandson, Asfandyar Wali Khan, is a member of the Awami National Party, a largely secular but historically Marxist (and atheist) organization, which is currently the elected government of the NWFP (and ironically a strong supporter of negotiated truces with the Taliban). President Hamid Karzai of Afghanistan is an adherent to the Naqshbandiyah order of Sufism, underlying the alternatives to the Deobandi-inspired Hanafi tradition of the Taliban.[33] Gulbadin Hikmatyar, one of the original Islamist revolutionaries who triggered the civil war in Afghanistan in 1974–75, and who opposed the Taliban for their lack of indignity, has re-emerged as one of the main opponents to the Western presence.[34] It was in an interview with a Western journalist that Hikmatyar conceded that at the root of all Pashtun movements is not religion, but nationalism.[35]

Pakistan has relied on this diversity to neutralize both Pashtun nationalism and Afghan support for this nationalism. Beginning with Partition in 1947, Pakistan backed religious leaders such as Sardar Ibrahim, who usually reject narrow nationalist definitions of identity, to offset the Pashtun resistance to the formation of Pakistan.[36] In 1973, following the coup of Daud Mohammad in Kabul (who had a history of supporting irredentism among the Pashtun), Pakistan backed militant Islamists to destabilize Afghanistan.[37] Pakistan continued to support the Taliban after the defeat of the Afghan communists to counter Indian interests and to undermine Afghan proclivities to influence the Pashtun in Pakistan.[38] Pakistan continues to indirectly support the Taliban, fearing that its total defeat in either Afghanistan or Pakistan would lead the Pashtun to successfully consolidate their nationalist claims, and to more immediately counter Indian interests, which Western agencies have admitted are providing aid to Baloch resistance against the Pakistan government.[39]

Second Scenario: The Jihadist Revolution

Some Islamist proponents, such as ex-ISI Director General Hamid Gul, have described an Islamic revolution in Pakistan as inevitable.[40] Such a revolution would erupt from a jihadist insurgency coordinating a mass of disaffected citizenry, brushing aside an illegitimate and disorganized state and military. To have a chance of success, it would have to erupt from within the Punjab, Pakistan's demographic, industrial, military and political core, and would have to appeal to the Punjabis, who constitute nearly two-thirds of the army's officers and half of its soldiery.[41] Its nucleus could be any one of a number of Punjabi movements, and augmented by Pashtun jihadists, who have had links with Punjabi militants since at least the 1980s.[42] In fact nearly 10 percent of militants in the NWFP and nearly half of those in Kashmir are Punjabis trained by these groups.[43] These include the Tableeghi Jama't or Lashkar-e-Tayyiba, both of which have a strong presence in the Punjab, the Harakat-ul-Mujahideen Al-alami group (believed to be responsible for the assassination attempts on Pakistan President Pervaiz Musharraf in 2002 and 2003), or the Tehreek-e-Nifaz-e-Shariat-e-Muhammadi, which seeks to emulate the Taliban, Lashkar-e-Jhangvi, or the Jama't ul-Fuqra, all of which espouse some form of totalitarian theocracy.[44] They may be inspired by the jihad of Maulana Muhammad Qasim Nanautawi, a Deobandi scholar, who took up arms against the British, or the Wahhabist Ahl-e-Hadith, who are followers of Syed Ahmad.[45] These jihadists are emboldened by the apprehension within the military that disarming these sectarian militias could provoke an uprising.[46] Nor may the military resist them if the recent trend continues of recruiting officers from the Islamist urban south of the Punjab rather than from the conservative rural north.[47]

A violent Islamic revolution seeking to impose a theocracy in Pakistan, along the lines of events in Iran in the late 1970s, is unlikely because at present there is no force able to unify the assorted Islamist groups, which are often in rivalry.[48] One estimate suggests there are approximately 245 religious parties in Pakistan: 215 have their own seminaries, 104 focus on jihad (mostly non-violent), 82 are sectarian, 20 are oriented towards tabligh (preaching) and 28 take part in the political process, of which the most significant are the Barelwi Jamiat-i-Islami, and the Deobandi Jamiat-e-Ulema. The most significant cleavages preventing Islamist solidarity are between Sunni and Shia (there are over 40 million Shia in Pakistan, predominantly in the Punjab, Sindh and around Peshawar), among the Hanafi Sunni it is the cleavage between

Barelwi (60 million) and Deobandi (20 million), and finally the Sindhi, who number 30 million, practice a form of syncretic Islam offensive to most of the Salafist organizations. Pakistan President Zia ul-Haq, with funding from overseas Pakistanis and Gulf Arab states, strengthened Sipah-e-Sahab, (SSP) a counter-revolutionary and anti-Shia organization, to offset shock waves from the Islamic Shia revolution in Iran.[49] Nearly 4,000 Shia have died in sectarian violence since then, more than have been killed in Pakistan by the Taliban.

The Taliban is itself inspired by the Deobandi tradition whose foundation in 1867 was in order to inspire Muslims to organize against British occupation of South Asia in the wake of the defeated Great Mutiny. It has displaced the Barelwi's in Kashmir and Afghanistan, but because of its strong support among the Pashtun, it has little legitimacy in the Punjab or the Sindh.[50] Jamiat-i-Islami, the most socially influential religious organization in Pakistan, and Barelwi, faces a similar problem since most of the senior leaders are Pashtun, and therefore have limited appeal among the Punjabi majority of Pakistan (despite its vociferous condemnation of the Taliban).[51] Similarly, Lashkar-e-Tayyiba, for all its prominence as a terror group and lavish support from the Pakistani Diaspora and the Gulf Arab states, is based on the Ahl-e-Hadith sect that has no more than 4 million adherents.[52] The most effective sectarian organization in Pakistan is the MQM (Muttahida Quomi Movement), which is defined by ethnicity (Muhajir) and language (Urdu) rather than religion (though it paradoxically espouses the most widely supported conception of Pan-Islam in Pakistan). It is responsible for approximately 1,500 deaths over the past 20 years, fought the Pakistani army to a standstill in Karachi in the 1990s, and continues its electoral dominance of Karachi, Pakistan's largest city.[53]

Furthermore, many Islamist groups depend on the Pakistani intelligence services, specifically the Joint Intelligence Bureau of the ISI, for financial support.[54] Some were promoted by the military in the 1970s to counteract perceived threats of Zulfikar Ali Bhutto's socialism, the shock of the Iranian (Shia) revolution, to mobilize resistance to the Soviet occupation in Afghanistan, and later to generate recruits for Kashmir.[55] To counter Bhutto populist socialism, the military backed the formation of the Islami Jamhuri Etihad (IJI), led by conservative non-Islamist politicians, but with its ideology defined by Jamaat-e-Islami.[56] Pakistan came closest to a radical political movement, albeit a secular one, with the anti-Western-oriented socialist government of Zulfikar Ali Bhutto, who believed that only a mass social movement could counter the army's power. He even attempted, unsuccessfully, to create a parallel militia, the Federal Security Force, to oppose the military. It was largely in response to this threat that the military encouraged the counter-mobilization of religious fundamentalists, and ultimately removed Bhutto from power.[57]

In conclusion, there is no single organization that can at present lead an Islamic revival in Pakistan or the Punjab, none that has the broad public appeal of the Taliban, and no prospect of a coalition creating the critical mass able to challenge the state.[58] If a revolt were to occur, it would most likely originate among the Barelwis and would need to somehow accommodate the Deobandi, the Shia and the syncretic practices of the Sindhis, an almost insurmountable task.

Setting aside the problem of a viable Islamist movement, even were an uprising to occur, it would be challenged by a military whose pervasive power is measured not only by its overwhelming coercive power, but also by its experience in subduing large-scale popular movements, such as in East Pakistan in 1971, Balochistan, and since 1947 in the NWFP. The military is particularly sensitive to the threat posed by mass social movements, often stirred by political parties, against its primarily feudal political case.[59] The military emerged from the barracks to manage domestic disturbances in East Pakistan in 1952, 1954, 1956 and 1958, and ultimately suppressed 75 million Bengalis with 40,000 troops in 1970–71, killing 300,000 and forcing 10 million refugees to flee to India.[60] In West Pakistan, the military intervened against domestic disturbances in 1953 in Lahore and Karachi, again in Karachi in 1957, and imposed order in Karachi during the Muhajir-Sindhi civil disturbance in the 1980s and 1990s.[61] Thousands were killed in the Baloch case in the mid-1970s. The use of force is a routine method of control of the more remote parts of the NWFP. More recently, the Pakistan state has repeatedly demonstrated its willingness to confront the Islamists by repeated successful quashing of mass protests, especially in the Punjab and Sindh.[62] In 2007 it dispatched the SSG (Special Services Group) commandos to suppress Islamist militants holding out in the Red Mosque, despite the political fallout.[63]

The conclusion is that it becomes difficult to envision at present any of the religious organizations or movements finding enough common ground to form even a rudimentary, uneasy alliance capable of threatening the Pakistani state.[64] Nevertheless, new social conditions may set the conditions for a revolution if the state's ability to foster socio-economic development falters on the same scale as Iran in the late 1970s.

Third Scenario: Electoral Islamism

The third scenario is that Islamist candidates are swept to a majority in the legislature, and once in control of government, overturn the electoral process and impose a theocracy, as almost occurred in Algeria in 1992.[65] The Islamist parties would then gradually secure control of the media, educational curricula and judiciary, thereby supplanting all of the secular institutions of Pakistan.[66] Former Prime Minister Benazir Bhutto warned the US that the MMA (Muttahida Majlis-e-Amal) (an umbrella of some of the 58 religious parties in Pakistan) could seize control of the Federal Senate and use it to transform Pakistan into an Islamist state.[67] Following the 2002 elections there was widespread concern of a surge in political support for Islamist parties, particularly as the MMA held an absolute majority in both the NWFP and a plurality in Balochistan.[68]

The reality is that Islamist parties in Pakistan have historically won a smaller share of seats than any equivalent religious party in Algeria, Egypt or Turkey. Religious parties in Pakistan typically win between 5 and 8 percent of the popular vote and most of these are in the NWFP.[69] What success the religious parties have had in the elections of 1970, 1988, 1993 and 2002, has largely been the result of assistance from the military and its intelligence services, primarily the ISI.[70] The military often relies on religious parties to counterbalance the dominance of secular parties, which it tends to view as corrupt, ineffective at national governance, and a threat to its autonomy.[71] Since the 1970s, the greatest ideological threat to the military is Zulfikar Ali Bhutto's left-leaning Pakistan Peoples' Party (PPP) (led also by Benazir Bhutto and Ali Asif Zardari).[72] The military's preference is for partyless elections, which Presidents Ayub Khan and Zia ul-Haq held in 1962 and 1985 respectively, but which both eventually resulted in a reassertion of party organization and influence.[73]

Unaided, religious parties do poorly for the simple reason that the secular parties, the largest currently being the PPP and the PML-N (Pakistan Muslim League — Nawaz Sharif), are far better organized.[74] The unprecedented national success of the MMA in the October 2002 elections (gaining 11 percent of the popular vote and 20 percent of the seats) was largely the result of the military's suppression of the PPP and PML-N by altering voter registration and candidate qualifications requirements.[75] In fact the PPP is capable of defeating almost any religious-based party that chooses to run in its constituencies, unless its candidate is physically detained by the Pakistani authorities.

Pakistan's best-organized religious party, Jamaat-e-Islami, is primarily based in the urban middle class (much like the Islamic brotherhood in Egypt), though organized like a Communist party with democratic centralism, a vanguard, a centralized, consultative and computerized membership, and enforced policy discipline. Precisely because it is so well organized, the ISI has maintained an alliance with it to counter the candidates of the more secular parties, the PPP and the Muslim League.[76] However, Jamaat-e-Islami has consistently performed poorly in all national elections since Partition because most issues in Pakistan are defined ethnically, ideologically or feudally, not religiously.[77] There is thus the paradox that while 60 percent of Pakistanis polled wanted religious leaders to play a larger role in politics, and 78 percent believed schools should put more emphasis on Islam, they don't vote for them in elections.[78] Even if the religious parties were to succeed, the military is as likely to intervene against them as they are against the secular parties.[79]

The 2008 elections reinforce the consistently poor performance of the Islamist parties. The Jamaat-e-Islami and the Jamiat-i-Ulema both declined to even field candidates. At the federal level, and out of a total of 342 seats, the Islamist coalition MMA's number of seats plummeted from 59 in 2002, to six in 2008. The PPP, a primarily Sindhi and left-leaning party, but with strong showings in nearly every province, thereby making it a true national party, increased its seats from 80 to 120. The PML-N, a regional Punjabi party, surged from 18 to 90 seats. The military's loyalist party, comprising mostly feudal territories throughout Pakistan, and which has since fragmented, dropped from 118 to 51 seats. The influential MQM, which controls every seat but one in Karachi, increased its share from 17 to 25. There were no other Islamist candidates at the federal level able to achieve party status. Even in the provincial elections in the NWFP, the MMA, with ten seats, had its majority broken by the Awami National Party, with 31 seats, and the PPP, with 17. In effect, without the active support of Pakistan's military, religious parties do poorly. With military support, they still cannot manage more than one-fifth of the seats in the Federal Assembly, though they do tend to alternate majorities with the secular parties in the NWFP. There is therefore little prospect that Islamists can impose a theocracy through the electoral process.

Conclusion

I demonstrated that the three populist paths to an Islamist Pakistan are illusory. First, the Islamist civil war scenario, a provincial challenge to the state, is too remote to be able to affect the Punjabi and Sindhi core of Pakistan. There is no historical evidence suggesting a Pashtun offensive towards this core has any likelihood of succeeding given Punjabi antipathy towards the Pashtun and the presence of the army. Second, the Islamist revolutionary scenario shows that the existing Islamist organizations in the Punjab lack the religious or political consensus, or the broad support, to lead a revolt. Furthermore, they have neither the power to confront the Pakistan military, nor the appeal to neutralize the military's leadership. Third, the Islamist electoral scenario has shown that without military support, and even with military support, the religious parties are unable to compete with the popularity and organization of the largest secular parties. The strength of Pakistan's bureaucracy combined with the autonomy of the military and its intelligence services render all three scenarios unlikely.

A more likely path to an Islamist seizure of the Pakistani state could be through a military coup d'etat. This I have treated and I have also concluded it is unlikely for two reasons.[80] First, historically, coups in Pakistan during both civilian and military governments have been planned through semi-official channels of consultation among the senior military leadership and in consultation with key members of the bureaucracy and/or the traditional Punjabi elite.[81] No coup has succeeded without the approval of the majority of the members of this process. Any Islamist movement would have to navigate this process of consultation. Without broad support, a dedicated Islamist movement would not win acceptance among the military unit commanders and would not therefore survive. The internal transparency of the military command structure therefore makes it difficult for an Islamist conspiracy to penetrate and then play off different internal factions to seize power. Second, despite alarmist claims that Islamist sympathizers have gained a foothold within the army, any disaffection in the military's ranks does not as yet appear to be wide or deep enough to cause institutional fractures or trigger intra-organizational conflict. The military thus far has been able to dismiss extremists and suppress domestic Islamist threats without much consequence to the allegiance of its members.[82] Those Islamists that remain don't have access to the institutional controls necessary to conduct a coup, even if they could convince whole battalions, brigades or even divisions to participate. Finally, for the reasons that Islam has little electoral or revolutionary appeal, a strict Islamist regime imposed by the military would quickly erode its political base.

Notes

1   Elisabeth Bumiller, "Petraeus Warns About Militants" Threat to Pakistan," *The New York Times*, April 1, 2009.

2   Ben Arnoldy, "Why the Taliban won't take over Pakistan," *Christian Science Monitor*, June 7, 2009, www.csmonitor.com/2009/0607/p06s07-wosc.html?page=1 (accessed August 3, 2009).

3   David Sanger, "Obama's Worst Pakistan Nightmare," *The New York Times*, January 8, 2009; Ben Arnoldy, op. cit.

4   The Fund for Peace, Failed State Index 2009, www.fundforpeace.org/web/index.php?option=com_content&task=view&id=391&Itemid=549 (accessed August 3, 2009).

5   I examine the possibility of coups elsewhere. See Julian Schofield and Michael Zekulin, "Appraising the Threat of Islamist Take-Over in Pakistan," *Notes de recherches du CEPES*, no. 34, March 2007.

6   Ben Arnoldy, op. cit.

7   Comprising the Federally Administered Tribal Areas (FATA), Provincially Administered Tribal Areas (PATA), the NWFP and northern Balochistan.

8   IISS, *The Military Balance 2009*. London: IISS, 2009, pp. 329–330.

9   Thomas Johnson and M. Chris Mason, "No Sign until the Burst of Fire," *International*

Security Vol. 32, No. 4 (Spring 2008), 41–77, 55; Zahid Hussain, *Frontline Pakistan*. New York: Columbia University Press, 2007, p. 148.

10   Ahmed Rashid, *Descent Into Chaos*. London: Viking, 2008, p. 385.

11   C. Christine Fair and Peter Chalk, *Fortifying Pakistan*. Washington, D.C.: USIP, 2006, p. 13.

12   C. Christine Fair and Peter Chalk, *Fortifying Pakistan* (Washington, D.C.: USIP, 2006), 48; Shuja Nawaz, *Crossed Swords* (Karachi: Oxford University Press, 2008), xxxiii.

13   Veena Kukreja, *Contemporary Pakistan* (New Delhi: Sage, 2003), 51; Owen Jones, *Pakistan* (New Haven: Yale University Press, 2002), 139.

14   Shuja Nawaz, *Crossed Swords*. Karachi: Oxford University Press, 2008, p. 571; Adam Roberts, "Doctrine and Reality in Afghanistan," *Survival* Vol. 51, No. 1 (Feb–March 2009), 29–60, 33; Thomas Johnson and M. Chris Mason, "No Sign until the Burst of Fire," *International Security* Vol. 32, No. 4 (Spring 2008), 41–77, 65.

15   IISS, *The Military Balance 2009*. London: IISS, 2009, pp. 329–330.

16   Adam Roberts, "Doctrine and Reality in Afghanistan," *Survival* Vol. 51, No. 1 (Feb–March 2009), 29–60, 53–54.

17   Sabrina Tavernise, Richard A. Oppel Jr. and Eric Schmitt, "United Militants Threaten Pakistan's Populous Heart," *The New York Times*, April 13, 2009; IISS, *The Military Balance 2009*. London: IISS, 2009, p. 330.

18   Ahmed Rashid, op. cit., p. 379.

19   Ben Arnoldy, op. cit. Jane Perlez and Pir Zubair Shah, "In Pakistan, Guile Helps Taliban Gain," *The New York Times*, April 25, 2009.

20   Syed Minhaj ul Hassan, "Tribal Areas of NWFP: Politics of Survival," in Syed Farooq Hasnat and Ahmad Faruqui (eds.), *Pakistan — Unresolved Issues of State and Society*. Lahore: Vanguard, 2008, pp. 209–236, 211.

21   Josef Korbel, *Danger in Kashmir*. Oxford: Oxford University Press, 2002, p. 73.

22   Robert Crews, "Moderate Taliban?" in Robert Crews and Amin Tarzi (eds.), *The Taliban and the Crisis of Afghanistan*. London: Harvard University Press, 2008, pp. 238–273, 243.

23   Ahmed Rashid, *Descent Into Chaos*. London: Viking, 2008, p. 36; Mansoor Akbar Kundi, "The Tribal Setup and Elections 2002 in Balochistan," in Syed Farooq Hasnat and Ahmad Faruqui (eds.), *Pakistan — Unresolved Issues of State and Society*. Lahore: Vanguard, 2008, pp. 237–256, 238.

24   Adam Roberts, "Doctrine and Reality in Afghanistan," *Survival* Vol. 51, No. 1 (Feb–March 2009), 29–60, 31; C. Christine Fair, *The Madrassah Challenge*. Washington, D.C.: USIP, 2008, pp. 10, 36; C. Christine Fair and Peter Chalk, op. cit., p. 11; Ayesha Jalal, *Partisan of Allah*. London: Harvard University Press, 2008, p. 275.

25   Abdulkader Sinno, "Explaining the Taliban's Ability to Mobilize the Pashtuns," in Robert Crews and Amin Tarzi (eds.), *The Taliban and the Crisis of Afghanistan*. London: Harvard University Press, 2008, pp. 59–89, 76–78, 85; IISS, *The Military Balance 2009*. London: IISS, 2009, p. 330.

26 IISS, *The Military Balance 2009*. London: IISS, 2009, p. 331.

27 Ahmed Rashid, op. cit., p. 7.

28 John W. Warnock, *Creating a Failed State — The US and Canada in Afghanistan* Halifax: Fernwood Publishing, 2008, p. 42.

29 Ayesha Jalal, *Partisan of Allah*. London: Harvard University Press, 2008, p. 90.

30 Ibid., p. 210.

31 Robert Wirsing, *The Baluchi's and Pathans — Report No. 48*. London: The Minority Rights Group, 1987, p. 5; Hugh Pettigrew, *Frontier Scouts*, pp. 2–3, 73–74, 100; Collin Davies, *The Problem of the North-West Frontier 1890-1908*, pp. 19–20, 119, 141, 149–150, 180; Sara Haroon, *Frontier of Faith*. New York: Columbia University Press, 2008, pp. 7–8; Ayesha Jalal, *Partisasn of Allah*. op. cit., p. 87.

32 Hussain Haqqani, "Insecurity along the Durand Line," in Geoffrey Hayes and Mark Sedra (eds.), *Afghanistan — Transition Under Threat*. Kitchener: Wilfrid Laurier Press, 2008, pp. 219–237, 234.

33 Ahmed Rashid, op. cit., p. 10; Seth G. Jones, "The Rise of Afghanistan's Insurgency," *International Security* Vol. 32, No. 4 (Spring 2008), pp. 7–40, 27.

34 Hussain Haqqani, op. cit., pp. 219–237, 232–233.

35 Weaver, pp. 80–81.

36 Agha Humayum Amin, *The Pakistan Army Till 1965*, p. 88.

37 Ahmed Rashid, op. cit., pp. 221–222; Thomas Johnson and M. Chris Mason, "No Sign until the Burst of Fire," *International Security* Vol. 32, No. 4 (Spring 2008), pp. 41–77, 53; Shuja Nawaz, *Crossed Swords*. Karachi: Oxford University Press, 2008, p. 368.

38 Ahmed Rashid, op. cit., pp. 25, 68; Abdulkader Sinno, *Organizations at War in Afghanistan and Beyond*. Ithaca: Cornell University Press, 2008, pp. 134–135, 233.

39 Seth G. Jones, op. cit., pp. 7–40, 32–33; Ahmed Rashid, op. cit., p. 286.

40 Robin Wright, "The Chilling Goal of Islam's New Warriors." (*LA Times*), [Online June 6, 2005).] available from http://www.angelfire.com/a14/terror/article22.htm

41 Sabrina Tavernise et al. op. cit.; Aslam Pervez Memon, "Political Behaviour in the Sindh Province," in Syed Farooq Hasnat and Ahmad Faruqui (eds.), *Pakistan — Unresolved Issues of State and Society*. Lahore: Vanguard, 2008, pp. 198–208, 204; Shuja Nawaz, *Crossed Swords*. Karachi: Oxford University Press, 2008, pp. 570–571.

42 Sabrina Tavernise et al. op. cit.

43 Ayesha Jalal, op. cit., p. 287; Sabrina Tavernise et al. op. cit.

44 Hassan Abbas, *Pakistan's Drift into Extremism*. London, M.E. Sharpe, 2005, pp. 201–202; SATP. Terrorist Groups of Pakistan: Harakat-ul-Mujahideen Al-alami. [Online June 9, 2005] available from http://www.satp.org/satporgtp/countries/pakistan/terrorist outfits.htm; IISS, *The Military Balance 2009*. London: IISS, 2009, p. 355.

45 Ayesha Jalal, op. cit., pp. 64, 75, 123.

46 Ibid., p. 284.

47 Shuja Nawaz, op. cit., p. 571.

48   Stephen Phillip Cohen. "The Nation and the State of Pakistan," p. 114.

49   Ayesha Jalal, op. cit., p. 278; Hassan Abbas, op. cit., p. 204; SATP. Terrorist Groups of
      Pakistan: Sipah-e-Sahaba. [Online June 9, 2005] available from http://www.satp.org/
      satporgtp/countries/pakistan/terroristoutfits.htm

50   Ayesha Jalal, op. cit., p. 276, 279; C. Raja Mohan. "What if Pakistan Fails?" *The
      Washington Quarterly* 28:1 (2004), p. 119; Jessica Stern. "Pakistan's Jihad Culture."
      Foreign Affairs (November 2000). [Online June 9, 2005] available from www.hks.har-
      vard.edu/fs/jstern/pakistan.htm; United States Institute of Peace. "Islamic Extremists:
      How Do they Mobilize Support?" (2002). [Online June 6, 2005] available from http://
      www.usip.org/pubs/specialreports/sr89.html; Hassan Abbas. op. cit., p. 228–229; Ajai
      Sahni. "A New Government Takes Charge." [Online June 9, 2005] available from http://
      satp.org/satporgtp/sair/Archives/1_19.htm#assessment1

51   Christophe Jaffrelot, ed., *A History of Pakistan and Its Origins*. London: Anthem, 2002,
      p. 140 (114); Stephen Cohen, "Pakistan's Fear of Failure," *The Asian Wall Street Journal*
      (Oct 23, 2000); Robin Wright. op. cit.

52   Ayesha Jalal, op. cit., pp. 276, 279.

53   SATP. Terrorist Groups of Pakistan: Mutahida Quomi Mahaz. [Online June 9, 2005]
      available from http://www.satp.org/satporgtp/countries/pakistan/terroristoutfits.
      htm

54   Maloy Krishna Dhar, *Fulcrum of Evil*. New Delhi: Manas, 2006, pp. 48, 51; Arvin Bahl.
      "India, America, Musharraf, And War." South Asia Analysis Group (2002). [Online
      June 6, 2005] available from http://www.saag.org/papers5/paper479.html

55   C. Raja Mohan, op. cit., p. 121.

56   Hussain Haqqani, op. cit., p. 276.

57   Stephen Phillip Cohen, op. cit., p. 119–120.

58   Rodney Jones. "The Prospect of State Failure in Pakistan." (2001): http://www.policy
      architects.org/pdf/Pak_statefailure_Exsumm.pdf#search='islamic%20extremist%20
      groups%20in%20pakistan (accessed September 6, 2005).

59   Zamindars, Vadayrays, and the minority communities in the non-Punjabi states that
      most recently coalesced around the PML-Quaid-e-Azam party. Mary Anne Weaver,
      Pakistan. New York: Farrar, Straus, and Giroux, 2002, p. 180; Owen Jones, *Pakistan*.
      New Haven: Yale University Press, 2002, pp. 244–247.

60   Lawrence Ziring, *The Ayub Khan Era — Politics in Pakistan 1958–1969*. Syracuse:
      Syracuse University Press, 1971, p. 7; G.W. Choudhury, *The Last Days of United
      Pakistan*. Bloomington: Indian UP, 1974, p. 156.

61   *Dawn*, May 16, 1953, cited in K.L. Kamal, *Pakistan — The Garrison State*. New Delhi:
      Intellectual Publishing House, 1982, p. 52; Lawrence Ziring, op. cit., p. 7.

62   Stephen Phillip Cohen, op. cit., p. 117; Samina Ahmed. "The Myth of the Good
      General Musharraf." [Online June 6, 2005] available from www.crisisgroup.org/home/
      index.cfm?id=2241&1=1; Issue Brief. "Nuclear Watch: Pakistan." (2004). [Online May

30, 2005] available from http://www.nti.org/e3_38b.html; Mark Katz. "What if Islamic Revolution Occurs in Pakistan?" January 26, 2005. [Online June 19, 2005] available from http://www.eurasianet.org/departments/insight/articles/eav012605a_pr.shtml

63   Ambassador Tariq Fatemi on Pakistani Politics after Lal Masjid. (August 9, 2007). Carnegie Endowment for International Peace.

64   Isaac Kfir (2007). "The Crisis of Pakistan: A Dangerously Weak State." *Middle East Review of International Affairs* 11(3); p. 78.

65   Mohammad Shehzad, "Fighting Words, Hidden Pact." [Online June 9, 2005] available from http://satp.org/satporgtp/sair/Archives/3_46.htmASSESSMENT2

66   "Factors Underlying Religious Extremism in Pakistan." [Online July 7, 2005] available from http://www.usip.org/pubs/specialreports/sr89.html

67   Hassan Abbas, op. cit., p. 201; Anwar Iqbal. "Analysis: Setback for Pakistan Extremists." United Press International (2003). [Online June 6, 2005] available from http://www.upi.com/view.cfm?StoryID=20030224-081836-1627r

68   Ajai Sahni. "A New Government Takes Charge." [Online June 9, 2005] available from http://satp.org/satporgtp/sair/Archives/1_19.htm#assessment1

69   Hussain Haqqani, op. cit., p. 95; Owen Jones, op. cit., p. 5.

70   The Pakistani Army and Post Election scenarios (February 13, 2008). Carnegie Endowment for International Peace; Frederic Grare (2006). South Asia Project — Islam, Militarism and the 2007–2008 Elections in Pakistan. Carnegie Papers 70: Carnegie Endowment for International Peace; Ahmed Rashid, op. cit., 39–40; Syed Minhaj ul Hassan, op. cit., pp. 209–236, 221.

71   Hussain Haqqani. "The Role of Islam in Pakistan's Future." The Washington Quarterly 28: 1 (Winter 2004): p. 91; Hasan Askari Rizvi, "Electoral Process in Pakistan," in Syed Farooq Hasnat and Ahmad Faruqui (eds.), *Pakistan — Unresolved Issues of State and Society* (Lahore: Vanguard, 2008), pp. 1–21, 7–8; Shuja Nawaz, *Crossed Swords*. Karachi: Oxford University Press, 2008, p. xxxiii.

72   Stephen Phillip Cohen, op. cit., p. 119.

73   Hasan Askari Rizvi, "Electoral Process in Pakistan," in Syed Farooq Hasnat and Ahmad Faruqui (eds.), *Pakistan — Unresolved Issues of State and Society.* Lahore: Vanguard, 2008, pp. 1–21, 8.

74   Hasan Askari Rizvi, op. cit., pp. 1–21.

75   Hussain Haqqani. "The Role of Islam in Pakistan's Future." *The Washington Quarterly* 28: 1 (Winter 2004), p. 91; Frederic Grare (2007). Rethinking Western Strategies Toward Pakistan: An Action Agenda for the US and Europe. Carnegie Endowment for International Peace; p. 28, 34 (pp. 4–55).

76   Owen Jones, op. cit., p. 6, 240; Christophe Jaffrelot, ed., *A History of Pakistan and Its Origins* (London: Anthem, 2002), p. 225; Ayesha Jalal, op. cit., p. 277.

77   Newsmax.com Wire Service. Analysis of Pakistan's Nuclear Weapons. September 19, 2001. [Online May 29, 2005] available from http://www.newsmax.com

78 Robin Wright, op. cit.

79 K. Alan Kronstadt. "Pakistan's Domestic Political Developments." (CRS Report for Congress 2004): Congressional Research Service, the Library of Congress. P. CRS-9; Hasan Askari Rizvi, op. cit., pp. 1–21, 11–12.

80 Julian Schofield and Michael Zekulin, "Appraising the Threat of Islamist Take-Over in Pakistan," *Notes de recherches du CEPES*, no. 34, March 2007.

81 B. Raman. "Pakistan: The Mullas" Blue Eyed General." South Asia Analysis Group (2000). [Online June 6, 2005] available from http://www.saag.org/papers2/paper146.html; A. H. Amin. "Possible Coup in Pakistan." (2003). [Online July 6, 2005] available from http://www.satribune.com/archives/feb_24mar1_03/opinion_coup.htm

82 Issue Brief. "Nuclear Watch: Pakistan." (2004). [Online May 30, 2005] available from http://www.nti.org/e3_38b.html

"We are the soldiers of Islam"[1]: Tehreek-e-Taliban Pakistan and the Ideology of Terror

Simon R. Valentine

Abstract

This chapter attempts to understand the psyche of Tehreek-Taliban Pakistan (TTP). Placing TTP in its geo-political context, the emergence of Islamic extremism in Pakistan is considered, and the origins of TTP as a distinct faction. In so doing the involvement of the CIA and the ISI in the emergence of such extremism is highlighted. Following a consideration of the organization and influence of TTP, the chapter assesses the group's ideology and beliefs, particularly its teaching on jihad; its attitude towards the American and Pakistan governments, and the implementation of Sharia. Specific attention is given to the Takfiri doctrine and the teaching of Ibn Taymiyyah, Syed Qutb, Syed Abul Ala Maududi and Abdullah Azzam. Despite claims that with the death of Baitullah Mehsud on August 5, 2009 TTP is now defunct and broken, the author concludes that, under the leadership of his successor, Hakimullah Mehsud, its ideological capacity to influence is far from over.

Introduction

On December 27, 2007, hundreds of police officers manned security checkpoints around Rawalpindi's Liaquat Bagh Park. Benazir Bhutto, the 54-year-old ex-prime minister of Pakistan, addressed thousands of her supporters in an election campaign rally. Eloquent and dignified, she declared to the crowd: "I put my life in danger and I came here because I believe this country is in danger." After speaking she left the podium protected by guards, and climbed into a waiting armoured car. As the car made its way through the city, cheered by her followers, she raised herself from her seat, lifting her head through the sunroof to salute the crowd. Minutes later she was dead. A gunman stepped out onto the road and, having shot Mrs Bhutto in the neck and shoulder, detonated a bomb that damaged her car and killed many bystanders.[2] Covered with blood, Mrs Bhutto was pulled from the wreckage of her vehicle and rushed to a nearby hospital where, despite emergency surgery, she died. Although President Musharraf made a request for people to remain calm, as news of the killing spread, protests erupted throughout Pakistan. There were no immediate claims of responsibility for the attack.[3] Although Baitullah Mehsud, leader of Tehreek-e-Taliban Pakistan (TTP) denied involvement, Musharraf was quick to name him as the culprit. Interior Ministry spokesman, Brigadier Javed Cheema, claimed the suicide bomber had been an al-Qaeda operative belonging to TTP.[4] "We have an intelligence intercept recorded this morning," he declared, "in which Baitullah Mehsud congratulated his people for carrying out this cowardly act." Guilty or not, the very fact that Musharraf saw fit to blame Baitullah for Benazir Bhutto's murder illustrates the importance of TTP as one of the main extremist groups in contemporary Pakistan.

The Tehreek-e-Taliban Pakistan: Origins and Development

TTP (Students' Movement of Pakistan in English) is a loosely connected conglomerate of jihadi tribesmen, operating mainly in the South Waziristan agency of the Federally Administered Tribal Areas (FATA) of Pakistan. Linked to, and financed by, al-Qaeda, TTP, as seen in its terrorist activities, possesses a significant supply of military and telecommunications equipment. Described by Pakistan's Interior Minister, Rehman Malik, as "the front face of al-Qaeda,"[5] TTP's main aims are the removal of foreigners (mainly American and other Western non-Muslims) from Pakistani soil and the establishment of a Sharia state.

In order to assess the origins and development of TTP it is important to stress how, to a great extent, Islamic extremism in Pakistan has been a product of CIA and ISI financing and encouragement.[6] The ISI, accused by some of being "a state within a state," working beyond the government's control and pursuing its own security interests, sponsored militant activity against the Red Army in Afghanistan. Covert support has also been given by the ISI to various groups fighting to free Kashmir from Indian rule, groups such as the Jammu and Kashmir Liberation front (JKLF) and Hizb-ul Mujahideen (HuM). Due to the significant influence of hard-line mullahs, a madrassah system, which trains terrorists, and sporadic support by government and army officials for militant activities, the ISI has also supported terrorist groups operating in Pakistan, namely Lashkar-e-Jhangvi (LeJ), Lashker-e-Tayyiba (LeT), and Jaish-e-Muhammad (JeM). The ISI maintains links with the Afghan Taliban as a "strategic hedge" to help Islamabad gain influence in Kabul once US troops leave the region.[7] India has claimed ISI support for the banned militant group LeT, the group believed to be responsible for the terrorist attacks in Mumbai in November 2008.[8]

Many of the jihadists recruited by TTP, as with Islamic extremists generally in Pakistan, were originally trained and "indoctrinated" by the CIA, to fight the Soviet Union in Afghanistan.[9] "After all," remarks Jessica Stern, "the US government helped to design and fund the strategy of employing violent Islamist cadres to serve as 'volunteer' fighters in a war that seemed critically important at the time, but left those cadres to their devices once they were no longer important for achieving US strategic goals."[10] Maulvi Nazir, Amir of the Taliban Mujahideen in South Waziristan, expressed similar views when he stated that militant Islam in that region as elsewhere is "CIA from start to finish," part of the "Western crusade" to "save the gods of Wall Street."[11] In a lengthy interview given in April 2009, Nazir explained how in his opinion "the entire Taliban/al-Qaeda operation from start to finish was a massive genocidal plot" created by Washington "to sacrifice nation after nation (beginning with the Soviet Union), in order to preserve American capitalism." "The 'jihadi' ideology," he continued, was a US invention manufactured "to salvage 'free market' ideology from the eventual consequences of its own unrestrained freedom to pursue profit."[12] TTP has its origins in the residue of the Mujahideen, left redundant after the withdrawal of the Soviet Union from Afghanistan. Such fighters, trained and eager for jihad, established numerous militant groups in Afghanistan, Kashmir and Pakistan, groups that contributed to the emergence of later extremist factions, including TTP.[13]

If the CIA and the ISI gave birth to Islamic extremism in Pakistan, the

Pakistan government rocked the cradle. Zulfikar Ali Bhutto, President of Pakistan (1971–73) and prime minister (1973–77), used Islamic militants from Afghanistan who had taken refuge in Pakistan, including Gulbadin Hikmatyar and Ahmad Shah Masud, to destabilize the Daud government in Kabul.[14] General Zia-ul-Haq, having led a coup d'état against Bhutto, and appointing himself President in 1978, undertook a policy of Islamization of Pakistan, in which he promoted the madrassah system, a system which was becoming the breeding ground for Islamic extremism. He also encouraged right-wing militant groups, particularly Maududi's organization, the Jamaat-e-Islami, so as to gain the support of the mullahs, thereby bolstering his position. With the support of the Pakistan government, the 1990s and beyond witnessed the further mushrooming of madrassahs all over Pakistan, many of which, sponsored by Saudi petro-dollars, taught a strongly anti-West Wahhabi ideology. Wanting an ally against India and Iran, the Pakistan government helped the Taliban in Afghanistan to consolidate its rule, providing it with military and financial support. Reliable sources state that, by 2002, there were about 24 "jihadi groups" operating in Pakistan.[15]

Mainly a Deobandi Sunni organization, TTP officially emerged as a group on December 14, 2007.[16] Baitullah Mehsud, regarded by the US as the "root cause of all evils,"[17] one of the most "odious and dangerous people" in the region[18] and a "key al-Qaeda facilitator,"[19] was appointed TTP Amir. Due to his effectiveness as a jihadist leader and terrorist, the US offered a $5 million reward for his capture.[20] Maulana Hafiz Gul Bahadur from North Waziristan was appointed the senior Naib Amir (senior vice chief) for TTP, while Maulvi Faqir Mohammad, from the Bajaur agency, was appointed third in command.[21] Baitullah, described by special envoy Richard Holbrooke as "a terrible man, a great danger to Pakistan, to Afghanistan,"[22] had emerged as a jihadist early in 2005. By killing off rivals and by sheer force of personality, within a short period of time, he had managed to spread his influence in all seven tribal agencies of FATA, virtually establishing an independent zone in parts of South Waziristan.[23] After nominating commanders in each agency, Baitullah began to extend his influence in neighboring North-West Frontier Province (NWFP), gaining support from various groups, especially the Afridi, a Pashtun clan, in Darra Adam Khel.[24] By killing many of the tribal leaders on charges of being US spies, TTP has established itself as the de-facto leadership replacing the traditional jirga (the tribal assembly of elders).

Early in 2008, Maulana Fazlullah, leader of the Tehreek-e-Nifaz-e-Shariat-e-Muhammadi (TNSM) in Swat, nicknamed "Mullah Radio" due to the regular interviews he gave, linked with TTP and declared his allegiance to Baitullah. TTP also formed strong links with the jihadi faction led by Asmatullah Shaheen Bhittani. In February 2009, Baitullah joined with certain sections of the Afghan Taliban, mainly Maulvi Nazir, to form the Shura Ittihadul Mujahideen (SIM), also known as the Shura Ittihadul-Mujahideen and the Council of United Mujahideen, announcing their allegiance to Mullah Omar as their Amir-ul-Mumineen.[25] In a written statement, the leaders of this group affirmed that they would put aside differences to fight American-led forces, and declared their allegiance to Osama bin Laden.[26] On February 14, 2009, the NWFP government agreed to a peace accord with the TNSM, effectively conceding the area of Swat to the Taliban, of which TTP forms a major part. This accord was seen by many as "a capitulation by a government desperate to stop Taliban abuses and a military embarrassed at losing ground after more than a year of intermittent fighting."[27] A temporary ceasefire was agreed by the Taliban, while the government agreed to allow the implementation of Sharia in the region once violence had stopped. Ten days later, on February 24, Muslim Khan, spokesperson for TTP, publicly announced that TTP would observe an indefinite ceasefire.[28] On April 13 President Zardari signed the Nizam-e-Adl regulation with the Taliban, effectively giving it control of the Malakand Division.

On August 5, 2009 Baitullah Mehsud was killed with one of his wives in South Waziristan, by a missile fired from a pilotless US drone.[29] Twelve days later the capture of Mullah Omar, leading spokesperson for TTP, was another major set-back for the group.[30] News reports about the present state of TTP have been contradictory. Maulvi Faqir Muhammad, TTP's deputy, stated on August 19 that he had taken over as acting head of the group in Pakistan, but denied reports that Baitullah Mehsud had been killed.[31] On August 22 he announced that Hakimullah Mehsud had been nominated as the new head of the group,[32] and later claimed that both Maulvi Nazir and Hafiz Gul Bahadur were happy with the decision.[33] It was only on August 26 that TTP publicly announced that Baitullah had died.[34] Faqir Muhammad announced the appointment of Tariq Azam (known also as Hafiz Noor Said) as TTP spokesman.

Hakimullah Mehsud, a man believed to be "a ferocious fighter" and "a ruthless enforcer of loyalty,"[35] is regarded by some merely as "a trigger-happy thug."[36] Analysts depict him as a "rash strutting fighter who has led dozens of major terrorist operations not only against the Pakistani security forces but also against the NATO supply trucks."[37] Shortly after the death of Baitullah Mehsud reports claimed that Hakimullah had also been killed in an armed clash between rival factions of TTP (during the shura meeting to elect a new chief).[38] However, Hakimullah, "a tenacious fighter, young, energetic and perhaps more violent than his mentor Baitullah,"[39] brushed aside those reports with a media tour and is proving to be a force to be reckoned with.

TTP: Organization, Activities and Influence

TTP, unlike the Afghan Taliban movement, which is older, more entrenched, and possessing a broader geographical presence, lacks a strong infrastructure and organization. It consists of a loose connection of several tribal groups held together by shared goals and ideals, a devotion to its own brand of radical Islam and an adherence to oligarchic Pashtunwali, a tribal code of honour emphasizing, inter alia, courage and pride.[40] The structure is led by several figures. Loyal to Hakimullah Mehsud, Maulvi Faqir Mohammed, also known as Ustade Fidayeen (Leader of the Intrepid), is a member of the Mohmand tribe and is the deputy commander of TTP. Qari Hussain Mehsud, "father of suicide bombings in Pakistan," inspired by the Basiji child martyrs of Shia Islam in Iran, allegedly organizes training camps for children to become suicide bombers.[41] Among other activities Qari Hussain is presumed to be the man responsible for the terrorist attack in Lahore in March 2008, and the attack on the ISI Rawalpindi's offices in November the previous year.[42] In a recent interview he stated that he had formed a group of suicide bombers known as the Fidayeen-e-Islam, claiming that the members of this team are "ready to give their lives if Pakistan proceeds with offensives in the tribal areas."[43] Other TTP leaders include Waliur Rehman, described as being "a very humble and intelligent man"[44] as well as a dedicated fighter. Rehman commands the TTP chapter in South Waziristan.[45] These men, and others, are in control of a formidable fighting force. Estimates vary as to the number of the men recruited by TTP. In 2008, shortly after the inception of the group, it was estimated that Baitullah Mehsud had 5,000 fighters.[46] By April 2009 it was claimed that this number had increased to somewhere between 20,000 and 30,000.[47] Even allowing for the official claims that many TTP fighters have been killed in recent fighting with security forces, a significant militia still remains. Reports also vary as to the make-up of this force. Some state that a significant percentage of the fighters belonging to TTP are non-Pakistani foreign elements including Uzbeks, Chechens, Afghani and Arabs.[48] Other reports claim that, unlike the Afghan Taliban, TTP has few, if no, foreign fighters amongst its ranks, and consists mainly of indigenous Pashtun tribesmen.[49] It is known for certain, however, that the membership of TTP is from all of FATA's seven tribal agencies as well as several districts of the NWFP, including Swat, Bannu, Tank, Lakki Marwat, Dera Ismail Khan, Kohistan, Buner and Malakand.

The terrorist activities carried out by TTP have had a devastating effect on Pakistan's society and abroad. Reference has already been made to the claim that TTP was responsible for the assassination of Benazir Bhutto in 2007 and the denial of that claim by the group. TTP has been blamed for many other attacks in Pakistan. It is believed that during the past two years they have been responsible for about 270 attacks, some of which were suicide bombings, others attacks with IEDs (improvised explosive devises)[50] that have killed more than 2,100 people across Pakistan, and the figure is growingly steadily.[51] Although Maulvi Nazir rejects the accusation, it is argued that TTP was part of the group that attacked Mumbai, India, on November 26–29, 2008.[52] TTP has been linked with the suicide attack in Chakwal in April 2009, although Mullah Omar denied responsibility.[53] Uncorroborated reports state that TTP was responsible for the murder of Qari Zainuddin, leader of the Abdullah Group, in June 2009.[54] Baitullah Mehsud claimed responsibility for the attack on the Manawan Police Academy in Punjab province in March 2009, which killed at least 13 people and wounded many more. Mehsud claimed responsibility for the attack, asserting that it was "in retaliation for the continued drone strikes by the US in collaboration with Pakistan on our people."[55] The former TTP leader also claimed responsibility for a suicide attack on a security convoy in Bannu that killed four security personnel and wounded nine others,[56] and the bombing of the Islamabad police station, both incidents occurring in March 2009.[57] TTP has been linked with the bombing of the Pearl Continental Hotel in Peshawar in June this year in which 17 people were killed,[58] and the killing of a prominent anti-Taliban cleric, Dr. Naeemi, in a suicide attack at Jamia Naeemia mosque in Lahore in the same month.[59] As well as suicide bombings, in 2008 it was reported that TTP kidnapped 70 people throughout Pakistan, including Karachi and Lahore, mainly as a revenue-boosting exercise.[60]

In light of the death of Baitullah Mehsud, and the alleged internal fighting taking place within the group, Ismail Khan is quoted as saying that "TTP will not be the TTP it was. Their time is up. We feel that the threat to national security is receding."[61] Despite such claims TTP has continued to be active and has a waged a renewed wave of terrorist attacks across the country under the leadership of Hakimullah Mehsud.

Beliefs and Ideology: Jihad, Jahiliyya and the Sovereignty of God

Critics of TTP have said: "it is not Islam, it is crime," that it's a group "making illegal money from warlords, and contractors by blackmail and extortion."[62] It is alleged that those belonging to the group are merely "paid brainwashed barbarians . . . Smugglers and criminals."[63] Although the majority of people would abhor the acts of terrorism carried out by TTP, and moderate Muslims would argue the beliefs and practices of the group are a misrepresentation of true Islam, in dismissing TTP in this way there is the danger of failing to see it as it is, a well-financed and fearless militia motivated by a coherent, if distorted, ideological world view. As declared by Maulvi Nazir: "We are the soldiers of Islam and we are Mujahideen, not some Pakistani horde."[64] Terry McDermott, in his study of the factors motivating three of the 9/11 terrorists, suggested: "we have no choice but to *understand them* in order to *stop them*."[65] If TTP and other extremist groups presently operating in Pakistan are to be stopped in carrying out their terrorist activities it is expedient for policy-makers and politicians alike to try and understand the mind-set that motivates and legitimizes its ideology of terror.

TTP's ideological framework is characterized by an aggressive doctrine of jihad, involving a poorly planned yet highly dangerous Islamic liberation theology aimed at the establishment of the hakimiyyah, or sovereignty of Allah in Pakistan, free from Western corruption, and the replacement of Takfiri rulers with a Sharia-based state. In refuting claims that TTP works for Mossad or the ISI, Maulvi Nazir asserted unequivocally: "We have rose [sic] for jihad and give sacrifices to establish the rule of Sharia."[66] Reminiscent of Abdullah Azzam's dictum: "jihad and the rifle alone: no negotiations, no conferences and no dialogues,"[67] Baitullah Mehsud stated that "only jihad can bring peace to the world."[68] "Jihad" and "peace" for TTP involves the removal, by force, of Western presence and presence from Pakistan, and apostate rulers from government. From what we can perceive from the official statements made by TTP, usually given by TTP members on the radio or on jihadist websites, the ideology of the group is firmly based on Syed Abul Ala Maududi's (1903–79) emphasis on hakimiyyah, the absolute sovereignty of God, and the argument that such hakimiyyah should be "for God alone, not for hakimiyyah al-bashariya, human sovereignty, law or the people."[69] A society without the rule of Allah is regarded as flawed and imperfect, tainted by jahiliyya (ignorance), the denial of "the overriding authority of the prophetic guidance in human life."[70] As such, it is fard'ayn, a religious duty, the "neglected obligation,"[71] for a Muslim to eliminate such jahiliyya and to fight so as to establish hukumat-i-ilahiyah (divine rule) in Pakistan, if not the entire world. Members of TTP, like extremists elsewhere, are bound together and motivated by mujahadah, the struggle (usually violent) by believers to establish the truth of Islam. In expressing jihad in this way TTP shares a common view with other militant factions in the NWFP. Hafiz Saeed, founder of LeT, expressed a similar idea when he declared; "for us jihad is sacred like praying and fasting that cannot be forsaken under any condition."[72]

Announcements made by TTP spokespeople make it clear that jihad is not seen merely as a localized conflict fighting against jahili forces in Pakistan, but it is an international struggle uniting Muslims worldwide. Pan-Islamism, the doctrine of "sacred space"[73] and the global victory of Islam, are ideals shared by militant Muslims throughout Southeast Asia. Such beliefs form the basis of statements made by TTP and other tribal factions in Pakistan. "We believe in the clash of civilizations," declared Hafiz Saeed, "and our jihad will continue until Islam becomes the dominant religion."[74] In reference to Afghanistan, and the American presence in Pakistan, Maulvi Nazir remarked: "our jihad is against Kufr, and to get back our lands that Kufr has occupied, and our jihad is meant to make supreme the word of Allah and to establish the system of Sharia."[75] Elaborating on this theme, Nazir remarked:

> We do not even accept these parting boundaries that "this shall be Pakistan" and "that shall be Afghanistan" . . . this is nothing but an inanity devised by the Jews and we reject it. All Muslims are our brothers, may they be in Saudi Arabia, Iraq, Palestine or anywhere in the world. It is impossible to create division between Muslims, and the present partitions are utterly rejected. Our jihad isn't limited to Pakistan or Afghanistan. Our jihad is a global jihad, and we aim to liberate Muslims throughout the world and obliterate tumult, oppression and mischief, and establish the system of Sharia all over the world. We want the Law of Allah on the Land of Allah.[76]

Officially, unlike most other jihadi groups operating in Pakistan, the Kashmiri issue is not one of the main aims of TTP. As Nazir affirmed: "The Kashmiri jihad does not help us forward in achieving our objectives," a statement reflecting the TTP's animosity towards the US rather than India.[77] Concerning Afghanistan, Maulvi Nazir maintains that rather than being disunited with the Afghan Taliban, TTP is actively supporting the war effort in that country against the US-led NATO ISAF forces. As he states: "we fight with them in Afghanistan too and are enemies of the occupation forces there."[78]

Suicide Bombings and the Cult of Martyrdom

The cult of martyrdom, although usually associated mainly with Shi'ism, beginning with the martyrdom of Hussain at Karbala in CE 680,[79] is also a significant strand of the jihadist ideology within Sunni Islam. Traditionally, Islam has taught that, as Allah is the only one who gives life and takes life, it is wrong for a Muslim to usurp that authority and commit suicide. Although suicide is apparently condemned in the hadith, which states: "Whoever kills himself (with a steel instrument or something else) will be punished in the same manner in the fire of Hell,"[80] TTP, as with militant Islamists generally, presents martyrdom as the supreme accolade for faithfulness as a Muslim, the surety of immediate entry on death into al-Janna, heaven, and subsequent reward therein. It is regarded as a supererogatory act cleansing the believer from all his sins. "To become a martyr," declares one member of LeJ, "is the dream of every Mujahid. It is a gift from God and will send a message to the enemy that a Mujahid would prefer to die in an interrogation cell rather than disclose any secret that could harm other Mujahids."[81]

In affirming the duty and value of martyrdom TTP follows the ideology of jihadists such as Abdullah Azzam (1941–89), who claimed that a major reason for jihad is the "hope for Martyrdom and a High Station in Paradise," and that martyrs will enjoy "seven special favours of Allah."[82] Islamic extremism has little difficulty finding Qur'anic and hadith support for martyrdom. Reference is made to Muhammad's declaration: "Lo! Allah hath purchased of the believers their persons and their goods. For theirs is the Garden [of paradise]: they fight in his cause, and slay and are slain."[83] Similarly, Abu Daud provides a hadith that pronounces: "he who is killed while protecting his property is a martyr, and he who is killed while defending his family, or his blood, or his religion is a martyr." In other hadith, such as that found in al-Bukhari, Prophet Muhammad is reported to have said: "I would love to be martyred in Allah's Cause and be resurrected and then get martyred, and then be resurrected again to be martyred again."[84]

In early April 2009, Mullah Omar, having condoned suicide missions, told reporters that suicide bombings would continue in cities throughout Pakistan until the US drone attacks ceased.[85] TTP, despite media reports of suicide bombings killing civilians, declares that it never intends to kill innocent civilians. In a recent interview, Maulvi Nazir stated:

> We are Mujahideen and we never carry out martyrdom operations in the vicinity of Muslims. It is the [Pakistan] Army upon which we execute such operations. The Army is our target because it has aided the Americans. We do carry out martyrdom operations throughout Pakistan but we renounce and condemn those of them in mosques and marketplaces. It is our enemy that does it.[86]

Attitude Towards America and the West

The philosophy of TTP is shaped by a polarized view of the world, a world torn between East and West, between belief and disbelief, between zalim (oppressed Muslims) and mustad'afin (the oppressor, the West). The West is seen as jahiliyyah-mahdiyya, civilization characterised by ignorance-materialism, godlessness, similar to the jahili society of pre-Islamic Arabia. Westerners, or more specifically Christians, Jews, polytheists and those who reject Islam, are regarded as being "the worst of creatures," immoral and decadent, worthy only of the perpetual fires of al-jahannam, Hell.[87] As well as being immoral, the West is generally regarded as the perpetual enemy of true religion, "the crusader-Zionists," whose aim is the destruction of Islam.

While regarding Western culture per se as jahili, ignorant and corrupt,[88] particular animosity is felt towards America. Muslims around the world deeply resent the "foreign policy of bloody and oppressive interventions" carried out by the US.[89] With the commencement of operation Enduring Freedom in October 2001, resulting in the US invasion of Afghanistan, tribes on the Afghan border (mainly the Mehsuds, Wazirs and Mohmands) revolted against their traditional tribal leaders and the Pakistan government because neither supported a struggle against what they regarded as unlawful US occupation of a Muslim land.[90] The US drone attacks against militants inside Pakistan are similarly seen as an unjustified interference in a Muslim country. Talking to Muslims at the Badshahi Mosque and other places in Lahore during a recent visit to Pakistan, I heard much that confirmed the animosity felt towards America, not only by extremists, but by moderate Muslims. As well as the killing of innocent civilians in missile attacks, and criticism of a foreign policy that seemed to serve US interests alone, Muslims I spoke to shared their concerns over the apparent Empire-building by America, the "McDonaldization" of their country and alleged US ignorance. It was with some humour that contacts I have in Peshawar, in email correspondence, criticized the way CNN, and the US media generally, calls Muslims, "Moslems," and in the mispronunciation of place names such as "Swot" instead of Swat (pronounced sa'wat). The "war on terror" is regarded by many Muslims, not just extremists, as a war on Islam itself.

With the above points in mind, the US is regarded by TTP as zalim, a tyrannical force that must be opposed; the Great Shaitan, Dajjal, or Satan, an evil eschatological power that will face the judgment of Allah, finally being overcome by a revived Islam.[91] As such, TTP, echoing the rhetoric of al-Qaeda and other radical groups, states it is the duty of all Muslims to "comply with

God's order by killing Americans and their allies."[92] The war on America is seen not only as being a struggle against US forces within Pakistan, but also on the wider, international level. Amir Waliur Rehman declared US President Barack Obama and his allies to be "our foremost enemy."[93] He has stated that TTP was committed to fighting foreign troops in Pakistan and was capable of hitting targets in London, Paris or Washington.[94] In a news statement broadcast on March 31, 2009, Baitullah Mehsud made a similar threat, stating his intention of launching an attack on Washington that would "amaze everyone in the world." He boasted: "The maximum they can do is martyr me. But we will exact our revenge on them from inside America."[95]

Criticism of the Pakistan Government

The Pakistan government and its leaders, particularly President Musharraf and his successor Asif Ali Zardari, are criticized by Pakistani militants as being "lapdogs," "cronies of America,"[96] and for supporting "America's dirty war" in Afghanistan. TTP believes that many of Pakistan's leaders work for the American government, and regards the ISI as an extension of the CIA.[97] Musharraf's U-turn in policy towards the Taliban by fully supporting the US military campaign in Afghanistan following the events of 9/11 angered many of the tribesmen of the NWFP. In January 2004, to the chagrin of militants throughout Pakistan, Musharraf, under pressure from the US, made an agreement with Atal Bihari Vajpayee, the Indian prime minister, agreeing that Azad Kashmir would not be used to support terrorist activity against India.[98] The Musharraf-Armitage agreement, made in June 2002, had supported the notion that the Pakistan government was merely a lackey of US foreign policy. Further anger was aimed at the Pakistan government in March 2009 with the announcement of the new Af-Pak policy by the Obama Administration. Amongst other things, for the purpose of fighting the Taliban, this policy treats the border regions of Afghanistan and Pakistan as one, and expects Pakistan to complement US military exercises in Afghanistan with a security operation in its own tribal areas.[99] For the reasons outlined here TTP has openly condemned the Pakistan government, accusing it of nifaq (hypocrisy), when a Muslim claims allegiance to Islam but doesn't live up to its principles. In November 2008 Hakimullah Mehsud declared to media that President Zardari was on his hit list, along with many other government officials, for their "pro-American" policies.[100] He warned that if Pakistan continued its support of NATO in its effort to flush out terrorism, it would have no choice but to storm Peshawar and other cities and eventually take over the entire country.[101] He also accused members of the central and provincial governments of "working to break up Pakistan in collaboration with the US." Due mainly to its links with America, the Pakistan government and its administrative and diplomatic proposals are regarded as "suspect" by the TTP. Maulvi Nazir, for example, rejected the separate peace deal signed between the TNSM and the authorities as a "deception to divide the organization [TNSM] and the militant groups waging war against India in Kashmir, using all as tools of the ISI."[102] With the above points in mind the Pakistan government, manifesting a nominal adherence to Islamic values, was criticized by Nazir for using "Islamic politics" merely to bolster and legitimize its position.

The Takfiri Doctrine and its Application

Adopting the *Takfiri* doctrine of the Medieval jurist Taqi ad-Din Ahmad Ibn Taymiyyah (1268–1328), later revived by the twentieth-century theoretician Syed Qutb (1906–1966), TTP justifies its stance of fighting other Muslims, and opposing a government that claims to be Muslim, yet fails to act according to Islamic principles.[103] Classical Sunni tradition regarded an existing Muslim regime as legitimate as long as the ruler did not publicly reject Islam by preventing Muslims from practicing their faith. It was argued that even a "bad" ruler is better than fitna (disorder and chaos). As Ibn Hanbal remarked in the ninth century, "you should obey the government and not rebel against it. If the ruler orders something which implies ma'siya [sin against God] you should neither obey nor rebel. Do not support the fitna," he opined, "neither by hand nor by your tongue."[104] As Emmanual Sivan remarks, "deligitimisation and the right for revolt are thus virtually alien to Sunnism."[105] However, contradicting such classical teaching, in adopting a theory of resistance against illegitimate power, TTP maintains that jihad should be waged against those considered to be Takfiri, those who do not follow the teachings of Islam, and the unjust Muslim ruler must be opposed.[106] Therefore, under Takfiri teaching, the Pakistan government, due to its allegiance to western Kufr states, is regarded by TTP as ridda (apostate or non-Muslim). Political figures are condemned as Takfir al-Hakim and fasidah, corrupt and apostate, rulers corrupted by ghazw fikri, the enchantment of Western ideas. Similarly, the Pakistan army is not regarded as a Muslim army, but "a mercenary army on the payroll of the US."[107] As one alim explains: "Islam views Takfir as a serious allegation. Takfir means to term a person as an infidel, or to practice as an act of infidelity."[108] Consequently TTP wages what it terms "defensive jihad against the Pakistan army" and the government.[109] Baitullah Mehsud argued that Pakistanis who cooperate with Westerners "are not true Muslims, they are collaborators of infidels, and deserve to be killed."[110] Hakimullah Mehsud, adopting a similar stance, has made strong-worded statements against leaders of the Pakistan Peoples Party (PPP), Awami National Party (ANP) and Mutahida Qaumi Movement (MQM), threatening attacks against them.[111]

The Strict Application of Sharia

TTP applies a rigid and strict exegesis of Sharia. In the opinion of TTP, as it is enacted under the legislative and judicial bodies in present day Pakistan, Sharia is a weakened, and therefore impious, form of true Islamic Law. Muslim Khan, formerly the chief spokesperson for TTP, said that "the [Pakistan] constitution itself was not completely Islamic. The Taliban does not accept any constitution other than Sharia."[112] Maulvi Nazir expressed similar views when he remarked:

> With these individuals remaining in power [the present government in Pakistan], it is ridiculous to think that Sharia would ever be as it should be. These are cronies of America. Pakistan has the British law implemented in it, and its educational system is that devised by Lord Macaulay. With this at hand, we cannot accept the supposed Sharia. The Supreme Court remains imposed upon our heads and then they say: "We donate the Sharia to Waziristan while they work under us" . . . sorry, we can't accept this.[113]

As mentioned above, TTP regards secularist Western culture in the Qutbian sense as jahiliyya, that is, "a psychological state which rejects the guidance of God."[114] Like other Muslim extremists, TTP, believing it to be the new jahiliyya or barbarism, condemns Western values and modernity, stressing their incompatibility and corrupting influence on Islam. Reminiscent of Ayman al-Zawahiri and his influential booklet "Knights Under the Prophet's Banner,"[115] in which he elaborated the teaching of al-wala wal-bara, — "loyalty" and "separation," "friendship" and "enmity" — TTP has emphasized how Western civilization, corrupting the Islamic world, is the root cause of all its ills and therefore is to be rejected. The stance manifested by TTP against the West is characterized by cognitive dissonance, a rejection of Western culture as jahili and corrupt, yet adopting an uncritical use of the West's technology, particularly telecommunications, computers and weapons. Other rules adopted by TTP seem nothing less than ethics of necessity and convenience. Qari Hussain, for instance, issued a "fatwa" declaring that it is permissible to rob banks because they are un-Islamic, and to rob minorities because they do not follow Islam.[116] Despite such inconsistencies, the social ethic of modernism, allegedly atheistic, pluralistic, and individualistic, is contrasted with the fundamental norms of a Muslim society, which is religious, God-fearing, and Sharia based. The principle of manhaj Allah, the way of Allah in all areas of life, and al-Manhaj al-Elahi, acknowledgment of the divine plan, forms the bedrock of extremist ideology and practice. The teaching of TTP reflects the Maududian notion of iqamat-i-deen,[117] "the establishment of religion," and the idea that society and the state should be subjected entirely to Sharia. TTP, in its reaction against modernity and the West, claims to search for a "pure" society based upon Sharia law, a society which, to use a phrase coined by Qutb, "grows in the shade of the Qur'an."

Believing that the "religious" and the "secular" cannot be separated, there is a call by TTP for tatbiq al-Sharia, "application of Muslim law" in every area of life. The implementation of Sharia involves a rejection of that which is not considered Islamic. As one journalist recently commented: TTP condemns those "who adopt a western outlook and lifestyle. Women, in particular, are the object of their hatred because they seek education, economic empowerment and dress in 'un-Islamic clothes.'"[118] In April 2009, TTP declared the imposition of Sharia in the Bajaur agency and other localities in the NWFP.[119] Since then it is believed that TTP members have set fire to TV sets, photos, paintings, audio and video cassettes and other things deemed offensive to

Islam in the Buner valley area. Manifesting the usual Deobandi rejection of Barelwi beliefs and practices as "bida" (superstitious innovations), the shrine of Pir Baba at Pacha Kili was locked, and followers of the wali (saint) were prevented from visiting the site.[120] TTP has destroyed numerous schools that catered for the education of girls, restricted women's employment and visibility in public spaces, killed those opposed to their version of Islam, banned the shaving of beards and prevented people from availing themselves of the Benazir Income Support Programme, a government project to provide financial aid to women.[121] It is also reported that TTP pressured doctors of public sector hospitals in Peshawar to wear traditional shalwar-qameez instead of Western suits. Similarly, female doctors were directed to observe purdah (decency, modesty, segregation from men) and cover their face from their male colleagues. TTP has denied making these threats.[122] The implementation of Sharia by TTP and its treatment of Kufr as second-class citizens has led to the persecution of minority groups. TTP, like other extremist Sunni groups such as Sipah-e-Sahab and its splinter group LeJ, is strongly anti-Shia. There have been reports of the maltreatment of Shia, regarded as zindique (heretics) by Sunni Muslims, due to doctrinal and ritual differences. Hakimullah Mehsud is known for his ruthless anti-Shia campaign in the Kurram agency, where the presence of TTP zealots led to fierce persecution of the Shia minority Pashtuns.[123] The application of Sharia has also led to the banishment of the few surviving native Christians, Sikhs and Hindus from the frontier province.[124] Such persecution, and the terrorist actions, has given rise to a major displacement of population, estimated at 3 million people to date.[125]

Conclusion

Since the death of Baitullah Mehsud, the official media line has claimed that the "Pakistani government has indeed broken [the] back-bone of the TTP" and "their leaders are hiding or have gone underground."[126] With alacrity it has been proclaimed that "Taliban sponsored terrorism in Pakistan has lost its sting."[127] Brigadier Mahmud Shah, former security chief of the NWF tribal areas, confidently stated that Baitullah's death had been "a great loss to the extremists," causing "infighting between the different groups." In his opinion it had "finally resulted in the division of power and authority in TTP."[128] Such claims seemed to be corroborated by the rumour that Hakimullah Mehsud had been killed in disputes with rival succession claimants. It was suggested that Hakimullah's lookalike brother, Kalimullah Mehsud, had been presented to the media in his place, to prevent further fissures within the group. Kalimullah himself was killed in a shoot-out with the Army in mid-September.[129] The capture and killing of other leading figures within TTP has given further credibility to the belief that the group is broken and dysfunctional. During September, for example, Pakistan Security forces captured Muslim Khan, Sher Muhammad Qassab, Mohammad Shah (alias Mamay, a close aide to Hakimullah)[130] and Abu Faraj.[131] Qari Tahir Yuldashev, one of the founders of the Islamic Movement of Uzbekistan (IMU), who had strong links with TTP, was killed by an American drone missile.[132] If government reports are to be believed, about 1,700 militants have been killed in Pakistan's northwest since Pakistan security forces launched operation Rah-e-Rast in April in the Malakand division.

Although some believe that "TTP remains a diminished force,"[133] recent events in Pakistan have indicated that such optimism may be premature. As Maleeha Lodhi rightly observes, "the Taliban movement survived the death of its leaders in the past, so it is too early to say [that Baitullah's death] is a decisive blow."[134] Having the men, weapons and motivation to fight, it would be reasonable to suggest that although TTP's institutional capacity may have received a set-back, its ideological capacity to influence is far from over. Hakimullah Mehsud has stated that "if the Pakistan government continues with its policy of following American diktat [sic] [some day] we can even try to capture Peshawar, Hangu, and even Islamabad, we have the strength to do it."[135] In response to media claims that TTP was a spent force, Amir Waliur Rehman boasted "We have thousands of suicide attackers, who can destroy their targets anywhere."[136] "Our movement has gained more strength," declared Qari Hussain, "after the martyrdom of Baitullah Mehsud. We are united."[137] The terrorist acts carried out by TTP since Hakimullah's appointment as leader would seem to indicate that these are not empty threats. It is a matter of conjecture as to the strength of support TTP may have amongst Pakistan's population generally, many people viewing the jihadists as freedom fighters, "standing up to the Americans."[138]

TTP, as with other terrorist groups in Pakistan, must be neutralized. As well as the suffering and strife caused by such terrorism within Pakistan itself, and the threat of terrorist activity planned in that area occurring in other parts of the world, it has been argued that there is also the danger of extremists taking control of a country such as Pakistan, which possesses a nuclear deterrent. Faced with such awful possibilities some may question the ability of the Pakistan army to perform the task of eradicating militancy. Likewise, it is argued that the Pakistan government needs to end its "double game" of officially condemning TTP and other militant groups, while unofficially supporting them in its anti-Indian and Soviet jihads. Others would suggest the adoption by the US of a more transparent, and less self-interested, foreign policy. Although military action is imperative it would be reasonable to say that the problem presented by TTP and other extremist groups in Pakistan cannot be overcome by military means alone. Military intervention has often given rise to *more* militancy rather than eradicating it. It has been a catalyst for further anger and despair and anti-West and anti-US sentiments. A reduction, if not an end, of the "collateral damage" caused by US air strikes would go a long way to the winning of hearts and minds. As such, as well as the use of military force, there is a need for social, economic and administrative policies. There is a need, for example, to monitor the curricula taught in the madrassahs, where young Pakistani men are "inculcated with a distorted version of Islam, and instead of learning to read and write they [are] taught how to kill people."[139] With large numbers of the population in Pakistan illiterate, assistance is needed in providing better education for the masses. The seriousness of the situation cannot be ignored. Hassan Abbas reminds us: "In this troubling scenario, dismantling TTP and bringing its leadership to justice is critical for Pakistan's internal security as well as for tackling the Taliban insurgency in southern Afghanistan."[140] As one journalist emphasizes the ensuing battle between TTP and the Pakistan government: it "is a fight for the very future of Pakistan."[141]

Notes

1 The words of Maulvi Nazir, interview, As-Sahab, Al-Qimmeh Media, March 14, 2009, http://www.alqimmah.net/showthread.php?p=10251 (accessed March 19, 2009).

2   "Benazir Bhutto killed in attack," BBC News, December 27, 2007, http://news.bbc. co.uk/1/hi/world/south_asia/7161590.stm (accessed December 27, 2007).

3   See "Benazir Bhutto assassinated at political rally in Pakistan," *Times*, December 28, 2007, http://www.timesonline.co.uk/tol/news/world/asia/article3099534.ece? token=null&offset=12&page=2 (accessed December 31, 2007).

4   Free Republic, August 10, 2009, http://www.freerepublic.com/focus/f-news/2312299/ posts (accessed August 16, 2009).

5   "Interview: Pakistan still considering options," Reuters, September 28, 2009, http:// in.reuters.com/article/worldNews/idINIndia-42746220090928 (accessed September 29, 2009).

6   The Inter-Services Intelligence, or ISI, is the largest intelligence service in Pakistan. See Pakistan Defence official website, http://www.defence.pk/forums/strategic-geopolitical-issues/551-isi-pakistan-inter-services-intelligence.html (accessed July 12, 2009).

7   "The ISI and Terrorism: behind the accusations," Council on Foreign Relations, May 28, 2009, http://www.cfr.org/publication/11644/ (accessed June 2, 2009).

8   Ibid.

9   J. Stern, Foreword, H. Abbas, *Pakistan's Drift into Extremism, Allah, the Army and America's War on Terror*. East Gate, New York, 2005, p. xlii.

10 J. Stern, H. Abbas, op. cit., p. xlii.

11 See Interview by Peter Chamberlin with Maulvi Nazir, As-Sahab, "Paramilitary Pretense, Who Controls the Predators?," http://www.uruknet.info/?p=53340 (accessed May 18, 2009).

12 Interview with Mullah Nazir, As-Sahab, "Paramilitary Pretense, Who Controls the Predators?," op. cit.

13 H. Abbas, op. cit.

14 Ibid., pp. 80f. Daud refused to accept the Durand Line, the border established by the British in 1893, as the border between Afghanistan and Pakistan. He argued for the merger of the NWFP with Afghanistan due to a shared Pashtun ethnicity.

15 Abbas, op. cit., p. 201.

16 The name "Tehrik-i-Taliban" had been used prior to the December 14 announcement. An organization with a similar name emerged in FATA's Orakzai agency in 1998, see Pakistan Defence Forum, http://www.defence.pk/forums/pakistans-war/32311-disintegrations-ttp-what.html (accessed September 14, 2009).

17 J. Ismail, "All Things Pakistan," August 4, 2009, http://pakistaniat.com/2009/06/15/ decisive-offensive-against-baitullah-mehsud/ (accessed September 6, 2009).

18 *The Daily Times Online*, July 24, 2009, http://www.dailytimes.com.pk/default. asp?page=2009\07\24\story_24-7-2009_pg1_1 (accessed August 2, 2009).

19 See page on Baitullah Mehsud, Rewards for Justice Website, http://www.rewards forjustice.net/index.cfm?page=mehsud (accessed June 3, 2009).

20   Ibid.

21   *The International News*, August 28, 2009, http://www.thenews.com.pk/daily_detail. asp?id=195420 (accessed August 29, 2009).

22   US special envoy Richard Holbrooke's message to India when he met Indian officials in New Delhi on April 8, 2009, "US envoy invokes India's help in fighting Mehsud," IBN Live, April 9, 2009, http://ibnlive.in.com/news/us-envoy-invokes-indias-help-in-fighting-mehsud/89828-2.html (accessed April 10, 2009).

23   See S. Nasir, "Baitullah Mehsud: South Waziristan's Unofficial Amir," *Terrorism Focus*, vol. 3, July 5, 2006; H Abbas, "A Profile of Tehrik-i-Taliban Pakistan," *CTC Sentinel*, January 2008, vol. 1, issue 2, pp. 1–4. http://belfercenter.ksg.harvard.edu/publication/17868/profile_of_tehrikitaliban_pakistan.html (accessed February 3, 2008); Raja, *Asian Tribune*, July 10, 2009, http://asiantribune.com/07/10/time-for-baitullah-mehsud-to-give-up-militancy/ (accessed July 13, 2009); K. C. Azar, Insurgent Profile: Baitullah Mehsud, May 4, 2009, www.theanalysiscorp.com/Mehsud%20profile.pdf (accessed May 14, 2009).

24   Bill Roggio, "Pakistani Taliban unites under Baitullah Mehsud," *Long War Journal*, December 15, 2008. http://www.longwarjournal.org/archives/2007/12/pakistani_taliban_un.php (accessed February 11, 2008).

25   "Taliban form Shura Ittihadul-ul-Mujahideen in Waziristan," Geo-Pakistan, February 22, 2009, http://www.geo.tv/2-22-2009/35712.htm (accessed February 27, 2009).

26   This union effectively came to an end on August 15 when 17 associates of Maulvi Nazir and Gul Bahadur were gunned down in the Mehsud dominated Salae Roghae region of the Ladha sub-division, see Waziristan Power Politics, Dawn.com, September 13, 2009, http://www.dawn.com/wps/wcm/connect/dawn-content-library/dawn/news/pakistan/provinces/04-waziristan-power-politics-qs-02 (accessed September 14, 2009).

27   J. Perlez, "Pakistan Makes a Taliban Truce, Creating a Haven," *The New York Times*, February 16, 2009, http://www.nytimes.com/2009/02/17/world/asia/17pstan.html (accessed February 16, 2009).

28   J. Perlez, "Taliban Accepts Pakistan ceasefire," *The New York Times*, February 24, 2009, http://www.nytimes.com/2009/02/25/world/asia/25pstan.html?_r=1 (accessed February 25, 2009).

29   *The Times Online* August 8, http://www.timesonline.co.uk/tol/news/world/asia/article6742384.ece (accessed September 9, 2009). For Baitullah Mehsud see Sohail Abdul Nasir, "Baitullah Mehsud: South Waziristan's Unofficial Amir," *Terrorism Focus*, vol. 3 (26), July 5, 2006; H Abbas, "A Profile of Tehrik-i-Taliban Pakistan," CTC Sentinel, West Point, NY 1 (2), pp. 1–4. http://belfercenter.ksg.harvard.edu/publication/17868/profile_of_tehrikitaliban_pakistan.html. vol. 1, issue 2, January 2008; http://www.jamestown.org/terrorism/news/article.php?articleid=2370054 (accessed February 11, 2009). Asif Haroon Raja, Asian Tribune, July 10, 2009, http://asiantribune.com/07/10/

time-for-baitullah-mehsud-to-give-up-militancy/, (accessed July 12, 2009); Azar, Insurgent Profile: Baitullah Mehsud, May 4, 2009, op. cit.

30 August 17, 2009, SANA, South Asia News Agency, http://www.sananews.com.pk/english/2009/08/19/top-ttp-spokesman-held-in-mohmand-agency-officials (accessed September 19, 2009).

31 See August 20, 2009, Reuters, http://www.reuters.com/article/topNews/idUSTRE 57H0L220090820 (accessed August 20, 2009).

32 "Hakimullah new TTP chief," August 23, 2009, http://www.nation.com.pk/pakistan-news-newspaper-daily-english-online/Politics/23-Aug-2009/Hakimullah-new-TTP-chief (accessed 23/08, 2009).

33 Pakistan News, August 23, 2009, http://www.nation.com.pk/pakistan-news-news paper-daily-english-online/Politics/23-Aug-2009/Hakimullah-new-TTP-chief (accessed August 23, 2009).

34 *People's Daily Online*, September 1, 2009, http://english.people.com.cn/90001/90777/90851/6745550.html (accessed September 3, 2009).

35 Zahid Hussain, "Killings Rattle Pakistan Taliban," *The Wall Street Journal*, http://online.wsj.com/article/SB125103758449251853.html (accessed August 23, 2009).

36 "Pak Taliban: At odds with each other as well as civilization," *Despardes*, September 1, 2009, http://despardes.com/wp/2009/09/01/pak-taliban-at-odds-with-each-other-as-well-as-civilization/ (accessed September 4, 2009).

37 *The International News*, August 28, 2009, http://www.thenews.com.pk/daily_detail. asp?id=195420 (accessed August 29, 2009).

38 "TTP leader Hakimullah Mehsud dead: Pak media," *Hindustan Times*, September 2, 2009 http://www.hindustantimes.com/News/pakistan/TTP-leader-Hakimullah-Mehsud-dead-Pak-media/Article1-449442.aspx (accessed September 2, 2009); *People's Daily Online*, September 1, 2009 http://english.people.com.cn/90001/90777/90851/6745550. html (accessed September 3, 2009).

39 September 3, 2009, http://teabreak.pk/troops-brace-for-decisive-offensive-221/25137/ (accessed August 30, 2009).

40 Pashtunwali encourages such fighters to practice aziz/azizwale (loyalty to the clan) and to show nang (Honour), tureh (courage) and ghairat (pride) in the way they fight and live their lives. Splits often occur within the group, or disagreements with other tribes, due to Terbor/Terborwali, (cousin and tribal rivalries). See S. E. Ali, *Cultures of the World: Afghanistan*, New York: Marshall Cavendish, 1995 and "'Pashtunwali': the Pashtun Way," terroristplanet.com, http://www.terroristplanet.com/pashtun.htm (accessed July 12, 2009).

41 *Long War Journal*, September 25, 2009, http://www.longwarjournal.org/threat-matrix/archives/2009/09/taliban_suicide_bombing_master.php (accessed September 28, 2009).

42 *Times Now*, September 2, 2009, http://www.timesnow.tv/No-Hafiz-Saeed-in-Paks-most-wanted-list/articleshow/4326310.cms (accessed September 4, 2009).

43 *Long War Journal*, September 25, 2009, op. cit.

44 Profile of Waliur Rahman September 2009, The NEFA Foundation, www.nefafoundation.org/miscellaneous/ . . . /nefa_rehman0909, (accessed October 1, 2009).

45 *Times Now*, op. cit.

46 H Abbas, "A Profile of Tehrik-i-Taliban Pakistan," *CTC Sentinel*, (West Point, NY: Combating Terrorism Center) 1 (2): 1–4. http://belfercenter.ksg.harvard.edu/publication/17868/profile_of_tehrikitaliban_pakistan.html. vol. 1, issue 2, January 2008.

47 See "US commander consults Pakistan on anti-Taliban campaign," *Reuters*, July 14, 2009, http://www.reuters.com/article/homepageCrisis/idUSISL213431._CH_.2400 (accessed July 18, 2009).

48 Jauhar Ismail, "Decisive offensive against Baitullah Mehsud?," *All Things Pakistan*, August 4, 2009, http://pakistaniat.com/2009/06/15/decisive-offensive-against-baitullah-mehsud/ (accessed September 6, 2009).

49 Comment made by Col. J. Spizser, the US commander for troops in north-eastern Afghanistan, "US Commander: Swat Valley Offensive Helping in Afghanistan," Antiwar.com, June 23, 2009, http://news.antiwar.com/2009/06/23/us-commander-swat-valley-offensive-helping-in-afghanistan/ (accessed June 29, 2009).

50 An improvised explosive device (IED) is a homemade bomb constructed and deployed in ways other than in conventional military action.

51 *Pakistan Views*, http://www.pakistanviews.com/hakimullah-mehsud-s-brother-killed-officials/ (accessed October 1, 2009).

52 Interview with Maulvi Nazir, As-Sahab, www.worldproutassembly.org/archives/2009/04/ (accessed October 1, 2009).

53 See *Daily Times of Pakistan*, www.dailytimes.com.pk (accessed April 7, 2009).

54 *Daily Times*, June 24, 2009, http://www.dailytimes.com.pk/default.asp?page=2009%5C06%5C24%5Cstory_24-6-2009_pg1_3 (accessed June 26, 2009).

55 *Reuters*, March 31, 2009, http://changinguppakistan.wordpress.com/2009/03/31/beitullah-mehsud-claims-responsibility-for-manawan-police-attack/ (accessed April 1, 2009).

56 *Daily Times*, March 31, 2009, http://www.dailytimes.com.pk/default.asp?page=2009%5C03%5C31%5Cstory_31-3-2009_pg7_2 (accessed April 2, 2009).

57 CBS News, March 23, 2009, http://www.cbsnews.com/stories/2009/03/23/world/main4884632.shtml, 30th and March 23 respectively (accessed March 24, 2009).

58 June 9, 2009, see BBC News, June 10, 2009, http://news.bbc.co.uk/1/hi/world/south_asia/8092147.stm (accessed June 11, 2009).

59 June 12, 2009, BBC News, http://news.bbc.co.uk/1/hi/world/south_asia/8096776.stm (accessed June 12, 2009).

60 Ismail Khan, Dawn.com., http://www.dawn.com/wps/wcm/connect/dawn-content-library/dawn/news/pakistan/provinces/08-Fight-for-spoils-splits-Taliban-ts-06 (accessed August 21, 2009).

61 Ibid.

62 Words of Air Marshall Ayaz Ahmad Khan, "Terrorism: the changed dimension," September 11, 2009, http://strategist-7777.blogspot.com/2009/09/terrorism-changed-dimension.html (accessed September 11, 2009).

63 Ibid.

64 Interview with Maulvi Nazir on the Islamic site As-Sahab, Al-Qimmeh Media, March 14, 2009, op. cit.

65 T. McDermott, *Perfect Soldiers, The hi-jackers, who they were, why they did it.* HarperCollins Publishers, New York, 2005, p. 14.

66 Interview with Maulvi Nazir on the Islamic site As-Sahab, April 10, 2009, op. cit.

67 A. Azzam, Quoted by P. Bergen, *Holy War: Inside the secret world of Osama bin Laden.* London: Phoenix, 2003, p. 56.

68 Abbas, "A Profile of Tehrik-i-Taliban Pakistan," op. cit.

69 S. V. R. Nasr, *Mawdudi, and the making of Islamic Revivalism.* Oxford, Oxford University Press, 1996, p. 167.

70 Mawdudi, Jihād fi sabil Allah, jihad in Islam, 1962, cited by Ahmad, K. and Z. Ishaq Ansari, K. (ed.) *Islamic Perspectives: Studies in honour of Maulana Sayyid Abul A'la Mawdudi*, Leicester, Islamic Foundation, 1979, p. 13.

71 Title of a tract written by Muhammad al-Farag, see J. J. C. Janson, *The Neglected Duty.* New York, Macmillan, 1986.

72 Cited by Z. Hussain, *Frontline Pakistan: the struggle with Militant Islam*, New York, Columbia University Press, 2007, p. 59.

73 The idea that any area once gained by Muslims is considered sacred and should belong to the *Umma* for ever, any area lost must be regained.

74 Interview by Hussain with Saeed, January 2001, see Z. Hussain, *Frontline Pakistan: the Struggle with Militant Islam*, op. cit., p. 53.

75 Interview with Mullah Nazir, on the Islamic website As-Sahab, April 10, 2009, www.worldproutassembly.org/archives/2009/04/, (accessed April 15, 2009).

76 Ibid.

77 Ibid.

78 Ibid.

79 J. L. Esposito, *The Oxford Dictionary of Islam.* London, Oxford University Press, 2003.

80 A tradition of the prophet Muhammad recorded by Bukhari and Muslim.

81 Z. Hussain, *Frontline Pakistan: the struggle with Militant Islam*, op. cit., p. 95.

82 A. Azzam, "Reasons for Jihad," *Join the Caravan*, Second English Edition, 1988, Azzam Publications, London, http://www.islamistwatch.org/texts/azzam/caravan/preface.html (accessed April 4, 2007).

83 A. Y. Ali, *The Holy Qur'an, Text, translation and Commentary, Amana Corporation*, Brentwood, Maryland, USA, 1989, *surah* 9:111.

84 Al-Bukhari, narrating the words of Abu Huraira.

85 Interview with Maulvi Nazir, op. cit.

86 Maulvi Nazir, interview, As-Sahab, Al-Qimmeh Media, March 14, 2009, op. cit.

87 Surah 98:6.

88 *Jahiliyya*, Arabic term meaning "ignorance," usually used in reference to pagan idolatrous religion in pre-Islamic Arabia, see J. L. Esposito, *The Oxford Dictionary of Islam*, op. cit., sv.

89 W. Blum, Rogue State: *A Guide to the World's only Superpower.* Zed Books, London, 2006, p. 42.

90 Anti-war.com, http://news.antiwar.com/2009/04/19/us-drone-strike-kills-up-to-eight-in-south-waziristan/ (accessed April 19, 2009).

91 Shaitan, a reference to Satan the Devil or Dajjal, "the deceiver," the Antichrist who is supposed to appear during the age of injustice preceding the end of the world, causing corruption and oppression to sweep over the world. See Esposito, J. L. The Oxford Dictionary of Islam, op. cit., sv, "antichrist."

92 Statement made by the International Islamic front against Jews and crusaders, cited by Z. Hussain, *Frontline Pakistan: the struggle with Militant Islam*, op. cit., p. 73.

93 "Pak Taliban: At odds with each other as well as civilization," Despardes, September 1, 2009, http://despardes.com/wp/2009/09/01/pak-taliban-at-odds-with-each-other-as-well-as-civilization/ (accessed September 4, 2009).

94 Thaindian News, August 26, 2009, http://www.thaindian.com/newsportal/south-asia/taliban-can-hit-europe-us-says-rebel-commander_100238018.html (accessed September 1, 2009).

95 Sindh Today.net, April 1, 2009, http://www.sindhtoday.net/pakistan/81844.htm (accessed April 3, 2009).

96 Interview with Maulvi Nazir, As-Sahab, op. cit.

97 Ibid.

98 Z. Hussain, *Frontline Pakistan*, op. cit., pp. 102, 104.

99 "What does Obama's Af-Pak policy say?," Rediff India Abroad, March 27, 2009, http://www.rediff.com/news/2009/mar/27obama-speech-on-new-policy-on-afghanisthan-and-pakistan.htm (accessed March 30, 2009).

100 "Hakimullah Mehsud: the new face of terror," *Geo Tau Asiay*, September 8, 2009, http://www.geotauaisay.com/2009/09/hakimullah-mehsud-the-new-face-of-terror (accessed September 9, 2009).

101 "Taliban: we will take over Pak soon," *Pakistan News*, December 2, 2008, http://www.apakistannews.com/taliban-we-will-take-over-pak-soon-93079 (accessed December 12, 2008).

102 An interview with Maulvi Nazir, on the Islamic site As-Sahab, April 10, 2009, op. cit.

103 See E. Sivan, *Radical Islam: Medieval Theology and Modern Politics.* New Haven/London, Yale University Press, 1985, pp. 90f.

104   Ibn Hanbal, *kitab al-Sunna*, cited by Sivan, *Radical Islam: Medieval Theology and Modern Politics*, op. cit., p. 91.

105   Sivan, *Radical Islam*, ibid., p. 91.

106   See Al-Mawardi, Al-Ahkam al-Sultaniyya, The ordinances of Government and Ibn Taymiyyah, Al-Siyasa al-Shar'iyya, Political Jurisprudence, see E. Sivan, op. cit., pp. 90f.

107   *Pak Tribune*, op. cit.

108   See Muhammad Haniff, "Takfir: declaring a person as an infidel," http://counterideology. multiply.com/journal/item/36/Takfir_Declaring_a_Person_as_an_Infidel_Part_1, (accessed April 5, 2008).

109   Pakistan Defence Forum, nd., op. cit.

110   Pak Tribune, nd., http://www.paktribune.com/news/print.php?id=216877, (accessed April 12, 2009).

111   *The Times of India*, August 22, 2009, http://timesofindia.indiatimes.com/news/ world/pakistan/Hakimullah-Mehsud-appointed-as-new-Pak-Taliban-chief/article- show/4922755.cms (accessed August 23, 2009).

112   *The Daily Times*, ANI, April 17, 2009, http://yuvaz.com/blog/now-taliban-demands- repeal-of-un-islamic-provisions-in-pak-constitution/ (accessed April 17, 2009).

113   Interview with Maulvi Nazir, on the Islamic site As-Sahab, April 10, 2009, op. cit.

114   S. Qutb, *Milestones*, Damascus, Syria Dar-al-Ilm, 1962, p. 11. See also A. Salahi (trans.) *In the Shade of the Qur'an*. Leicester, Islamic Foundation, 6 vols, 2002.

115   Al-Zawahiri, *Al-Fursan Taht Rayah Al-Nabi* (Knights under the Prophet's Banner). Casablanca, Morocco: Dar-al-Najaah Al-Jadeedah, 2001.

116   *Daily Times*, June 5, 2009, http://www.dailytimes.com.pk/default.asp?page=2009% 5C06%5C24%5Cstory_24-6-2009_pg12_1 (accessed June 8, 2009).

117   Mawdudi, The Islamic State, Islamic Foundation, London, 1984, passim.

118   Rasheeda Bhagat, "Mehsud goes, but not his ideology," *Hindu Business Line*, August 11, 2009, http://www.thehindubusinessline.com/2009/08/11/stories/2009081150050800. htm (accessed August 17, 2009).

119   *The Hindu*, Saturday April 11, 2009, http://www.thehindu.com/holnus, op. cit.

120   *The Hindu*, Saturday April 11, 2009, http://www.thehindu.com/holnus/001200904 111453.htm (accessed April 15, 2009).

121   Radio broadcast by Maulvi Faqir Mohammad, *The Hindu*, Saturday April 11, 2009, http://www.thehindu.com/holnus/001200904111453.htm (accessed April 15, 2009.

122   *International News Online*, May 9, 2009, http://www.thenews.com.pk (accessed May 9, 2009).

123   "Hakimullah Mehsud: the new face of terror," *Geo Tau Asiay*, September 8, 2009, http://www.geotauaisay.com/2009/09/hakimullah-mehsud-the-new-face-of-terror, (accessed September 9, 2009); *The Times of India*, September 4, 2009, http://

timesofindia.indiatimes.com/news/world/pakistan/Hakimullah-Mehsud-alive-insists-Pak-Taliban/articleshow/4973129.cms, (accessed September 4, 2009).

124   *The Hindu Times*, Saturday April 11, 2009, op. cit.

125   *The Hindu Times*, April 11, 2009, ibid.

126   Mian Iftikhar Hussain, Provincial Information Minister of Pakhtoonkhwa province, talking to Media, September 27, 2009, "Blasts in Peshawar and Bannu," Ground Report September 27, 2009, http://www.groundreport.com/World/Blasts-in-Peshawar-and-Bannu/2908240, (accessed September 27, 2009).

127   "Terrorism: the changed dimension," September 11, 2001, http://strategist-7777. blogspot.com/2009/09/terrorism-changed-dimension.html, (accessed September 12, 2009).

128   *The News PK*, August 26, 2009, http://www.thenewspk.com/2009/08/pakistan-taliban-threatens-to-avenge-leaders-death/, (accessed August 28, 2009).

129   "Top Commander Captured," *Pakistan News*, September 12, 2009, http://www.pakistan views.com/swat-taliban-mouthpiece-top-commander-captured/ (accessed September 13, 2009).

130   "Hakimullah's close aide arrested in NWFP," http://blog.taragana.com/n/hakeemullah-mehsuds-close-aide-arrested-in-nwfp-183858/ (accessed October 1, 2009).

131   "Suicide bombing mastermind apprehended," *Asian Tribune*, September 23, 2009, http://www.asiantribune.com/news/2009/09/22/suicide-bombing-mastermind-apprehended (accessed September 23, 2009).

132   "Yuldashev: end of a regional terrorist," Pakistan Defence Forum, October 2, 2009, http://www.defence.pk/forums/pakistans-war/35645-thank-you-usa.html (accessed October 3, 2009).

133   Quote from "After Baitullah, TTP loses support at home and abroad," *The National*, September 7, 2009, http://www.thenational.ae/apps/pbcs.dll/article?AID=/20090907/ OPINION/709069944/1080 (accessed September 7, 2009).

134   The *Wall Street Journal*, August 8, 2009, http://online.wsj.com/article/SB124961 991813313685.html (accessed August 17, 2009).

135   "Terrorism: the changed dimension," September 11, 2001, http://strategist-7777. blogspot.com/2009/09/terrorism-changed-dimension.html (accessed September 12, 2009).

136   GEO Pakistan, "Baitullah is alive, says TTP Amir in SWA," August 24, 2009, http://www.geo.tv/8–24–2009/48136.htm (accessed August 25, 2009).

137   "Blasts in Peshawar and Bannu," Ground Report, September 27, 2009, http://www.ground report.com/World/Blasts-in-Peshawar-and-Bannu/2908240 (accessed September 27, 2009).

138   Pervez Hoodbhoy, "Pakistan: Intolerance running riot," April 12, 2009, http://paktea house.wordpress.com/2009/04/12/pakistan-intolerance-running-riot/ (accessed April 16, 2009).

139   H. Abbas, op. cit., p. 204.

140   H. Abbas, "A Profile of Tehrik-i-Taliban Pakistan," CTC Sentinel, vol. 1, issue 2, January 2008.

141   J. Ismail, op. cit.

CHAPTER ELEVEN

Women in Jihad: Emerging Discourses in Pakistan

Samina Yasmeen

Abstract

The literature on militancy in Pakistan, and elsewhere, mostly focuses on the role of men. This ignores the agency of women in promoting such ideas by virtue of being nurturers in the family structures organized along orthodox lines. This chapter looks at how women in Pakistan have gradually contributed to notions of divine will being paramount in determining social and political structures, and in the process promoted orthodox understandings of Islamic identities and jihadist ideologies. It looks at groups such as the Al-Huda Academy and literature published by militant Islamic organizations to discuss gender-based contributions to growing militancy in the country. It also asks the question of how these ideas can be countered using more nuanced understandings of women's agency in a country like Pakistan.

Introduction

The rise of militancy in Pakistan has earned the country the dubious title of being the epicenter of terrorist networks, which pose a threat to world security. Attempts to understand the causes of this militancy, and possible strategies designed to counter militant/jihadi strands, have focused on the issue in gender-specific terms. Militancy in Pakistan is viewed as a phenomenon controlled and executed by men. While this assumption is not clearly articulated, the literature and coverage of acts of militancy play in down the agency of women in jihad. The tendency stands in contrast to the growing recognition of women's role in jihadi activities in other Muslim societies, including Palestine, Iraq and Algeria. It also fails to take into account the processes that have characterized the rise of Islamism in Pakistan.

This chapter aims to explore the agency of women in jihad with reference to emerging discourses in Pakistan on Muslim womanhood and their rights and responsibilities in Islamic spaces. It argues that, against the background of increasing Islamization and Arabization of religious identities in Pakistan, women in Pakistan have gradually contributed to notions of divine will being paramount in determining social and political structures. In the process they have supplemented the male agenda of promoting orthodox understandings of what it means to be a "true Muslim" in Pakistan. This, in turn, has created space in which militants have promoted notions of women's role as supporters of jihad as well as active participants in the duty to fight the enemies of Islam. While currently the impact of these discourses is not fully appreciated, it is likely to impact upon the future of militancy in Pakistan. The argument is developed in four parts: the first part provides a framework in which Islamization in general can be understood and its links to domestic and international contexts. The second part focuses on the gradual evolution of the context that has created space for discourses on women's agency in jihad. The third part discusses the roles assigned to women in jihadi discourses and the last part explores its possible impact on Pakistani society.

Islamization, Dynamics, Contexts and Agents

The phenomenon of Islamizm and the rise of militancy among some groups in the Muslim community can be understood in terms of the primacy assigned to divine will versus human will in determining the structures of Islamic/Muslim societies and communities.[1] Those who assign primacy to divine will generally subscribe to the view that the message contained in the Qur'an and the set of Ahadith or narrations of prophetic tradition provide the primary source for understanding the meaning of "being a Muslim." The relevance of these injunctions is considered to exist independent of time and geographical location(s): the correct way of being a Muslim, in other words, does not alter with moving times or shifting the locale of one's nationality. Essentially, the text is considered as fixed with limited or no space available for the reader(s) of the text to interpret the religious injunctions in the light of changing circumstances. While those occupying this end of the spectrum do not share identical views, sufficient consensus exists among them to be categorized as orthodox/traditional Muslims.

The opposite end of the spectrum includes Muslims who view religious injunctions in terms of the primacy of human will. This emphasis is not aimed at denying the primacy of God or His injunctions. Rather those subscribing to this end of the spectrum view the primacy of human will in line with God's identification of human beings as His best creation. Endowed with the ability to think and analyze, human beings are assigned the right and the responsibility to ascertain the most appropriate meanings of being a Muslim in line with changing circumstances. In their capacity as the reader(s) of religious injunctions in a primary position, Muslims are acknowledged to have the capacity and the right to interpret Qur'anic and/or prophetic traditions in line with the time and geographical locations. The approach employs a flexibility that enables the readers, and those who agree with these ideas, to shift meanings assigned to ideas and practices away from those agreed to be the norm during different stages in Islamic history.

The simplicity of the spectrum, however, is compromised by the willingness of some on the divine will end to acknowledge a role, even if limited, in shaping how Muslim communities could live their lives. Similarly, some of those committed to the idea of human will as paramount may also accept the possibility and necessity of incorporating divine will in determining the structures, operations and roles of different sections in Muslim states and societies. The picture is further rendered complex by the fact that understandings among Muslim communities and societies do not remain fixed on either end of the spectrum. Rather, a constant process of negotiation and renegotiation of Muslim identities occurs that moves Muslims from one end of the spectrum to another. The possibility also exists of them shifting their views in terms of the relative admissibility of human and/or divine will in shaping the structures and processes of their societies.

This complexity can be understood, at one level, in terms of the state-sponsored and societal Islam: while in the first category, the state retains the right to interpret what it means to be a Muslim and guides the society in the directions considered appropriate, the societal Islam leaves the initiative with societal groups as the arbiters and determiners of Muslim identities. In some respects, state-sponsored Islam and societal Islam reinforce each other: the particular understandings and meanings assigned by the state to being a Muslim, for example, could result in the introduction of rules, regulations and ideas that shift a society from one end of the spectrum to another. Similarly, societal groups may introduce understandings of Muslim identity that put pressure on the state structures to reflect these ideas in marked contrast to the history of the community. But the picture is rendered even more complex by the fact that different sections in a society/state may subscribe to different views at the same time on the merits of assigning primacy to divine or human will. Hence, for example, while the state may prefer the primacy of human will as primary determinant of social and political structures, sections within the bureaucratic/political institutions may opt for a slightly or radically different view in this respect. Similar differences may also exist in the societal sector with multiple views coexisting on the meanings of being a Muslim.

The role of women in Muslim societies can be placed within this complex context of spectrum of identities combined with the multiplicity of agency. As Muslims, these women both articulate their views and shape the contours of the spaces in which members of their respective communities give meanings to their Muslim identities. They can be agents of change shifting societies from the human will end of the spectrum to the divine will as much as they can play a role in moving the communities in the opposite direction(s). Also, by subscribing to divergent understandings of being Muslim, different women's groups operating at societal and/or state levels may empower competing views of these identities.

This complexity also provides the space in which Muslim women develop and articulate their views on the need and appropriateness of jihad. Such articulation, it needs to be pointed out, does not exist in isolation from the views being held by male members of respective societies. Rather, a constant sharing of ideas across the gender divide contributes to the articulation of views on the need and acceptability of jihad. It also determines the parameters in which gender-specific roles are discussed with reference to jihad. The relevance of this context and multiplicity can be appreciated with reference to gradually unfolding discourses on women's roles as Muslims and their contribution to jihad in Pakistan.

Islamization and Women in Pakistan

The notions of Muslim womanhood in Pakistan have evolved within the parameters determined by a combination of its socio-political history and interaction with cultural influences that either originated from the Indian subcontinent or have been introduced from other regions. A mix of orthodox, Sufi and liberal/moderate understandings of Islam has interacted with the emphasis on Pakistan's identity as an Islamic state, as well as the international debates on human rights. The resulting prescriptions of what it means to be a good Muslim woman in Pakistan have varied over the six decades of the country's existence, with some emphasizing the primacy of divine will to introduce ideas that limit a woman's ability to operate freely in the public space. Others, drawing influence from universalistic notions of Islam, have favoured approaches that combine human will and divine will in varying degrees to create spaces where women can operate in both private and public spheres.

The relative balance between the competing notions of womanhood, however, mostly remained in favour of liberal/moderate and Sufi traditions and approaches. This found expression in the pivotal role played by women belonging to the elite classes in the 1950s and 1960s to "modernize" Pakistan; educational opportunities for girls and employment opportunities for women were promoted by these elite woman. This implied the questioning of the norms limiting women's participation in the private sphere also impacted upon the dress codes: the tradition of wearing burqa, for example, declined in the major cities of the country.

The Indo-Pakistan war of 1971, which resulted in the dismemberment of Pakistan and the emergence of Bangladesh, gradually shifted the balance away from the moderate understandings of Muslim womanhood. The need to understand the causes of Pakistan's defeat energized orthodox Islamic parties operating in the country. As in Egypt in the post-1967 era, a new language emerged that blamed the defeat at the hands of the enemy — in this case the "Hindu India" — on the failure of the society to subscribe to true Islamic values. This, in turn, energized the groups that argued for the primacy of divine will in determining the context in which Pakistan could operate as a state and society. The process was hastened with the rise to power of General Zia-ul-Haq in July 1977; the alliance between the military regime and orthodox Jamaat-e-Islami created the space in which the state became the agent for moving the country towards orthodoxy. The Zia regime introduced a host of laws and administrative changes that were explained and justified in terms of the Qur'anic injunctions and prophetic traditions.

The references to the primacy of divine will in shaping the culture of Pakistani society impacted upon the position of women beyond the apparent abuse of their human rights under the Hudood Ordinance. They also privileged the discourses that either emphasized that women's primary area of operation is restricted to the family sphere, or qualified the conditions under which women could operate in the public sphere. The process did not cease with the onset of the era of democratically elected governments after General Zia's death in August 1988. On the contrary, against the backdrop of the continuing instability that led to frequent changes in government, Pakistani society experienced a proliferation of orthodox discourses on womanhood. Unlike in the past, these discourses did not remain limited to the rural areas or less economically privileged sections of Pakistani society. Women from the elite class also became active in accepting and disseminating the newly acquired knowledge of the "true Islamic identity" of a Pakistani Muslim woman. Societal groups effectively appropriated the state-sponsored Islam. While acting as agents of Islamization in its own right, however, these groups did not completely sideline the state. Instead, linkages were maintained that enabled the societal groups to promote their respective readings of what constitutes a good Muslim woman. The orthodox nature of these discourses and the linkages can be appreciated with reference to the Al-Huda in Pakistan.

The origin of Al-Huda dates back to 1994 when Dr. Farhat Hashmi set up the group upon her return from the UK.[2] The declared aim of the groups was to educate women about true Islam. From the outset, she received patronage from the President of Pakistan, Farooq Leghari — she was provided access to space in the Presidential residence, where she disseminated her message to the elite women of Islamabad. She also organized study circles, often held in five-star hotels, where the elite women were encouraged to understand Islam. Soon the group was able to establish its academies in the major cities, including Lahore. The process was facilitated by economically privileged women who donated funds and, in the case of Lahore, even access to a building for the academy.

The curriculum for the academy drew heavily upon the teachings propagated by the Jamaat-e-Islami Pakistan. The language used to communicate the message, however, was tailored to suit the needs of the women from the elite class. In addition to teaching them about the rights and responsibilities of "good Muslims," Al-Huda also conducted classes in which the students learnt Qur'an meanings. Willing graduates were encouraged to further disseminate the message to others after completing their courses. The ever-expanding circle of influence provided the space in which Al-Huda carved out a niche for itself. Gradually it also brought women from the lower economic classes into the network, thus creating a pool of women who are willing "converts" to the idea of gender-specific rights and responsibilities for women.[3] The message is now being communicated at the international level with the setting up of an Al-Huda Institute in 2001 in Canada. Claiming to provide "authentic Islamic knowledge" that can contribute to "find[ing] inner peace" and "effective interpersonal relations," the Institute offers structured courses, both on campus and online.[4]

The Movement has impacted upon women in ways that belie expectations. Emerging against the background of increasing emphasis on Islam at the international level, it has attracted women who want to learn about Islam while also making sense of their lives in a Pakistani and an international context. Most significantly, the exposure has literally brain-washed some women in their search for true Islamic knowledge. There is anecdotal evidence of women from economically privileged professional backgrounds opting to give up their jobs and adopt extremely orthodox practices. This is particularly evident in them opting for hijab and abayas as a true reflection of how a Muslim woman must dress. Taking place against the backdrop of growing Arabization of Pakistani society due to increased interaction with the Gulf States, these attitudes have resulted in an increasing articulation of women's place and role in terms of complementary gender roles.

Jihadi Discourses and Women

The articulation of what it means to be a "good and true" Muslim woman by orthodox sections in Pakistani society and political groups has inadvertently created the space in which jihadi organizations can promote their own understandings of "good" Muslim women. The literature published by these groups reveals a tendency to build on the attributes of good Muslim women as identified by the orthodox groups and add notions of the significance of jihad. Women are encouraged to play their role in the jihadi project to validate their Islamic identity. The discourse on the nature of this role, and the manner in which it is communicated, however, varies with the particular agenda of the jihadi group: sometimes the relevance of jihad is communicated subtly, and sometimes directly to women through a host of publications that have been traditionally easily available in the open market. Interestingly, women associated with jihadi groups are not always the articulators of these ideas. On the contrary, men considered to represent the authentic version of Islam often develop the ideas that are later repeated by women in subsequent publications, particularly magazines.

Women's role in jihad is essentially grounded in the context of complementarities of roles created by God for men and women. Replicating the ideas presented by orthodox notions of women's rights and responsibilities, jihadi literature also focuses on the need for women to accept and operate gracefully in the sphere allocated for them through divine will, i.e. the home environment. The primacy of the family sphere is identified as evidence of the special status assigned to women in Islam compared to other religious and cultural traditions. It is also linked to the stability and survival of the basic unit of human existence: the family. Women are identified as both capable of, and responsible for, the effective functioning of the family sphere. By drawing upon Qu'ranic verses and Ahadith, available literature reminds women of the value of being patient, loving, nurturing and focused on religious teachings. Referring to selected Ahadith that equate "taking care of family responsibilities" with jihad, Muslim women are reassured of the value of operating in the family sphere. Specifically, exemplary Muslim women are portrayed as appreciating the distinction between family and public sphere, and subscribe to traditional Islamic dress code while operating in the public sphere. The commitment to observing purdah is not limited to those who are not members of the extended family but extends to all non-mahram males, including in-laws.

These attributes are presented in an oppositional relationship to those of women who are either non-Muslim or influenced by Western traditions.

Specifically, the literature castigates Muslim men for encouraging or condoning the tendency among their women to move freely in the public space, follow Western traditions, and not observe purdah. Muslim women who question these ideas are also criticized for deviating from the authentic Islamic injunctions. But the possibility of them reverting to the true message is kept open by referring to stories of women who became aware of their follies and chose the righteous path.

The notion of restricted spaces for Muslim women, however, sits parallel to the right and responsibility for them to participate in Jihad. The idea of participation, at one level, is grounded in the understanding that women are not expected or enjoined to actively engage in jihad due to their inherent physical weakness.[5] Hence, they are to follow alternative paths to seek equivalent reward and recompense from God. An analysis of selected publications suggests that women's role as mothers and wives is privileged over other roles as the means through which they could engage in jihad. Essentially this involves them supporting and nurturing a family environment in which men can engage in jihad. As a wife, a woman is encouraged to be kind to her husband, taking into account his emotional, physical and spiritual needs. Given that jihad is assigned a special place as the main pillar of Islam, sometimes surpassing Hajj, a good Muslim woman is also expected and encouraged to support her husband in his commitment to actively participating in jihad. This commitment includes parting with jewellery and other valuables to raise funds for jihad, a willingness to happily accept long periods of his absence and the preparedness to celebrate his martyrdom.

As mothers, Muslim women are also assigned the responsibility of bringing up youth committed to the idea of jihad. A book entitled *Misali Ma'an* (iconic mother), for example, subtly introduces these ideas by discussing the value of motherhood for Muslim women. Identified as approved by Mufti Shamzai, known for his radical ideas, the author provides a series of suggestions on how a Muslim woman needs to deal with pregnancy and bringing up children. The need to create an appropriate environment in which children can grow up to be good Muslims, the author argues, requiring mothers to be well-versed in Islamic teachings and practices. This knowledge is to be utilized to ensure that children grow up to be individuals who are healthy, happy, confident, disciplined and respectful towards their elders. Mothers are also entrusted with the task of ensuring that children learn the Arabic language. They are also to inculcate an acceptance of gender-specific roles for girls and boys: girls are particularly to be taught not to strive to be equal to or copy male members of their family. Effectively mothers are entrusted with the task of creating an environment marked by "ample discussions of Iman and Yaqin, detachment from the world, passion for heaven and fear of hell." The ultimate aim of the nurturing, however, is to bring up children who shun the worldly life and grow up with the single aim of spreading the din throughout the world even at the cost of their lives, possessions, time and all energy.

The mother's responsibility of preparing Mujahids extends to the choice of educational institutions. For example, an iconic mother is portrayed as one who would ensure that the home environment is purely Islamic: children wake up early, say prayers and experience everyday living along Islamic lines. But a good mother is also entrusted with the responsibility of choosing schools that will turn their children into tomorrow's Mujahid.[6] The duty to support jihad does not end with the death of the mother either: she is encouraged to clearly mention in her will that her children "be brought up to be hafiz, students of religion and Mujahid."[7]

The agenda of willingly preparing martyrs for the future is justified with reference to early Islamic history, and examples from the region. The female companions of the Prophet Muhammad, it is pointed out, willingly sent their sons and husbands to jihad. The story of Hazrat Khansa establishes a mother's commitment to jihad by sending her four sons to fight kuffar.[8] Examples of Islamic warriors, such as Khalid bin Waleed, Umar bin Khattab, Muhammad bin Qasim, Mahmood Ghaznavi and Tippu Sultan, are presented as icons who can only be emulated if a Muslim mother inculcated the appropriate spirit in her children for jihad. These examples are often supplemented by generic stories that highlight and suggest the responsibility for a Muslim woman to remain committed to the project of jihad for the ultimate glory of their religion. A book entitled *Misali Aurat* (iconic woman) illustrates the attributes of good Muslim women by discussing the story of a woman who heard about the value of jihad. Once convinced of the beauty of the hoor (a virgin promised in heaven) that a martyred son would be eternally married to, she offered her son for jihad. So strong was her commitment that she awaited the returning soldiers and queried if she should be congratulated for being the mother of a martyr or be offered condolences for her son surviving the jihad.[9]

The preference for women playing a supportive role only is occasionally set aside in favour of a more active participation in the jihad project. As in the case of the supportive aspect, the validation for such a role is sought in historical examples. For example, references are made to Ayesha and Umm Salim carrying water for those engaged in active combat. Later Umm Salim is reported to have carried a dagger in the battle of Hunain, with the expressed intention of stabbing any kuffar who would dare to get near her. The propensity to use such historical references, however, varies with militant organizations: Lashker-e-Tayyiba, for instance, only sparingly acknowledges the role of women during the Soviet occupation of Afghanistan in the 1980s. In contrast, the literature published for women by Jaish-e-Muhammad, which was created in 2000, categorically refers to the desirability of them participating in campaigns.

Meaning and Impact On Actual Involvement in Jihad

The question arises as to what are the implications of such discourses that draw inspiration from and are situated in the emerging orthodoxy in Pakistan? Do they directly correlate to active participation of women in jihad in Pakistan?

At one level, it could be argued that these discourses remain in the domain of ideas and that they are not really translated into women's active agency in the project of jihad. This could be due to the overwhelming preference for men as agents of militancy in Pakistan, including suicide bombings. With one exception, where a mentally retarded woman was involved in a suicide bombing, women have generally remained absent from the militant space. This may be attributed to prevalence of orthodoxy and reluctance among even radical elements to draw women into the arena of militancy. In the North-West Frontier Province (NWFP), which has borne the brunt of suicide bombings, cultural norms oppose the idea of women using weapons and this accounts for their non-participation in militancy. There are also cases where young radicalized males have taken steps to distance their female siblings from any possibility of being radicalized and drawn into militant activities.

The situation hence stands in contrast to the situation in Palestine, where the militant discourse was followed by women actively participating in suicide bombings.

An alternative approach to the issue of participation, however, presents a different conclusion. If we extend the idea of participation to include a willingness to be actively engaged in Jihadi activities, even if it does not culminate in active participation, it could be argued that the available discourse has impacted upon the manner in which some women have approached the question of jihad. The saga surrounding the Lal Masjid (Red Mosque) and the involvement of women from Jamia Hafsa in 2007 falls in this category. The girls/women enrolled in the Jamia Hafsa belonged to the less-privileged economic classes, with a substantial number belonging to Swat, Kashmir and other areas.

From the outset, the young students enrolled in the Jamia were influenced by the orthodox understandings of Islam preferred by Maulana Abdullah, and then his sons Abdul Aziz and Abdul Rashid Ghazi. In the post-9/11 days, the push to clamp down on religious schools pushed the owners of the Lal Masjid and Jamia Hafsa towards increased orthodoxy. With the emphasis on the clash between Islam and the West, and emerging discord on appropriate foreign policy for Pakistan, the mosque adopted an increasingly defiant attitude towards the Musharraf regime. The increasingly pro-Western attitude of the ruling government was questioned through the use of language that focused on the primacy of the divine will, and the right and responsibility of every true Muslim to work for its implementation. It took the form of actions such as kidnapping a woman allegedly running a brothel close to the Mosque, and also kidnapping some Chinese women who owned a massage parlour. The stated aim of these actions was to force the miscreants to repent and to ensure that the Islamic nature of society was not compromised. As these and other challenges to the Musharraf regime intensified into an open conflict between the ruling government and the Ghazi brothers, the relevance of the ideas communicated to women became apparent.

Although it is not easy to find reliable information on what happened, it appears that some of the young women chose to stay in Jamia Hafsa as the showdown between the government and the Ghazi brothers became imminent. Their choice was couched in terms of a preference for martyrdom.

Similar language also surfaced in interviews with girls who survived the showdown due to early departure from the Jamia Hafsa. A young woman who left the Jamia before the army crackdown on July 10, 2007, for example, described her feelings as follows: "Everyone is coming to meet me. When they meet me I say: 'I wish I had been martyred.' Had these people visited us on my martyrdom, I would have been happier."[10] She also stated without prompting:

> They have martyred Lal Masjid and Jamia Hafsa. Now I wish that mosques like Lal Masjid and madaris like Jamia Hafsa be established across the country. Insha Allah (God willing), wherever I work, I will work with Jihadi passion. If not, I would soon open a Madrassah to impart Jihadi knowledge.[11]

Such views about the relevance of martyrdom continue to appear. Umm Ahsan, who reportedly took up arms towards the end of the encounter with the army in 2007, is reported to have remained committed to the idea of Shariat or shahadat (Sharia or martyrdom).[12]

Conclusion

The pernicious impact of the discourse exhorting women to play a role in jihad, however, exists more with reference to their role as nurturers. The declared duty to create environments in which male members are prepared for jihad and female members are committed to the idea of supporting men in their perceived religious duty has sown the seeds for a gradual increase in the number of men participating in militancy. Unless countered, Pakistan will have a generation who are more committed to the idea of jihad and feel compelled to perform their duty in this respect. The long-term impact of the jihadi discourse for women, therefore, is likely to be felt more indirectly than directly.

Any attempt to counter these discourses, however, requires careful strategies: a categorically contrapuntal discourse runs the risk of reinforcing the perception that the roles conceptualized for women in jihadi literature are valid. Instead, a counter-narrative needs to evolve that presents alternative understandings of women's role in an Islamic society, along the lines preferred by those who accept the need to incorporate human and divine will in structuring human societies. Given that the orthodox discourses are also receiving uncritical acceptance among some sections of the elite, the counter-narratives need to be developed in terms that appeal to a wider section of the society. Limiting it to the less-privileged classes on the assumption of a direct linkage between poverty and militancy may fail to plug the possibilities of militant discourses being accepted by a small section of the elite class in Pakistan.

Notes

1 This discussion draws upon the ideas developed by Ishtiaq Ahmed, *The Concept of an Islamic State: An Analysis of the Ideological Controversy in Pakistan*. Palgrave Macmillan, 1987.

2 Based on personal participation in a meeting and discussions with those who originally interacted with Dr. Farhat Hashmi.

3 For excellent coverage, see Sadaf Ahmad, "Identity Matters, Culture Wars: An account of Al-Huda (re)-defining identity and reconfiguring culture in Pakistan," *Religion and Culture*, 2008, 9(1): 63–80.

4 Al Huda Institute Canada, http://www.alhudainstitute.ca/ (accessed December 15, 2009).

5 See, for example, Maulana Mufti Mohammad Irshad Sahib-ul-Qasmi, *Jannati Aurat*. Karachi: Zamzam Publishers, 2009, pp. 167–168.

6 Mohammad Haneef Abdul Majid, Misali Maan, (Karachi, Bait-ul-Ilm Trust, 2009), p. 321.

7 Misali Maan, p. 405.

8 Misali Maan, pp. 258–262.

9 Mohammad Harun Muawiya, "Eik Bahadur Maan ka Waqiya" (story of a brave mother), *Misali Aurat*. Karachi: Darul Ishaat, 2006, pp. 571–574.

10 Mohammad Asghar Abdullah, "Ibn Maryam Hua Karey Koi," *Lal Masjid ka Lahou* (The Blood of Lal Masjid). Lahore: Nigarshat Publishers, 2008, p. 98.

11 Ibid., p. 99.

12 See, for example. Tariq Ismael Sagar, *Lal Masjid*. Laore: Tahir Sons Publishers, 2007, pp. 44–142.

Epilogue

Usama Butt

The all-encompassing question, that of an "existential crisis," is still in an evolutionary stage, as the recent carnage in the cities of Peshawar, Lahore and Multan has demonstrated. Each bloodbath is a firm reminder of the stark reality that Pakistan's quagmire is only deepening. At the beginning of the book I set out a list of questions and dimensions that I wanted this book to address, starting with the question of an "existential threat." I wanted this book to explore, through its valued contributors, the dimensions of security, strategy and the future of Pakistan and by doing so, the goal was to assess the current turmoil in its entirety with a critical and academic perspective. The overall aim set in the Introduction was also to assess the genesis of the crisis, review the current strategic discourses of both national and international actors by addressing all important phenomenona and then finally analyze and explore the future strategic discourses.

As stated in the Introduction, instead of following the current "norm" in the available literature, this book would differ, not only with the versatility of its contributors, which included both Western and Pakistani academics and experts, but also with the inclusion of the proponents and opponents of Pakistan's "war on terror"; this book has established a new "norm," a new style of perspective and enquiry, that doesn't only address issues that a particular set of readership would find stimulating but attempts to engage both a Western and a Pakistani readership, may they be academics, politicians, strategists or member of the general population.

As promised, each chapter has addressed a highly relevant phenomenon of this crisis though a critical spectrum of enquiry, although each contributor has of course drawn their own set of assessments of the crisis. This presents the readers with a variety of expert views on the matter that I hope have been stimulating enough to inspire readers to come to their own conclusions.

To start with the most critical question, that of an existential threat, one thing has been clear: this crisis is as close to an existential threat that Pakistan has ever gotten to, if not an existential threat in itself. Similarly the themes regarding the genesis of the crisis throughout the chapters include: the Afghan Jihad with full US backing, the threat of radical Islam as well as the ideological challenges, 9/11 and the US-led war on terror and the role of Pakistani establishment, whether civilian or military, with their mixed, hesitant and ambiguous responses on the matter.

Second, the book and its different chapters also presents a near unanimous opposition to the US policy in Pakistan and Afghanistan. Although the Obama Administration has somewhat broken with the total "coercive" tradition of its predecessor, which is commonly appreciated, the books contributors have, nonetheless, mostly questioned US strategy, particularly towards Afghanistan and India. While some chapters have gone as far as to define this crisis as a "US proxy war," the other "accommodating" views are not completely sympathetic either and a resentment and anxiety is visible towards the historic experiences in the US-Pakistan relationship, the US military and economic assistance, the state of Pakistan's economy, the discomfort towards US meddling within Pakistani affairs, i.e. the nuclear issue, and the undue pressure to always "do more." In short there is a lot more that remains to be done.

Third, the threat of militancy, which is one of the paramount ingredients of this quagmire, couldn't have been evaluated without a thorough assessment and analysis of the genesis, nature, ideology and operational capabilities of both national and transnational jihadist organizations. The book, therefore, has attempted to establish both ideological and operational discourses of the nationalists and transnationalist jihadists organizations, while evaluating the level of threat posed by these elements to Pakistan and beyond, against the capabilities of the state machinery and its security and military apparatus to contain it. The contributors, although of different inclinations, have agreed about the seriousness of this threat to the state of Pakistan and the urgent need to tackle it. The recommendations range from the most "accommodating" of the views, i.e. a complete collaboration with the US, to the complete opposite, of not playing a US proxy at all. There remains, however, a generalized sense of an urgent need for a "strategy review," mutually constructed by the civilian government and the army, through truly national reconciliatory efforts.

This leads us to examine the three aspects we set out in the beginning of the book, that of the "security," "strategy" and "future" of Pakistan. To start with the "security" aspect, as different chapters of the book have explored, the national security of Pakistan is indeed severely threatened by this turmoil, both internally and externally. The homegrown Taliban and the imported al-Qaeda are the security nightmare that Pakistan has woken up to since 9/11. Similarly, as many of the chapters pointed fingers toward the constant threat emancipating from Indian and the Afghan borders, the external front is no more secure, an issue that the newly formed US-Indian "friendship" only strengthens. The war in Afghanistan, as almost all of our contributors contended, has and will lead to further unrest within Pakistan. The "security" nightmare doesn't end there either, there are more international security concerns that Pakistan must attend to, which includes the question of its nuclear arsenal, its "export" of terrorism, and a pressure "to do more" in the "war on terror."

The "strategy" aspect, as briefly mentioned earlier, is somewhat contended among different chapters, but thoroughly explored and analyzed nonetheless throughout the book. There is a crucial need of a "strategy" review as the military solution will not be the ultimate solvent of this crisis. There is also a general realization of the fact that whether proxy or not, the "war" is now fought within Pakistani borders and its impacts are ideological, social and economical. Therefore there is the sense of an urgent need for a coherent strategy that not only addresses "international concerns," which at worst are exaggerated and at best overstated, but which also gives attention to hardcore economic and social realities. The book's chapters offer different paths — from overcoming the ideologically driven identity crisis to reviewing the "benefits" and "costs" of Pakistan's war on terror or eliminating the militancy by any military means possible. The fact remains, however, that all strategic options must be assimilated into a national reconciliatory effort to form a coherent and workable future strategy.

And finally, when considering Pakistan's future, the picture is at best blurred or at worst frightening. Stuck in this security and strategic quagmire, Pakistan cannot hope for a better and brighter future. For a glimmer of hope towards a securer future, Pakistan must overcome this crisis as quickly as it can. I shall be discussing Pakistan's "twenty years" crisis" in one of my forthcoming books, but will say here that whether proxy or not this "war" must end, but this isn't possible without an end to the conflict cross the border in Afghanistan. The Obama Administration's 18-month exit strategy from Afghanistan is at best too hopeful and at worst impractical. Pakistanis have also shown no real and positive signs of engaging in ending this war. The "jihad" of the Pakistani army (as interior minister Rehman Malik described it), has not been all "glorifying" and successful as the recently ended South Waziristan operation has demonstrated. Barely a day after its end, there is talk of a new frontier in another agency, which only proves that either Operation Rah-e-Nijat wasn't all that successful or the problem persists in a similar severity elsewhere too. And of course why stop in FATA, when militants have "known" strong bases within Punjab, NWFP and Balochistan, etc.

It is very clear then that this "war" is far from over and will drag on for years. There is no guarantee of the outcome of the US-led "war on terror" across the border. Al-Qaeda, with its handful of "core" members, can and already have found safe havens elsewhere, such places as Somalia and Yemen. Similarly, the crisis in the Middle East has only been increased since the US "democratic" onslaught in Iraq. The insurgency there has shown no sign of dying either, as al-Qaeda is now "franchised" and compartmentalized and is still capable of attacking all-important security targets within the highly secured "Green Zone." Similarly, the picture of the "real" epicenter of "terrorism," the Israel-Palestenian conflict, is ever bleaker; with the coalition of the right and far-right government in Israel, and Hamas, and Fatah's rivalry, the fire could ignite once again at any given time. Israel's massacre of civilians in both the Gazan and Lebanese conflicts and a complete deadlock on any negotiations only "proves" the jihadists point that "the only way" forward is their way of "jihad." No one can really tell how many recruits these two wars have provided to the jihadist causes within Palestine, Lebanon, Pakistan and beyond. With dictatorial, tyrannical and authoritarian Muslim regimes that the West fully supports, the Middle East is a volcano waiting to erupt again at any time.

It is a big wonder then that the Pakistani strategists find themselves immune to this "volcanic eruption," particularly when they are sitting right in the middle of it. How can Pakistan stay neutral in such crisis when a chunk of its own population sees jihad and militancy the only way forward, particularly to the backdrop of the fact that Pakistan is still unable to meaningfully suppress them? Is it really in Pakistan's interest to only use the military option, without further engaging in the political solution, particularly when an anti-Pakistani government is now installed in Afghanistan and a threat from India looks increasingly real?

The picture, therefore, is gloomy and bleak, which is a negative way to end a book. I need to remind the readers that this is not "just another" book, as this is not just another "war." Its repercussions are severe and both regional and global. Western readers know all too well that what happens in this region will affect their future security, but Pakistani readers also need to be reminded that it will affect the security of their children and grandchildren too. And finally, as President Obama in his December Af-Pak speech told American audiences, above all he is *only* concerned with the "security of American people." Is the "security" of the Pakistani population similarly important? And the immediate answer to this question, as this book has suggested, will be embedded in finding the best available escape routes from this quagmire; a path that the current military onslaught is only delaying. A political solution with the full backing of the general public, based on a realist national interest and coupled with the addressing of real hardcore questions regarding the role of religion, democracy and identity might drag Pakistan out from this bloody pit of a quagmire.

Glossary

Abaya	traditional over-garment wore by women in parts of the Islamic world
Ahadith	plural of Hadith
Alim	learned scholar or a religious cleric
Amir	leader
Badal	revenge
Baya	oath of allegiance
Burqa	Pakistani equivalent of Hijab
Fitna	chaos or disorder
Hadith	statement(s) of the Prophet
Haram	forbidden
Hukumat-e-ilahiyah	divine rule of God
Ijma	consensus
Jahiliyya	ignorance; the term is interchangeably used for both Pre-Islamic Arabia and the Western civilization
Kuffar	non-believers
Kufr	disbelief
Madaris	plural of "Madrassah"
Madrassah	religious schools
Mahram	male members of the family with whom a female is forbidden to marry, i.e. uncle, father, brother etc. (vice versa in the case of mahram for males)
Majlis-e-Shura	consultative council

Mohtarma	"respectable lady"; Benazir Bhutto was normally addressed with this title
Mussalmans	Muslims
Najaez	unlawful
Nifaq	hypocrisy
Nizam-e-Adl	justice system based on Sharia
Purdah	covering of face in presence of non-Mahram men
Qiyas	traditionalist frame of thinking that persisted before the tenth century
Rah-e-Nijat	"the way out" or "path to deliverance"
Shahadat	martyrdom
Sharia	Islamic system of governance based on the teaching of Qur'an and Sunna
Shura	consultation
Sulah	truce
Sunna	deeds and sayings of the Prophet
Tabligh	preaching
Takfir	excommunication
Tehsil	part of a "district," or simply a "town"
Ulema	plural of "Alim"
Umma	global Muslim community
Wajibul-lqatl	allowed to be killed
Yaqin	belief
Zalim	oppressor